THE HYMNS OF QUMRAN

SOCIETY
OF BIBLICAL
LITERATURE

DISSERTATION SERIES

edited by
Douglas A. Knight

Number 50
THE HYMNS OF QUMRAN
TRANSLATION AND COMMENTARY
by
Bonnie Pedrotti Kittel

Bonnie Pedrotti Kittel

THE HYMNS OF QUMRAN
TRANSLATION
AND COMMENTARY

Scholars Press

Distributed by
Scholars Press
101 Salem Street
Chico, California 95926

THE HYMNS OF QUMRAN
TRANSLATION AND COMMENTARY
Bonnie Pedrotti Kittel

Ph.D., 1975
Graduate Theological Union

Adviser:
Victor R. Gold

Library of Congress Cataloging in Publication Data

Kittel, Bonnie Pedrotti.
  The hymns of Qumran.

  (Dissertation series—Society of Biblical Literature ;
no. 50 ISSN 0145-269X)
  Selected hymns in English and Hebrew, commentary
in English.
  Originally presented as the author's thesis, Graduate
Theological Union, 1975.
  Bibliography: p.
  1. Thanksgiving scroll—Criticism, interpretation, etc.
2. Hymns, Hebrew—History and criticism. I.
Thanksgiving scroll. English & Hebrew. Selections.
1980. II. Title. III. Series: Society of Biblical Literature.
Dissertation series; no. 50.
BM488.T5K57   1980   296.1'55   80-11616
ISBN 0-89130-397-9 (pbk.)

Printed in the United States of America
1 2 3 4 5
Edwards Brothers, Inc.
Ann Arbor, Michigan 48106

To My Teachers

James Muilenburg and David Noel Freedman

TABLE OF CONTENTS

LIST OF TABLES

PRINCIPAL ABBREVIATIONS

Dead Sea Scrolls
- 1QS   The Manual of Discipline
- 1QM   The War of the Sons of Light with the Sons of Darkness
- 1QH   The Hodayot (The Psalms of Thanksgiving)
- 1QIsa^a First copy of Isaiah from Qumran Cave 1

Periodicals

BA	*The Biblical Archaeologist*
BJRL	*Bulletin of the John Rylands Library Manchester*
IEJ	*Israel Exploration Journal*
JBL	*Journal of Biblical Literature*
JNES	*Journal of Near Eastern Studies*
JQR	*The Jewish Quarterly Review*
JSS	*Journal of Semitic Studies*
NTS	*New Testament Studies*
RB	*Revue Biblique*
RQ	*Revue de Qumran*
RHR	*Revue de l'Histoire des Religions*
TLZ	*Theologische Literaturzeitung*
TS	*Theological Studies*
VT	*Vetus Testamentum*

CHAPTER I

THE HODAYOT: A SURVEY OF WHAT HAS BEEN ACCOMPLISHED

Among the scrolls discovered in a cave near Khirbet Qumran
in 1947 by the Taamira Bedouin was the scroll which came to be
known as *Hodayot*, or Thanksgiving Psalms. This scroll, with
several others, came into the possession of E. L. Sukenik in
1947 when the Bedouin were looking for buyers.[1] Sukenik, like
Brownlee, Trever, Burrows, and Albright, early recognized the
importance of these scrolls and their great antiquity. Although
in the early tumultuous days when the discovery of the scrolls
was announced there were numerous scholars who were doubtful of
their authenticity, only one or two have subsequently stubbornly
refused to admit that the scrolls date from the last centuries
B.C. and the first century A.D.

The Hodayot scroll was one of several nonbiblical manuscripts discovered at Qumran which were previously unknown. It
contains a number of psalm-like compositions prefaced, where
the scroll has not deteriorated, by the phrase אודכה אדוני ("I
thank thee, Lord") or ברוך אתה אדוני ("Blessed art thou"). From
the first of these phrases the scroll received its name, Hodayot,
or Thanksgiving Psalms. The name has stuck, and is generally
descriptive of the contents, despite the fact that these thanksgiving psalms are rather different than their Old Testament
counterparts. Millar Burrows has given a succinct summary of
the situation.

> Not everything in the scroll corresponds to this
> title....Elements of the type known as the individual
> psalm of complaint in the Old Testament are combined
> with the note of thanksgiving in some of the poems.
> Their prevailing tone, however, even in the descrip-
> tions of past trials or of future disasters, is that
> of thanksgiving for deliverance.[2]

In other words, the Hodayot represent a "mixed form" judged by
OT standards, and this typology with the attendant difficulty
of determining the Sitz im Leben is typical of the problems en-
countered in studying the Hodayot.

The question of the literary type of the Hodayot points to
a central problem in dealing with this material. It is non-
canonical; it is later than OT poetry and is rather difficult,
as predicted by scholars on the basis of other poetry from the
intertestamental period. Nevertheless, when dealing with this
material, writers have tended to try to fit the Hodayot into
the scheme of development they have already discerned on the
basis of OT evidence. There were, of course, other late Hebrew
poems known before the discovery of the Hodayot, chief of which
were Ben-Sira and the Psalms of Solomon. The latter, however,
is known only in Greek translation, and the Hebrew fragments of
Ben-Sira, until Yadin's discovery of a Ben-Sira scroll at
Masada recently, were considered dubious evidence for the
original Hebrew.[3]

The Qumran discoveries, then, presented a challenge to the
schemata of OT literature as worked out by scholars. On the
one hand, they were welcome and helped to prove numerous hypo-
theses; on the other, they were occasionally somewhat bewilder-
ing and where they did not fit OT standards, were often judged
inferior. This has especially been the case with the Hodayot;
discussions of form criticism, Sitz im Leben, obscure terms,
and poetic structure all rely for terminology on that developed
for OT poetry. To a certain extent this is necessary and
valid. The problem has been that certain distinctive features
of the Hodayot are obscured, or considered baffling, or judged
inferior because terminology is inadequate.

This study is primarily concerned with exploring the
poetic structure of the Hodayot, and thereby contributing to
the solution of this terminological problem. It is worthwhile
in passing, however, to note some of the problems and suggested
solutions in the area of form criticism. In general, most of
the psalms of the Hodayot show the threefold development which
Gunkel outlined for thanksgiving songs: the description of the
author's distress, the cry for help, and the description of
deliverance.[4] The customary thanksgiving formula appears also
at the beginning of the psalm, just as in canonical poetry.
Few, if any, of these psalms represent a pure type, however.
There are elements of the lament or complaint, of penitence, of

petition, and of hymnic praise, and other sections of apocalyptic character quite unlike any in the psalter. This in itself is not too disturbing to form critics; Gunkel had already discerned this development toward a mixed type in late poetry.[5] Most scholars find it convenient and helpful to delineate these psalms according to the classic scheme, pointing out the additional elements.

Two recent writers, however, have suggested a division of these psalms into two categories: thankoffering songs and hymns.[6] Since all the psalms have similar openings, and since the body of the psalms all contain disparate elements, the distinction is made chiefly on the basis of the content and what is judged to be the central theme. Subjective as this standard is, both Morawe and Holm-Nielsen, working independently, show almost complete agreement in the division between the two types. Morawe is more categorical in the assignment of his types than Holm-Nielsen, who is content to leave the matter open in some cases.[7]

In fact, Holm-Nielsen occasionally refers to a psalm by both terms, making it difficult to know which category he really intends.[8] He has a purpose in distinguishing between the two types, since he later suggests that the hymn type in particular was used in the cult of the Qumran community. He cites some persuasive examples from his hymn category as evidence of this.[9] Attractive as his arguments are, and poetic analysis would seem to support his case in a number of instances, the haziness of his criteria for delineating the two types mars his discussion. Furthermore, Morawe also hedges his division of these psalms into two types with the qualification that the hymn type actually stands within the thankoffering song type and shares many elements with it.[10] The problem of delineating two types of poetry in the scroll is further underscored by Mansoor's title "Thanksgiving Hymns" for the entire scroll.[11]

An attentive reading of the Hodayot does suggest that, despite the formal adherence to the "thankoffering song" scheme, there are a number of psalms that are definitely "different"; and any listing would surely include many or all of those sections called hymns by Holm-Nielsen and Morawe. A number of

these sections fall within the material selected for analysis
in the following chapters, and the poetic and thematic devices
used to set off these psalms will be discussed. In particular,
three passages selected for analysis share a number of poetic
features and devices which can be described quite accurately
and which differ somewhat from techniques employed elsewhere in
the scroll.[12] These techniques offer some objective evidence
for a hymn form, differing from the thankoffering song. It
would appear, then, that the latest form critical work is far
from complete, and would be greatly aided by additional evidence from poetic analysis.

Nor is the Sitz im Leben of the Hodayot easy to determine.
As Holm-Nielsen has commented, this question has been obscured
in most discussions so far by the more intriguing question of
authorship--the "I" of the psalms.[13] As he has remarked, no
definitive answer can ever be reached in regard to authorship
on the present evidence, particularly possible authorship by
the Teacher of Righteousness. Such discussions do not, in any
case, answer the question of the use intended for these psalms,
which cannot be determined by appealing to a hypothetical author. Holm-Nielsen's discussion of the Sitz im Leben problem
is a cogent summary and critique of the various positions ad-
vanced by scholars. He goes straight to the heart of the problem: the Sitz im Leben of the Hodayot cannot be determined
simply from the form employed.

The thankoffering song was originally intended for use by
individuals or a community in the temple. The Qumran community
had rejected the temple worship of its day as impure, yet con-
tinued to employ the literary form of the thankoffering song.
Clearly, other than form critical evidence must be used to ar-
rive at the use of these psalms. By reviewing what is known of
the Qumran sect, Holm-Nielsen arrives at the conclusion that
some, at least, of these psalms could have been employed in the
ceremony of covenant renewal. Those most likely to have been
so used are the hymns he has previously identified, for in
several of these clear references to the sect are made. He
therefore suggests that the whole collection was made for cultic use on special occasions, not all of which must necessarily

correspond to the original Sitz im Leben which influenced the
development of the literary form of the thanksgiving song.[14]

Many scholars do not share Holm-Nielsen's views, believing
that the Hodayot represent "private" poetry, intended for medi-
tational or instructional use, rather than use in worship.[15]
As evidence, they point to the style, considered obscure and
unwieldy for cultic use, and they tend to emphasize the view
that the psalms are a product of a great *teacher* of the sect,
and are therefore meant to be for personal meditation and in-
struction. The evidence drawn from the poetic structure in these
poems supports Holm-Nielsen's view, at least for the hymn types
he has identified, and this matter is touched on briefly in the
concluding chapter of this paper.

Aside from the form critical research, the work done on
the Hodayot can be divided into the following categories.

1. Editions of the text, with or without notes.
2. Articles dealing with the physical characteristics
   of the scroll: date, number and type of scribes,
   condition of the text. (This work is discussed
   in Chapter II.)
3. Translations of the text, usually with notes or
   other commentary.
4. Discussions of the theology and imagery of all
   or parts of the scroll.
5. Investigation of the poetic structures of the
   psalms.

The bulk of the work by far falls into categories three
and four; most of the work published has involved translations
of all or part of the scroll with interest either in textual
problems or theological problems, or a combination of both.
Studies of the poetry of the psalms, or more precisely, of the
structure, style, and poetic devices, are very few. None of
these studies has presented a full scale investigation of these
matters, although three scholars have attempted a poetic over-
view of the scroll. Translators have been content to note a
few general comments on the poetry, or to put their translations into bicola and stanzas without commenting on the process.

Yet, as Frank Moore Cross has observed, these psalms and
others in the Qumran material form the bridge between OT and NT
poetry. Although they are composed in Hebrew, and employ many
phrases from the Psalter, they are quite different from even

the latest canonical psalms; they bear many resemblances to
hymns in the NT.[16] Holding such an important place in the history of biblical poetry, they would seem to offer much valuable
evidence, and to be worthy of more detailed exploration in the
area of prosody. At the same time, it can be said that the
translations and theological studies of the Hodayot, valuable
as they are, need the evidence which a thorough study of poetic
structure and technique can offer. In a number of cases an
understanding of the poetic structure solves or helps to solve
textual problems of the translator, and deepens the understanding of the theology of these poems.

These two reasons are quite sufficient for, and in fact,
demand, a complete study of the poetry of the Hodayot. A less
impelling, but aesthetically satisfying reason for such a poetic exploration comes from immersing oneself in these psalms.
The prevailing judgment of these hymns has been that they are
poor imitations of canonical poetry. Licht, for example, comments on the scroll:

> It makes rather awkward use of a great many biblical
> phrases, and although some passages have a bizarre
> grandeur, DST [the Hodayot scroll] is on the whole
> rather humdrum, and does not seem to possess any high
> degree of literary merit. It is also very repetitive,
> to the point of monotony.[17]

Holm-Nielsen uses the term "biblical mosaic" in character-
izing the structure of at least one psalm.[18] Kraft, attempting
to deal with the poetic structures more directly, uses the term
"chaotic" several times in reference to meter or poem organization.[19] Translators such as Carmignac and Bardtke who have
worked a great deal with the texts tend to be less than enthu-
siastic about the hymns. Gaster alone seems to be an exception,
but his translations are so elliptical and paraphrastic that
they offer no real evidence in themselves. Much of this low
opinion of the psalms is due to a lack of understanding of the
poetic forms used at Qumran and to modern distaste for apocalyptic imagery. When these barriers are overcome, the power of
the imagery and the subtleties of the poetic form can speak for
themselves. This study represents an attempt to surmount these
barriers, and a conviction that the poetry of the hymns can
stand alongside the other poetry of the ancient world.

With these aims in view it is well to review what has been
accomplished in the study of the Hodayot. The edition of the
text most in use today is that of Sukenik, who has provided
both plates and transcriptions in '*wsr hmgylwt hgnwzwt*.[20]
Sukenik's transcription has been followed in this study, except
where noted. Other editions of the text were published by
Licht and Habermann, and most recently by Delcor, each with
introductory material and annotated text. Habermann has also
provided vocalization.[21] A vocalized text is also found with
Lohse's translation and a minimal number of notes in *Die Texte
aus Qumran*.[22]

Translations of the Hodayot, separately or with other
Qumran texts, abound. Best known of the translations of the
collected Qumran writings are those of Vermes, Dupont-Sommer,
Burrows, and Gaster,[23] but there are others.[24] Among the
translators of the Hodayot alone are Bardtke, Holm-Nielsen,
Mansoor, Molin, van Selms, Wallenstein, Carmignac, Delcor, and
van der Woude.[25] Most of these scholars have provided their
translations with copious notes on textual and syntactical
problems. All translate the eighteen extant columns, dividing
them into a series of psalms by following hints in the text and
their own judgment. The collected works meant for popular use
generally have fewer notes than the others, and the studies by
Mansoor, Holm-Nielsen, and Wallenstein, intended for scholarly
use, provide the most detailed and complete comments.

These works represent a wide spectrum in types of translation. Gaster probably represents one extreme; his translation
is the most poetic by modern standards, but this poetry is
often achieved by elliptical and paraphrastic renderings, and
occasional unexplained emendations or transpositions. Burrows'
translation, which does not cover the whole scroll, is indicative of the other extreme: a translation as close as possible
to the literal which is understandable in English. The other
translations fall between these poles, although on the whole,
they tend to be closer to the standards of Burrows than Gaster.

In this study of the poetic structure, the valuable textual, lexicographical, and syntactical work done by these translators has been utilized many times. The problems of the translator, however, are not the problems of the study of poetic

structure. There is some overlap, of course, since an understanding of the language and syntax is vital to both. But
English (or French or German) translations can never fully indicate the poetic conventions of the Hebrew, nor allow a full
appreciation of them. Translations can often smooth over
problems in understanding poetic structure so that they apparently disappear, and conversely, translations can create problems where there were none for the original hearers. A scholar
who tries to deal with problems of poetry in conjunction with
translations without a clear delineation of his problem often
creates unnecessary problems for himself, as can be seen in the
critique of two writers which follows. The translations provided with the analysis of the hymns in this study are provided
for the reader's convenience. Each translation reflects the
matters discussed in the analysis, and while it is as accurate
as possible in lexicographical matters, it also attempts to re-
tain those organizational features important to the original
hearers of the poem.

Translations generally do not exist for their own sake.
Many translators and commentators have had theological inter-
ests in these psalms which they have attempted to elucidate.
The theology of the Hodayot appears to be generally the same as
that of the other Qumran sectarian documents. The same great
eschatological theme of warfare between the preordained forces
of good and evil leading to a final judgment by God is present
in the Hodayot as it is in the Manual of Discipline and the War
Scroll. There are also some noteworthy differences from the
other scrolls.

1. There are no historical references in these psalms.
    (Moses is mentioned once in connection with a
    scriptural law, 17:12.) This is in great contrast
    to the pesharim and the War Scroll.
2. There are no references to the coming of the
    Messiahs and/or a Prophet. It was thought in the
    early days of Hodayot studies that 3:3-18 referred
    to the birth of a Messiah but later studies have[26]
    shown this to be a misunderstanding of the text.
3. There are references to the sect in these psalms,
    but always from the viewpoint of the speaker ("I").
4. The Hodayot scroll, in fact, is the only one of
    the scrolls found so far written from the viewpoint
    of the first person, and describing intensive
    suffering and the experience of salvation.

The most commonly held view among those who have worked
with the theology of this scroll is that these observations
point to authorship by a prominent teacher of the cult, namely
the Teacher of Righteousness (Bardtke, Hyatt, Glanzmann, Molin,
Carmignac). He is seen as the natural author of a collection
of writings in the first person which was apparently cherished
by the community. The miseries and troubles described in the
psalms fit well with the persecutions described in the Habakkuk
pesher. The lack of historical references then falls away as
the psalms are read as personal descriptions of incidents in
the Teacher/author's life.[27]

Attractive as this view is, it is built on a fallacious
assumption and circular argument. While the Teacher of Righteousness is a figure known from the other Qumran scrolls, all
descriptions of him are couched in the apocalyptic language of
an eschatologically ordered community. With the use of outside, controlled data, such descriptions can be related to per-
sons and events otherwise known in history, but much of what
appears to be specific description is actually the application
of formalized, scriptural language which provided the stamp of
authenticity to the community's interpretation of their experiences as in the "last times." Cross, who has worked extensively
with these documents, sums up the problem.

> Theoretically the allusions in biblical commentaries
> can be utilized in reconstructing the history of the
> sect. On the other hand, the elusive character of
> the data suggests that we can achieve sound historical
> results only by utilizing outside controls to limit
> the framework within which our sources operate. Con-
> cretely this means that we must approach the problems
> relating to the historical interpretation of our texts
> by first determining the time period set by archaeo-
> logical data, by paleographical evidence, and by other
> more objective methods before applying the more sub-
> jective techniques of internal criticism.[28]

Cross concludes that the Teacher of Righteousness will
always remain a shadowy figure on the basis of the descriptions
from these documents. It would seem that in the case of the
Hodayot the problem is compounded by the absence of the historical references of the other scrolls. Undaunted by such sober
warnings, many scholars have concluded that since the Teacher
of Righteousness is described as suffering and persecuted, and

the author of the Hodayot also speaks of suffering, the two
must be the same. Once having made this identification, they
see the distresses related in these psalms as events in the
life of the Teacher, and thus affirm by this circular argument
that he wrote them. In countering this latter argument, Holm-
Nielsen, who has done the most intensive study of the use of
the OT in the Hodayot, has commented:

> In each case it can be ascertained that the expression
> is borrowed from one or more places in the Old Testa-
> ment. For this reason, one must be especially careful
> in applying a concrete interpretation; if one first
> allows oneself to do this, it can easily become arbi-
> trary where one limits the interpretation;... As
> things stand now, one must conclude that the author,
> or authors, felt bound strongly to the Old Testament
> example even to the choice of words, but this means
> simply that he felt himself to be in the same situation
> as portrayed in the Old Testament. He drew therefore
> upon the portrayals of misery from the scripture and
> applied them to himself and to his own time. The main
> consideration is thus not that these expressions suit
> in detail his own life, but that the Old Testament
> portrayals are now fulfilled in his own experience.[29]

Because of the eschatological and apocalyptic viewpoint of
the scrolls, no identification of the Teacher as the author of
the Hodayot is possible. He may have been the author of some
or all of the psalms, but it is just as possible that another,
or several others of the sect, could have composed them. One
thing must be admitted; a collection of psalms, composed in the
biblical pattern, all belonging to one literary category, is
unusual and *may* point to an author or redactor with a highly
original viewpoint. Poetry of other types was composed at Qumran; other psalms are found both in the Manual of Discipline
and the War Scroll. Since the Hodayot seem to be more than
"private poetry," meant for meditation, this adherence to a
single pattern in the collection needs further explanation.

Holm-Nielsen's remarks on the application of scripture by
the community to itself buttresses his view that whoever the
author of these psalms was, the Hodayot could be used in cultic
worship at Qumran. The "I" of the psalms, and the intense
religious fervor of these poems, being based on such scriptural
language understood eschatologically, could be embraced by the

whole community as their experience, too. The personal thanksgiving psalms in the OT certainly came to be used and applied
by the community as a whole. Because canonical personal psalms
were, by the time the Hodayot were written, used in communal
worship, it is wise to be cautious of Jacob Licht's comment on
the basis of the personal flavor of the hymns that they are
"remarkably individualistic."[30]

Most discussions of the Hodayot's theology are arranged
topically. This is an arrangement commonly employed in works
on OT and NT theology, but Licht apparently felt it necessary
to further justify this systematizing. As a preface to his
topical recapitulation he states his belief that behind the
repetitious psalms there is a "conscious speculation" about "a
definite theological system."[31] His article, then, is only the
delineation of a system already present. While his arrangement
is more natural than most such systematic presentations, with
one topic flowing naturally into the next, there is not much in
the structure or content of the Hodayot that justifies his initial statement. Mansoor does not attempt to justify dealing
with the theology of the Hodayot theme by theme. His topics,
which include most of those Licht worked into his essay, are
those used in standard OT schemes, and also include topics
normally associated with apocalyptic writings: angelology,
dualism, spirit, resurrection.

Two other well-known scholars must also be mentioned here
for their similar treatments of the sectarian theology as a
whole: Nötscher and Ringgren.[32] Within these works the theology of the Hodayot takes its place as a contributing factor to
the total sectarian view. The one problem of this total approach is that the inconsistencies or contrary opinions of the
various Qumran authors fade from the scene and a synthetic over-
view of all the writers is achieved at this price. Not only do
the various Qumran writers hold quite different opinions on a
subject, but a writer himself may not be entirely consistent in
his view. Licht has noted this several times in his study of
the Hodayot's theology.[33] The psalms stress both the preordi-
nation of all things and man's choice to do good or evil. No
particular effort is made to resolve the contradiction; both

statements are considered true by the psalmist. Even Licht's
notation of inconsistencies is far from complete, and is simply
a reflection of the fact that systematic, topical arrangements
are far from the manner in which the Hodayot's author(s) were
accustomed to express their fatih.

A second approach to the theology of the Hodayot has been
to summarize, psalm by psalm, the themes of the poet. This
eliminates the artificial pattern of the topical arrangement,
and allows inconsistencies to stand. Both Mansoor and Holm-
Nielsen provide such summaries in their works. The problem
here is that no synthesis is offered, and a reader can get lost
in the repetition or play upon a theme.

As an introduction to the theology of the scroll, the
following brief remarks can be made. It seems clear now that
the Qumran sect, probably Essenes, were a true branch of Judaism in the last centuries B.C. and the first century A.D.
They stand out from the rest of Judaism in the intensity of
their eschatological and messianic hopes, their separation from
the rest of society, which they considered impure, and their
extreme emphasis on the election of man to salvation or damna-
tion. These beliefs were incorporated into a unique day-to-day
life pattern in the Qumran community, a pattern including every
aspect of life, cultic or mundane.[34] The theological themes of
the Hodayot represent one (possibly more) individual's discern-
ment of God's working with man in what this community considered the last times.

Three summary statements bring out the central thrust of
these psalms.

1. The focus of the poems is God and his attributes,
   always seen in relation to man and to God's world
   plan, with an emphasis on the final judgment.

2. All the psalms are set in the context of thanksgiving to God for his deliverance from sin,
   distress, and evil men.

3. The author(s) thought naturally and characteris-
   tically in terms of contrast: God--man, purity--
   sin, life--death, salvation--damnation.

This latter characteristic is usually considered as a
separate topic, "dualism." The connotations of this term,
however, are usually limited simply to the "doctrine of the two

spirits" and the consequent division between the sons of light
and the sons of darkness. Though the importance of the war
between these two elements is frequently stressed, this theme
by no means exhausts the contrasting powers and values introduced in the Hodayot. Due to the prevalent use of contrast in
the hymns, it could be called a poetic device, but this too
seems to be less than a full appreciation. Whether we call it
dualism or contrast, it seems better to see this attribute as a
major way of classifying (and mythologizing) the world on the
part of the author of the hymns, and perhaps of the whole Qumran sect. It has much in common with the theological outlook
of Deuteronomy, and not surprisingly, Deuteronomic quotations
and references are frequent in all the Qumran writings.

The imagery in which the author's faith is couched is
apocalyptic, a mixture of metaphors drawn from the OT and
placed on the vaster plain of the ultimate struggle between God
and the forces of evil. The theology and imagery of the individual poems is explored in the following chapters as each
psalm is analyzed. These explorations are not intended to be
exhaustive, but to indicate the main lines of theme development
and the way in which an understanding of the poetic structure
enhances meaning.

Before reviewing the work already done on poetic structure, one other work on the Hodayot must be mentioned. Svend
Holm-Nielsen has not only given a translation of these hymns,
but has painstakingly surveyed the OT backgrounds of each hymn.[35]
He has done this in two ways. First, in his notes to his translation he has explored the syntactical and lexicographical usage
of the poet in terms of OT vocabulary and syntax. Following
these notes he writes of the allusions and quotations from the
OT in the hymn. The information so presented often overlaps in
the two sections, of course, but the arrangement is logical.
Holm-Nielsen's work is so far unique in the field in this re-
spect. Other scholars have tried to point out OT syntax, allusions, and quotations in their work, but Holm-Nielsen alone gives
this information systematically and with some attempt at completeness.

Two criticisms must be made of Holm-Nielsen's work, however. First, he does not define what he means by "allusion,"
"inspiration," and "quotation"--the three terms most frequently
employed in his analysis. Although there would seem to be
quite a difference between these terms, the usage of them is
often fuzzy and rather subjective. What is often labeled a
"quotation" is the use of one or two words occurring in the
same form somewhere in the OT. Except in rare cases, this
would seem rather to be an "allusion," or even, in a few cases
a coincidence, since the thought of the Qumran poet is usually
quite different than the OT passage in question. At best,
"quotations" refer not to the modern practice at all, but to
paraphrase or quoting from memory.

A second problem with Holm-Nielsen's work is that it seems
he is often misled by vocabulary or morphology. When a rather
unusual Hebrew word appears in a hymn, he is inclined to see
the hymn passage as "inspired by," or "alluding to" the OT passage where a similar word or form is found, even though other
OT passages are far closer in general content or even vocabulary
than the one he has chosen. For example, the occurrence of the
word ויתמוגגו in Hodayot 3:34 leads him to assign the inspiration of the passage to Psalm 107.[36] Yet the themes of these
two passages are quite different; in fact, the theme and
vocabulary are far closer to Nahum 1:5, where the form התמגגו
occurs. Holm-Nielsen's work, then, must be used with some
caution.

Finally we come to those who have written on poetic style
and structure of the Hodayot. The earliest of these scholars
was Charles F. Kraft.[37] He apparently intended a full scale
study of poetic technique, but never completed this, and his
article represents in some ways a "bare-bones" outline of the
larger study. Kraft's method, like the method of this study,
was to isolate for study first of all the complete poems in the
Hodayot. His criteria were slightly different than those outlined in the next chapter, but most of the units he chose coincide with the ones I have delineated.[38] After selecting these
units he analyzes three of the poems in some detail, and briefly summarizes the chief features of the others.

Kraft's article offers a number of observations on poetic
organization in the Hodayot which are valuable starting points
for further investigation, and his plan of looking for objective criteria as a starting point is not only the logical one,
but the necessary one. However, numerous problems arise with
Kraft's viewpoint. Kraft, like many others, came to the Hodayot with the assumption that OT poetic conventions were the
categories with which the Hodayot must also be analyzed. His
analysis of meter and parallelism in the hymns show clearly
that he had little question that current understandings of OT
poetic conventions were the categories with which the Hodayot
could and should be explored. When OT conventions break down
in the hymns, Kraft, rather than speculating on different techniques which might be current at Qumran, simply concludes:

> The variety of metrical structure in these poems seems
> to amount almost to metrical chaos. Either the meter
> is completely adjusted to the flow of the poet's ideas
> or, perhaps, meter is really considered to be of no
> consequence.[39]

> The parallelism is basic, not rigid. In line after
> line there seems to be no hesitation about adding a
> stichos of dependent comment or piling up additional
> words in successive stichos or even lines....Most
> likely this freedom in the use of parallelism is due,
> not to imitation, but to the sense of the liberty to
> express whatever the free mind of the poet wishes
> with no rigid rules cramping one's style.[40]

Not only does Kraft fail to appreciate the possibilities
of a different type of poetry at Qumran, but he is somewhat
weighted with terminology and criteria for Hebrew poetry which
has come under question in the years since his article was completed. While his understanding of meter in canonical poetry
is perhaps still the generally accepted one, and therefore
workable, his assumptions on the strophe in Hebrew poetry are
definitely open to challenge. Kraft believes that in canonical
poetry, the strophe is composed of a "couplet"--either two bicola (or tricola) or three bicola (or tricola).[41] When this
assumption is brought to the study of the Hodayot a number of
difficulties arise. Kraft admits that in many cases the scheme
will not work, and there are overhanging parts. He offers some
valuable terminology for dealing with these sections (e.g.,

"envelope form").[42] However, the problems arise not where he
has seen difficulties with his scheme, but where he has not
seen difficulties. In many cases he has set out lines as bicola or tricola which are not parallel to each other, and which
can be shown by other rhetorical features to belong structurally with different lines. The reader cannot always be certain
what Kraft intends here because he has chosen to show his poetic schemes in English translation rather than with the Hebrew
original.

To illustrate the difficulties of working with a translation, his analysis of 2:25-28 may be cited. Kraft analyzes
these lines, strophe 4 of his hymn, as a triad (three sets of
bicola or tricola): a tricolon, a second tricolon, and a final
bicolon. His tricola are outlined here.

חנו עלי גבורים
סבבום בכל כלי מלחמותם
ויפרו חצים לאין מרפא

ולהוב חנית באש אוכלת עצים
וכהמון מים רבים שאון קולם
נפץ וזרם להשחית רבים

Rather than arguing his point from the Hebrew text, he appeals
to his English translation to show the relationships of the
tricola.

> There have encamped against me mighty men;
>> they have surrounded me with all their weapons of war;
>> and they have loosed arrows without healing.
> And the spear's flashing is with fire consuming trees;
>> and as the roar of many waters is the noise of their
>> voice;
>> a tempestuous cloudburst destroying many.[43]

The English translation carries the weight of his argument that
there are two tricola as opposed to any other arrangement here.
But the translation, which for the first tricolon is almost
literal,[44] becomes paraphrastic at the beginning of the second,
implying a syntactical difference not in the original. This
points up the dangers of working with translations in delineating poetic structure.

A more objective look at poetic conventions in these hymns
is provided by Jean Carmignac.[45] He has organized his article
around increasingly larger units in Hebrew poetry, as understood
from the canonical books, exploring first the stich, then the

couplet, and finally the strophe. At each level, he makes
some observations about the meter and parallelism as well. Not
so freighted with assumptions about the possible usage of these
categories as Kraft, Carmignac observed that, at each level,
the tendency of the Hodayot author was for longer units than
those preferred by biblical authors.[46] Carmignac was willing
to accept, without a prior judgment on quality, the idea of a
stich of seven or eight words, and even suggests that a couplet
may be as long as eleven or twelve lines.[47] (Kraft's outside
limit was nine.) Furthermore, rather than identifying such a
couplet with the stanza or strophe, Carmignac looked basically
to the manuscript for his strophic identifications. He maintains that strophes in the Hodayot can be picked out in two
ways: (1) from spaces left by the copyist, where such spaces
are clearly not evidences of marginal fitting; and (2) by the
strategic use of the independent pronouns at the beginning of
new units.[48]

On the whole, Carmignac's comments are made with great
force, and even with a sense of delight at the ingenuity of the
author. His observations on certain stichs and couplets have
been of great aid to this thesis, as can be seen by the footnotes. Of his criteria for establishing strophic limits there
is much to be said. Unfortunately, the use of spaces by the
copyists is not as clear as Carmignac would have readers believe. Marginal fitting was practiced by Qumran scribes, and
has been observed in this scroll. However, it is not automati-
cally possible to ascribe a space left in the scroll either to
marginal fitting or else to strophic arrangement, as Carmignac
suggests.[49] His comments on the strategic use of independent
pronouns are greatly to the point, and indeed these are one of
the most valuable indicators of division between strophes or
stanzas.

Apparently Carmignac was not greatly interested in whole
poems, since his article closes with his comments on strophe
and his few comments on entire poems are relegated to footnotes.
If one general criticism of Carmignac's work can be made, it is
that he was content to deal with certain structures in Qumran
poetry, but did not attempt to put these in their full perspective. He concludes that the Qumran poet everywhere enjoyed

more amplitude in expression in comparison with his biblical
counterpart, and implies that this is the major difference between this late poetry and canonical psalms.

As far as Carmignac went in his investigations, his conclusion is both justified and correct. It is somewhat disappointing, however, that Carmignac chose to confine himself
to the traditionally recognized structures in canonical poetry.
As we are now beginning to see, delineations of stich or line,
bicola and tricola, even of stanzas, by no means exhausts the
stylistic repertoire of the canonical poet. The Hodayot, which
are admittedly different from canonical poetry, may be expected
to employ a similar wide range of structural and stylistic features. For this reason, Carmignac's work, valuable as it is in
studying the poetry of the Hodayot, has not provided the point
of departure for this investigation.

What Carmignac failed to do has been attempted by Barbara
Thiering in her article on the Hodayot.[50] Unlike older scholars, Thiering actually accepted in fact as well as theory the
idea that the Hodayot were different from canonical poetry.
Rather than seeing the hymns as poor imitations of the biblical
style, or more amplified in form--conclusions which result from
studying the Hodayot with only canonical criteria in mind--she
looked for a structural characteristic which would provide a
key to the passages long considered chaotic and monotonous.

> When the Hodayot are examined with the purpose of dis-
> covering their own poetic conventions, alien as these
> may be, it becomes evident that they are written ac-
> cording to strong principles of form, and are in fact
> more formally constructed than most Old Testament
> poetry. Whether the elaborate nature of the forms,
> and the intricate way in which they are often inter-
> woven, constitutes literary merit, is a matter of
> opinion, but at least the impression of formlessness
> must be considerably revised as a result of these
> investigations.[51]

Thiering believed that an examination of the Hodayot to discover "their own poetic conventions" revealed that the "main
key to the formal structure of the hymns is *chiasmus*."[52]
Basing her work solidly on the work of Lund,[53] she traces this
key structure in the various hymns, along with two other "patterns" of structure: lists and gathering lines. The latter is

her term for a line of poetry which is composed chiefly of
words found earlier in the poetic unit under study. Such a
line "gathers" a word or two from several previous lines.[54]

It may be seen from the description just given, and from
her work itself that Thiering both succeeds and fails in her
objective to discover the hymns' own structure. In her willing-
ness to consider the importance of such stylistic features as
chiasmus, she has broken free of the major obstacle to appreci-
ating the hymns: the assumption, conscious or unconscious, that
standardly recognized canonical criteria are adequate for analysis of Qumran poetry. However, as might be expected from
her limitation of exploration to one major and two minor structural patterns, Thiering has failed at times to let the hymns
speak for themselves in structural matters. The chiastic
structures outlined often seem forced. Occasionally she imposes *chiasmus* on the hymns in a more rigid manner than the
original poet himself. In 12:4-7, the "Time Hymn," she trans-
poses two phrases in order to achieve perfect chiasm, but admits that the original order was probably that of the poet himself who preferred a chronological scheme to a chiastic scheme.[55]

The greatest problem with most of the structures Thiering
outlines is that she bases her understanding of chiasm on simple vocabulary repetitions, without regard to surrounding patterns of syntax, morphology, and rhetoric. Where she was able
to do so, she pointed out the total balance of units in theme
and style as well as word repetition--and these are her most
convincingly argued arrangements. Where no such balance occurs,
she rests her case on simple word repetitions. In many analyses of the latter type, she actually fails to recognize the
structural bases of the poem. For example, in the hymn in 2:
20-30 both Kraft and Carmignac have commented on the strategic
use of the independent pronouns, which apparently delineate the
stanzas of the poem. Analysis of other phenomena in the poem--
parallelism, even meter calculated by standard means--confirm
this stanza division. Thiering's chiastic structure totally
disregards the pronouns, and she has to admit that one section
in her analysis is "irrelevant to the main chiasm."[56]

An examination of Thiering's work reveals that several
"chiasms" should more accurately be called "inclusios." In
these cases, opening and closing motifs recall each other, but
the body of the poem has a different organizational pattern.[57]
This clears up many of the problems with Thiering's analysis
of 2:20-30, for example. In other cases, Thiering has failed
to recognize the importance of prepositions, or has been
trapped by the repetition of a single word frequently employed
in the psalms (e.g., נפש) into matching sections in a chiastic
arrangement.[58]

Where even determined effort fails to yield a chiastic
structure, Thiering labels the poem's structure as "baffling,"
even if she detects other balancing features.[59] By so doing,
Thiering reveals that she, like other scholars, has been trapped
by her own assumptions; in this case, that *chiasmus* is the
"main key" to the poetry of the Hodayot. If the study of canonical poetry offers any analogy, the stylistic devices and structures of the Hodayot may be expected to cover a range of accept-
able patterns, rather than employing only one or two devices.

Nevertheless, Thiering's work points the way for further
investigation. The hymns must be allowed to speak of their own
poetic conventions. Connections in style, language, and certain
structural devices to canonical poetry may be expected, but none
should be the standard by which the hymns are judged, nor the
procrustean bed into which these poems are fit at any cost. The
poetic analysis of this study leans toward the descriptive
rather than the definitive. It attempts as complete as possible
a study of poetic structures and devices, and yet does not maintain that all such patterns are discovered. Nevertheless, when
the description of the hymns has been made, it seems clear that
certain conclusions can be drawn as to poetic syntax, style,
larger structures and meter. These will appear at their proper
place after the study of the individual poems.

CHAPTER II

THE CONDITION OF THE TEXT AND THE METHOD OF ANALYSIS

The photographs of the Hodayot scroll, taken in the un-
rolling process, reveal quite clearly the miserable state in
which it came into Sukenik's hands. The scroll consisted of
two bundles, the first of which contained three sheets of
leather, each with four columns of text (columns 1-12). When
Sukenik received the scroll, two of the sheets were folded together with the third forced into the bundle. The photos of
these sheets unfolded indicate that originally they had been
sewn together and rolled up as the other scrolls were. The
bottom and the top of this roll had rotted away, as well as a
substantial portion of those columns on the outer part of the
roll. The second bundle was a crumpled mass of congealed
leather containing about seventy fragments. Among these fragments it was possible to piece together parts of six additional
columns. All eighteen columns suffered from numerous lacunae
and blackened leather.[1]

As expected from the above description, the text is poorly
preserved. Sukenik's plates show a copy hand which is easily
read but whose work is mutilated by ragged holes and blackened
leather. Infrared photography was used to produce these plates,[2]
but even so, there are many illegible letters. The amount preserved in each column varies from twenty lines in the more fragmentary columns to forty-one lines in the best preserved. The
top margin is missing completely, and part of the bottom margin
is visible only in columns 4, 7, and 8. In some cases the right-
or left-hand margin is missing for much of a column.[3]

The approximate date at which the scroll was written can be
determined from archaeological and paleographical evidence.
Ceramic and numismatic evidence from Cave I and from Khirbet
Qumran suggests that the scroll was deposited in the cave no
later than 68 A.D.[4] Carbon 14 tests of linen fragments from
scroll wrappings found in the cave give a date of about 35 A.D.,
plus or minus 200 years.[5] According to Birnbaum, who has done
the most extensive paleographical study of the Qumran scrolls,

21

the scripts of the Hodayot scroll come from approximately the
same period as the War Scroll and the Habakkuk pesher, which he
dates to the middle of the first century B.C.[6]

A precise date for the Hodayot scroll is not vital to an
examination of its poetic structure (though it would be of interest in the history of Hebrew poetry). It is sufficient to
note that the scroll certainly is tied to the Qumran sect, and
that this copy probably originated in the early decades of the
period of the chief occupation of Qumran (100 B.C.-68 A.D.).

The Hodayot scroll is certainly not an autograph copy by
the author. Evidence for this is quite clear. Scraps of several Hodayot scrolls have been found in Cave IV,[7] suggesting
that this scroll, like many others, was in popular use at Qumran. Furthermore, the Cave I scroll was copied by at least two
scribes, and was later corrected in a number of places. This
change of copyists and the corrections make it extremely unlikely that this was the original of the author's work.

When Sukenik edited the Hodayot, he commented on the two
copy hands which can be clearly discerned in the scroll. The
first copyist, designated A, is replaced by a second copyist,
B, in the middle of line 22 in column 11. In Copyist B's handwriting are columns 12 and 18 and some of the fragments as well.
Since Copyist A was responsible for columns 13-17, it was clear
that the numbering of the columns of the scroll did not represent their original order. Sukenik therefore remarked that the
order of the surviving columns would seem to be columns 13-17,
1-11:22 (A's work), followed by 11:22-12, 18 (B's work).[8] This
ordering has been accepted by the majority of scholars, and certainly cannot be far wrong as far as the relative ordering of
what has survived of the original work is concerned.

Modifications and challenges to Sukenik's view have been
offered. Malachi Martin believes that he can distinguish a
third copyist's hand in the scroll in 11:22-26 and in corrections in both A and B's work. Martin believes that this evidence, together with other scribal habits and the orthographical differences between A's work and the rest of the scroll,
suggests that the Hodayot were compiled from several sources.[9]
Svend Holm-Nielsen also believes a third copyist was involved

in writing the scroll, but he finds this copyist at work in the
sections assigned to Copyist A. Rather than drawing his conclusions from a wide variety of scribal phenomena, as Martin
does, Holm-Nielsen bases his argument on one feature: the existence of two different orthographical systems in the A sections.
These differences can be summarized as follows.[10]

Columns 1-11 use: Columns 13-17 use:

כה (2 m.s. suffix)   ך (2 m.s. suffix)

כיא   כי

לוא   לא

בלא   בלוא

כל   כול

On this evidence, Holm-Nielsen assigns columns 1-11 to one
copyist, and columns 13-17 to another. He admits that the
orthographical differences in the two sections are not entirely
consistent--that in both sections כיא and כי occur, but bases
his argument on the predominance of one form over the other.
He shows this predominance in percentage form: כיא is used in
20% of the occurrences of this particle in columns 1-11, and
only 13% of the instances in columns 13-17. Even on this basis, it might be asked whether such a finding is significant.
but Holm-Nielsen's whole argument collapses with Martin's observation that not a single column, nor a single hymn, employs
one form of this word without the other.[11]

Of interest to scholars also has been the attempt by Carmignac to determine the original limits of the Hodayot scroll.[12]
This has involved the examination of the fragments, not only
those published by Sukenik, but also those subsequently found
in Cave I excavation and published by Barthélemy and Milik.[13]
Many of these fragments are too small to yield more than a word
or two of text, and contribute little to the search. By com-
paring the shapes of the larger pieces Carmignac has been able
to make a guess at the number of missing columns, since two
fragments of approximately the same shape presumably belonged
to different columns of the scroll. As the scroll deteriorated,
layer after layer of the roll was penetrated by rot, so that the
jagged holes of the outer layers are mirrored in the shape of
the holes of the inner layers. Besides this clue, the fragments

in the handwriting of Copyist A obviously must belong to columns
missing early in the scroll, and those in B's handwriting to
the end of the scroll. To the fragmentary columns identified
in this manner by Carmignac, smaller pieces sometimes can be
fitted. Carmignac concludes that the original scroll contained
eight sheets of four columns each.

Sheet 1:	columns 13-16 (four columns to a sheet, as shown by photographs of the larger bundle).
Sheet 2:	consisted of four columns, the first of which is entirely lost, and the other three are represented by fragment 15, and columns I and II of Milik.
Sheet 3:	consisted of three missing columns and column 17.
Sheets 4-6:	columns 1-12, in order.
Sheet 7:	consisted of four columns represented by fragments 5, 1, 46, 58, column 18, fragments 62, 61, 57, 9, 50, and 6. (B's handwriting.)
Sheet 8:	consisted of four columns, the first three represented by 8, 2, 7, 3, and 4 of the numbered fragments. The final column is missing. (B's handwriting.)

Carmignac further suggested that sheets 1 and 2 represented
an earlier, separate scroll, to which sheets 3-8 were later
added. In his final article on this subject,[14] he suggested
that the differences in themes which he detected between these
two rolls were due to the author's experience of extreme suffering in the interim period, on which he reflected in his later
work. In Carmignac's view, this author was certainly the
Teacher of Righteousness. The analysis of the extent of the
original scroll is not dependent on Carmignac's comments on
authorship. The possible change in thematic matter, like the
orthographical differences pointed out by Holm-Nielsen, are
just as plausibly accounted for by a compilation of sources in
the scroll as by the changes in the life of the Teacher of Righteousness. While Carmignac's scheme of the whole scroll requires several assumptions as well as keen observation, it is a
logical analysis of the available data.

The work which has already been done in delineating the
poetic structure of the Hodayot has been outlined in Chapter I.
All of these studies represent partial explorations on this
topic, and leave many questions unanswered. A detailed analysis

of a large portion of the hymns seems desirable. Since so much
is missing of the text, however, it seems wise to set some con-
trol on the material for examination. The best and most complete texts are obviously desirable. Fortunately, the author(s)
and the copyists have provided us with some objective criteria
in determining the limits of a psalm.

The hymns employ a standard introductory phrase, אודכה
אדוני; and each time the formula appears, the copyist has indicated a new paragraph. Two types of paragraph spacing were
used. In some cases the formula appears at the right-hand
margin of a new line, and the previous line is completed some
distance before the left-hand margin.[15] In other places the
formula is indented to the middle of the new line, and the previous line is also completed before the left-hand margin.[16]
There are other paragraphing marks as well, but where the
thanksgiving formula and one of the above paragraphing marks
coincide it may be fairly assumed that a new hymn begins.

Due to the ravages of time, the formula may now be missing
in places, and the limits of some hymns may have to be guessed.
Sometimes the formula does not appear for several columns. This
may indicate very long hymns, but since the formula appears twice
in five of the columns, and in column seven appears three times,
it seems likely that the formula is now missing in several places.
Generally, scholars have guessed at the limits of the psalms in
these cases. Dupont-Sommer and Licht each divide the scroll into
thirty-two psalms in this way. They do not always agree on the
limits of these psalms. Mansoor has harmonized these two schemes
in his translation without attempting to solve their differences.[17] Holm-Nielsen follows Licht's numbering for columns 1-
12, but in 13-18 he sets his own limits for the psalms, with a
new psalm beginning at the top of each of the last six columns.[18]

In any case, none of these subjective divisions, convenient as they are for studying the scroll, are of value for a
more thorough examination of poetic structures. To guess at
the limits of a psalm on the basis of themes imposes modern
assumptions on the material at the outset, and may distort
other evidence. Those hymns which can be judged complete offer
the best evidence for inquiry. Complete hymns are those whose

beginning and end can be determined by the paragraphing conventions described earlier; where the opening thanksgiving formula can be seen at the start of the psalm and also observed at the beginning of the next psalm, and the lacunae are not so lengthy that such a formula could be missing, the psalm can be judged complete.[19]

A study of the scroll reveals nine psalms whose limits are quite certain: 2:20-30; 3:19-36; 5:5-19; 7:6-25, 26-33; 9:37-10:12; 11:3-14; 14:8-22; and 17:17-25. The last hymn has such a large number of lacunae that it is not a good candidate for poetic analysis. 9:37-10:12 has several lines missing at the beginning of the poem (at the bottom of column 9) but enough hints remain to judge it a complete poem by the method outlined above.

This study begins with an examination of each of these hymns in turn, according to the method outlined below. Following these analyses, there is a recapitulation of the chief techniques, forms, and syntactical phenomena which characterize this poetry, with some brief comparisons to canonical Hebrew poetry. In this way it is hoped that the structure of these psalms will be better understood, and that a more exact description of the techniques and devices used in this poetry can be made. It is hoped that an accurate picture is provided of the dependence on canonical Hebrew in language and form, on the one hand; and on the other, that the creativity and originality of the Qumran poet is given its full due.

In discovering the poetic structure of these psalms, the known has to provide the starting point for the exploration of the unknown. Objective observations rather than assumptions are desirable here. The first observation which can be made is that *parallelismus membrorum* is used in these psalms in many places. It is worth reviewing here the description of parallelism given by that early expositor, Lowth.

> The correspondence of one verse, or line, with another,
> I call parallelism. When a proposition is delivered,
> and a second is subjoined to it, or drawn under it,
> equivalent, or contrasted with it, in sense; or similar
> to it in the form of grammatical construction; these I
> call parallel lines, and the words or phrases, answering
> one to another in the corresponding lines, parallel

terms. Parallel lines may be reduced to three sorts:
parallels synonymous, parallels antithetic and
parallels synthetic.[20]

These statements of Lowth were elaborated early in this century
by Gray, who introduced the terms "complete" and "incomplete
parallelism" to describe the degree of correspondence between
two lines of biblical poetry.[21] Freedman has commented that if
all of biblical poetry were placed on a graph showing the degrees of parallelism from incomplete to complete, that a wide
variety of patterns in parallelism in canonical poetry would be
apparent.[22]

    If some of the earlier psalms in the Psalter are set aside
(those employing that pattern also found in Ugaritic poetry
where several lines vary in only a single word or term), the
parallelism of the Hodayot is quite similar in its completeness
(or incompleteness) to that of the Psalms and of the prophets.
That is, in a bicolon or tricolon, the lines employ synonymous
or contrasting terms, and identical grammatical constructions,
to express essentially the same thought twice. In lines in-
completely parallel, the different terms introduced in the
lines extend the thought introduced, and the full sense of the
bicolon must be derived from the combination of the two lines.
This parallelism is of most immediate help in understanding the
structure of the Hodayot, as it is in the Psalter.

    Lists, repetitions of phrases, and chiastically ordered
phrases are also objective evidence that can point up the
structure of the poems. Within some sections of these hymns,
these devices alone provide a clear indication of the structure.
More often, the total hymn structure is still amorphous even
when these devices are identified.

    As Carmignac has observed,[23] independent pronouns are often
set off in the scroll by spacing, and it seems logical to assume
as he does, that these words strategically mark off units within
the poem. Such words are similarly used in canonical poetry,
and therefore it may be asked if other words used at strategic
points in canonical poetry are not also so used in the Hodayot.
With canonical poetry in mind it seems best to consider such
frequently used words as לכן, כי, מי, מה, and הנה as possibly
strategically placed as well.[24]

One other fairly objective observation can be made in regard to possible structural indications. A reading of all the sectarian texts shows that infinitive constructions were extremely popular in both prose and poetry. Even in the prose texts they provide a certain rhythmical sound to the text. It seems likely that in the Hodayot, the occurrence of several infinitive phrases in succession may give some indication of a larger unit. In any case, the infinitive phrases will probably belong to the same unit.

It may be asked if the development of themes within the poem does not give an indication of the structure. Certainly theme development is tied to structure, but unfortunately, themes themselves provide little help in elucidating structure. Where there is a sharp distinction in themes, particularly where an extended simile breaks off, and another begins, some indication of structure is certain. But often this is not the case. Within any hymn there are certain phrases which thematically might belong with preceding matter or with what follows. Instead, it is usually a solid understanding of the poem's structure which elucidates the poem's theme and solves these problems.

Much attention is given to repeated words and phrases. It is assumed that these will often occur at key points in the poem. In many cases this assumption is corroborated by other evidence. The succession or change of finite verb forms as an indicator of units large or small is more problematic. In some cases, repeated forms clearly mark off a unit. More often the verb pattern is such that the analysis is made by feeling and must be confirmed by other data. The use of all these criteria in analyzing the poems has brought the discovery of other poetic techniques and structural devices, and confirmed the presence or absence of others already suggested.

What has been avoided in this exploration is any attempt to find a single structural device which is the key to all the hymns. Like Thiering and Carmignac, I have come to the conclusion that the poetry is not chaotic, but arranged according to its own conventions; but I have not seen any evidence that this order is dependent on a single structural pattern. Similarly,

since traditional methods of reckoning meter in Hebrew poetry
fail to yield much order in these hymns, it seems necessary to
conclude that meter or rhythm was reckoned in a different manner. Observable phenomena in regard to rhythm are of more
value than the simple statement that biblical meter is not used
(see "rhythmical balance," p. 30).

It was originally intended that each hymn would be presented in a single diagram showing all the poetic devices used.
It quickly became apparent that such a diagram would be impos-
sibly cluttered. Instead, the text of each hymn is first given
completely, divided into the stanzas suggested by structural
analysis. In the discussion which follows the text, a diagram
or description is given of each section to illustrate its devices and techniques. In the presentation of the total poem,
the column line numbers from Sukenik's transcription are given
in the left margin for reference. Where a poetic line contains
parts of two column lines, both are given in the margin. Although this system is not exact, it leaves the text uncluttered,
and provides adequate reference.

The introductory formula is set off from the rest of the
poem. In a few cases, a concluding formula has been attached
to the hymn, and it is also set apart. These formulae stand
outside the poem proper. The chief rhetorical or structural
mark of each stanza--the device by which a stanza unit can most
readily be recognized--is indicated in the hymn text in the
following ways:

1. Where a particle, pronoun or other single word
    marks the beginning of a new stanza, it appears
    set off from the rest of the stanza:

והמה סוד שוא ועדת בליעל
לא ידעו כיא מאתכה מעמדי
ובחסדיכה תושיע נפשי

2. Where a single word or syntactical phrase marks
    the beginning of a new stanza and is repeated
    at the beginning of successive bicola (tricola),
    it appears at the right-hand margin each time,
    with the other lines indented:

כי שמחה נפשי בצרור החיים
ותשוך בעדי מכול מוקשי שחת
כי עריצים בקשו נפשי
בתומכי בבריתכה

3. Where a list is a key structural device in a
    stanza, the members of the list are underlined.

4. In an extended prosaic section, the indentations
    of the text are meant to indicate rhythmical
    flow; they are not suggested divisions of the
    material into bicola.

5. In long stanzas, subsections are indicated by
    indenting the first word of the subsections
    only half the distance of the other lines in
    the unit.

To avoid confusion, I am appending the following list of
terms and signs which I use in the discussion of the text and
in diagrams (other technical terms are defined in the Glossary
of Terms).

bicolon/bicola: This is the standard term in use by American
    scholars of OT poetry. It is used to refer to sets of
    parallel lines. Tricola, sets of three parallel lines,
    also occur frequently in the Hodayot. I do not use this
    term to refer to lists which are not set within parallel
    constructions, or to certain types of more prosaic con-
    structions where no real parallelism occurs.

line: In reference to poetry, this is a line of poetry as I
    have shown it in my diagram. It may refer to a single
    line of a bicolon, or to a line in a list, or to a line in
    a more prosaic construction. It is a general, descriptive
    term, not intended to coincide with the definition of
    stich, hemistich or any other standardized unit delineated
    by studies of OT poetry.

stanza: I have chosen this term over others for the larger
    units of the poems. "Strophe" implies a standardized
    unit, which these larger units of the Hodayot are not.

rhythmical balance: This term is chosen rather than meter to
    avoid misunderstanding; under this term I have included
    all material relating to the perception (on our part) of
    rhythmic balance. In some cases, the traditionally dis-
    cussed meters, based on accentual systems, work in these
    poems. In almost all of the poems, however, the psalm
    seems to collapse into metric chaos in one or more sections
    when these systems are used, so that the poem as a whole
    defies metrical analysis. As it will be shown in the fol-
    lowing chapters, the syllable weight of these "chaotic"
    sections quite often balances another section of the poem.
    Combinations of stanzas syllabically balance each other,
    usually in accord with the poem's structure as determined
    by other means. Whatever the metric rules were for the
    author of the Hodayot may not be determinable in our pres-
    ent state of knowledge, but it can be shown that rhythmic

balancing is present by counting the syllables of the
bicola and stanzas. Such syllable counting does not claim
any validity as the metric system used in this period, but
it does offer a way to increase our perception of the
poem's balance and organization.
      Since the Hodayot scroll is unvocalized, counting
syllables may seem to be a risky business. There is a
general agreement among scholars that the text was vocalized in a manner approaching the Massoretic system, and
the two scholars who have vocalized this scroll both do
so with the Massoretic system.[25] To avoid the impression
that exact and rigid counting is involved in achieving
this balance, a minimum and maximum count is given for
most stanzas. This is done because there is some debate
over the way to count segolate nouns and half-open
syllables with shewa. The difference between minimum and
maximum counts is rarely more than six syllables in a
stanza, and usually less. Even with this leeway allowed,
the balance between stanzas is remarkably close in most
of these poems. Observation also suggests that there is
a mathematical relationship between the units in these
poems; more will be said of this in Chapter VI.

} is used to indicate parallel lines, that is, a bicolon.

[ ] are used to indicate restored text; the validity of indi-
    vidual restorations is discussed with each hymn. Gener-
    ally, only restorations which are fairly certain and
    agreed upon by most scholars are included in the poetic
    format.

CHAPTER III

AN EXAMINATION OF THREE HYMNS
WITH APOCALYPTIC IMAGERY

In order to facilitate the analysis of the eight complete hymns in the Hodayot, they have been divided into three groups, to be examined in the next three chapters. These groupings are largely a matter of convenience rather than indicative of major differences between the psalms. Three of the eight psalms (7:6-25, 9:37-10:12, and 14:8-22) have large lacunae that leave certain poetic (and theological) features in doubt. These three are examined last, in Chapter V, so that comments on some of their features can be made in light of the more certain structures of the other hymns. Of the other five complete hymns, three share an interest in apocalyptic imagery that is perhaps more marked than that in 7:26-33 and 11:3-14. These three hymns, then (2:20-30, 3:19-36 and 5:5-19), form the group analyzed in this chapter.

1. Hodayot 2:20-30 (Plate 36)

The text of this short psalm is in remarkably good condition, and is perhaps the best text in the entire scroll. There is a single lacuna, in the middle of line 21, where three letters at the most are missing. More likely, there are two letters missing. There are three other letters which are disputed, due to worn spots in the leather, but on the whole the text is quite legible. The psalm is set off by the usual paragraph indications; the formula in line 20 is indented, and after the closing words of the poem in line 30 the rest of the line is blank. The introductory formula of the next psalm begins on a new line, 31. There are no indications of paragraphing within the body of the psalm, but the coda is set apart by an extra long space in line 29. In two places, additions were made by a third hand some time after the copying of the scroll. The first of these, in line 23, was made in a space left by Copyist A; the second addition, at the end of line 29, begins just within the margin line and runs across the margin into column 3.

These additions and disputed readings are noted in the transcription of the text and are discussed in the pages that
follow.

Hebrew Text of Hodayot 2:20-30

20   אודכה אדוני

21	כי שמחתה נפשי בצרור החיים ותשוך בעדי מכול מוקשי שחת	Opening Stanza
21-22	[כי]ᵃעריצים בקשר נפשי בתומכי בבריתכᵇה	
23	והמה סוד שוא ועדת בליעל לא ידעו כיא מאתכה מעמדי ובחסדיכה תושיע נפשי כיא מאתכה מצעדי	A
23-24	והמה מאתכהᶜ גרו על נפשי בעבור הכבדכה במשפט רשעים	B
24-25	והגבירכה בי נגד בני אדם כיא בחסדכה עמדי	
25-26	ואני אמרתי חנו עלי גבורים סבבוט בכל כלי מלחמותם ויפרו חצים לאין מרפא ולהוב חנית באש אוכלת עצים	C
27	וכהמון מים רבים שאון קולם נפץ וᵈזרם להשחית רבים	
27-28	למזרות יבקעו אפעה ושוא בהתרומט גליהם	
29	ואני במוס לבי כמים ותחזק נפשי בבריתך והם רשת פרשו לי תלכוד רגלם ופחים טמנו לנפשי נפלו בם	Closing Stanza
30	ורגלי ᵉעמדה במישורᵉ מקהלם אברכה שמכה	Coda

ᵃThis is the restoration accepted by the largest group of
scholars. See p. 36.

ᵇFinal ך in a nonfinal position occurs several times in
the Hodayot in the writing of the second person suffix, and can
be considered a simple slip of the pen.

ᶜאתכה was added by a later hand, in a space left by the
first copyist.

ᵈSukenik's transcription does not show ו, but it is
visible in the Plate.

ᵉThese two words were added by a later hand, and run into
the margin between cols. 2 and 3.

Translation of Hodayot 2:20-30[A]

20   I thank you, O Lord,

        For you set my life in the bundle of the living,
21   And you protected me from all the snares of the Pit;
        [For] ruthless men sought my life
21-22   When I held fast to your covenant.

        And they--an assembly of wickedness and the
            congregation of Belial!
        They did not know that from you is my rank,
23   And that with your steadfast love you saved my life,
        For from you are my footsteps.

23-24   And they--forth from you they fought against my life,
        So that you might be glorified in the judgment of
            the wicked,
24-25   And that you might be declared mighty through me
            before the sons of men,
        For in your steadfast love is my stand.

25   And I, I said,
        Mighty men have encamped against me,
        Surrounding <me> with all their weapons of war;
        And arrows without healing have torn,
        And a flaming spear with fire consumes the trees.

27   And like the roar of the deeps is the sound of
            their voice,
        Torrents of rain for the destruction of many;
27-28   Terrible wickedness breaks forth, crushed out,
            in the cresting of their waves.[B]

        And I, when my heart melted like water,
        Then you strengthened my life in your covenant.
29   But they, the net they spread for me has captured
            their feet,
        And the snares they hid for my life, they fell
            in them.

        "But my foot stands on level ground,
30   From the assemblies I will bless your name."[C]

[A]The translations given for the hymns, although they are
placed after the transcription of the psalm for convenience,
reflect the matters discussed in the analysis of the psalm. To
aid the reader who may have questions about the translation,
notes in the translation refer to subsequent discussion of the
problem involved. These notes have been kept to a minimum, because an annotated translation is not the purpose of this study,
but rather poetic analysis.

    Since it is a major contention of this investigation that
poetic analysis aids proper understanding of these psalms, an
effort has been made in the translation to preserve important

Stanza Analysis

The structure of this poem is clearly marked by the recur-
ring independent pronouns, and once this device is recognized,
the balance and movement of the entire psalm can be perceived.[1]
The stanza which follows the customary introductory phrase has
a pattern which is characteristic of the majority of the opening lines of the Hodayot: כי followed by a second masculine
singular perfect verb. True to the form of the thankoffering
psalm, the opening bicolon gives a general statement of salvation from distress. In this poem, this general statement is
repeated and slightly amplified by the second bicolon. The
parallelism of this opening stanza, while not perfect, is certainly not far from the standard parallelism of the canonical
psalms, though the lines of the bicola are slightly longer.

> כי שמחה נפשי בצרור החיים
> ותשוך בעדי מכול מוקשי שחת
>
> [כי] עריצים בקשו נפשי
> בתומכי בבריתכה

The majority of scholars accept the reconstruction כי in
the lacuna before עריצים.[2] Wallenstein, one of the earliest
commentators, suggested the restoration ומעריצים,[3] but there is
a distinct space before עריצים, and this seems unlikely. כי is
the most probable reconstruction, but if the original text was
different, the larger structure of the stanza would remain the
same; the second bicolon could then be understood as subordinate to the initial כי.

---

organizational features--repeated verb forms or strategic
phrases, for example--as aids to understanding. Repeated forms,
chiastic arrangements, construct chains and other features of
Hebrew syntax which are key to the poetic organization are preserved where possible. Changes in word order or expression are
used to avoid awkward or un-English expressions, however.
    Where the text in the psalm has large gaps, the most com-
monly accepted restorations are supplied, or in a few cases
where this is not possible, the general sense required by the
passage is given. These restorations are bracketed, [ ]. In
the rarer cases in which a double duty pronoun or preposition
is employed in Hebrew, this is indicated by a translation
within < >.

BDiscussion of this line, in which there are several obscure expressions, is found on pp. 42-43.

CThe quotation marks are used because this coda was an
obvious borrowing of Ps 26:12. See p. 44.

In these two bicola, the perennial theme of the Hodayot (and indeed of all Qumran sectarian documents) is introduced: the war between the wicked and the righteous, and the corresponding battle between life and death. This use of contrast, found here in the double theme and the anticipated conclusion of the battle, is the chief thematic device of the poem, carried on in the next stanzas by contrasting independent pronouns.

It is interesting that the term ברית is found only in this stanza and the closing stanza, and does not appear in the body of the poem. It is this fact, and the repetition of נפש, on which Thiering bases her chiastic analysis of this poem. In Thiering's diagram, the body of the hymn is merely labeled as the center, with the chiasm confined to the first six lines and the last six lines.[4] The end of the poem does indeed return to the opening theme, including ברית, which is not specifically mentioned in the body of the poem. This device is more properly termed inclusio rather than chiasm, and is frequently employed in the Hodayot.

With the double battle theme introduced (death against life, the wicked against the righteous), the poet develops a strong contrast in the body of the poem. The enemy, the wicked, are consistently identified as "they." Rhythmatically and structurally the body of the poem falls into equal halves, the first focusing on this enemy ("they"), and the second on the author ("I").

The structure suggested for the body of the poem may at first glance appear to be rather irregular. However, the total balance between the halves of the poem is quite good, and, as in canonical poetry, shows an interest in variety as well as in symmetry of construction. In the "they" half of the poem, there seem to be two stanzas (A and B), each opening with the independent pronoun, while the second half has a single long stanza (C).

The four lines of stanza A have quite a different structure than does the opening stanza, but each word or expression in this stanza is as delicately balanced. Instead of two parallel bicola, there is a kind of envelope structure, with lines two and three parallel to each other, and lines one and four providing the frame, or envelope. The recognition of this device

helps to explain the repetitious כיא מאתכה מצעדי which closes
the stanza: taken in conjunction with the first line of the
stanza, which balances it, it summarizes the thought and thematic contrast of the stanza. It is also a kind of refrain
line, echoed in the last line of the next stanza which is
paired structurally and thematically with this one. It is interesting, too, that the rhythmic balance of this stanza apparently follows the structure: lines one and four balance lines
two and three in syllable weight.

The first line of the stanza pairs two common expressions
for the enemies of the Qumran sect. This kind of parallel expression within what is normally considered one line of a bicolon is found in canonical poetry, and is used frequently in
the Hodayot. There is no need to divide this line itself into
a bicolon because of this inner parallelism, as Kraft does.[5]
The proof can be seen in the first line of the following stanza
which begins the same way, and which is exactly the same length.
There is no question there that a single line of a bicolon is
involved. Parallelism within a single line of poetry is an ac-
ceptable stylistic variant at Qumran.

In lines two and three of this stanza can be detected also
the use of a double-duty verb, with a ballast variant (a term
whose weight balances its parallel and the double duty term) in
the following line. (כיא) לא ידעו is intended to be applied to
both lines: "they did not know that my steps are with you; they
did not know that with your *ḥesed* you saved my life." מאתכה
מעמדי is paralleled by a longer phrase in the next line to compensate for the double-duty verb in the previous line.

internal parallel

summary:
repetition

refrain line

רהמה סוד שוא ועדת בליעל
לא ידעו כיא מאתכה מעמדי
ובחסדיכה תושיע נפשי
כיא מאתכה מצעדי

Pronoun marks
new stanza

envelope
lines

The outline of Stanza B is like that of Stanza A: the introductory third masculine plural independent pronoun begins
the first line, the second and third lines are parallel, and
the fourth line is somewhat shorter and a virtual repetition of

the closing line of the previous stanza. There is one minor
textual problem here, however. Copyist A wrote only the מ of
the second word, מאתכה, and the rest of the word was filled
into the blank by a later hand. Since the word appears to be
somewhat awkward and prosaic in the phrase, and since it follows two other usages of the same word in a different expression, its authenticity is questioned.[6] The double use of מאתכה
in the previous stanza suggests an influencing of the blank.
The other two usages occur in strategic places; this occurrence
is not strategic. The thought expressed by the first line of
this stanza is quite in line with the theology of the Hodayot
and the Qumran sectarian documents in general, however. Elsewhere in the Hodayot, the poet speaks of his affliction as intended by God for his purification and God's greater glory; and
the strangeness of the syntax here is probably outweighed by
this consideration. No alternative reconstruction has been
offered by scholars.

The second half of the psalm focuses on the author. The
division is very clearly marked. The two stanzas of the first
half began with והמה; the new unit begins with an emphatic ואני.
It is easily seen that this second half of the poem is roughly
equal in weight to the first half. However, ואני comes only
once in this section in contrast to והמה used twice in the
first half; and other features which would clearly divide this
unit into two equal stanzas are missing as well. The text appears to arrange itself in seven lines, no matter how it is
divided (there are some obscure phrases here). Probably the
section should be regarded as one long stanza, although it is
possible to see a slight inner division between the fourth and
fifth lines that suggests the two-stanza pattern of the first
half. The battle imagery is carried through the entire section, however, with a new image in each line, suggesting a deliberate use of sevenfold structure for symbolic purposes.

There are several minor textual problems in this section
and several major problems of interpretation of unusual terms.
A recognition of the structure outlined above is of help in
some of these cases. Each line of the vivid battle imagery
builds on the previous line, extending the theme with a new

image. The figures of the first four lines clearly deal with
the battlefield: soldiers and weaponry apocalyptically employed.
The last three lines deal with water and its destructive power,
and this shift in imagery, as mentioned earlier, suggests a
slight inner division of the section. Viewed in more traditional terms, it could be stated that this stanza consists of
two bicola and a tricolon equal in length to the two bicola.

With this structure in mind, the problems in interpreting
the text can be examined. Sukenik's transcription of this text
reads סבבם in line 25, and this reading has caused many problems for commentators. Earlier translators (Bardtke, Licht,
Dupont-Sommer, Delcor) emended the text to סבבוני.[7] Mansoor
suggested that the מ was enclitic, but in the end emended the
text as the others do.[8] Carmignac reads סבבים (ו and י are
written identically in the manuscript), and has suggested it is
a Qal participle.[9] However, he is not completely satisfied
with the text and seems to believe, due to the lack of a first-
person object pronoun, that something has fallen out of the
text. There is no necessity for such an assumption. סבבים,
understood as a Qal participle, is almost certainly the correct
reading here.[10] It parallels the גבורים of the previous line,
and can be understood in the noun sense. The idea is clear
without the first-person pronoun--as every translator has
found--and the lack of the pronoun may be considered intentional. עלי, in the previous line, may be seen as supplying, in a
double-duty fashion, the missing pronoun.

In his original transcription of the manuscript, Sukenik
read ויירו for the word at the beginning of line 26 (the third
line of this stanza), and the root then would be ירה, "cast."
Wallenstein emended this to ויגרו taking the verb from the root
נגר, "pour out."[11] Later editions of Sukenik's work read ויפרו,
and the פ is quite distinct in the photographs of the manuscript.
The root is then believed by most scholars to be פרר, "shatter,
rend."

Kraft understands חצים, the following word, to be the object of ויפרו, perhaps emended to ויגרו.[12] In this case the
antecedent for the pronoun of the verb would be the גבורים in
the first line of the stanza. While this is not impossible, the

poetic structure suggests that it is better to understand חצים
as the subject of the verb. This removes Kraft's problem in
understanding ויפרו. Moreover, Kraft's translation of this
phrase is built on the assumption that סביט/סבבום needs to be
corrected to סבבוני, which then provides a previous reference
to גבורים in its pronoun subject. That, as has already been
demonstrated, is an unnecessary emendation. Furthermore, the
parallelism employed suggests two bicola. In the first bicolon
the soldiers and their weapons are the images evoked. The second bicolon pairs more specifically two "weapons" chosen for
their apocalyptic background and power: arrows which rend
flesh, and a flaming spear.

The imagery of the arrows employs a construction known
from late biblical Hebrew, לאין + a noun. This construction is
found several times in the Hodayot, and expresses with admir-
able brevity the complete impossibility of something. In this
case, there is no restoration for any hit by the arrows of the
enemy. The imagery of the flaming spear which is the climax to
this first set of battle symbols has a number of biblical ante-
cedents (see Excursus). Bardtke has suggested emending באש
אוכלת to כאש,[13] but there seems to be no need for this poeti-
cally or syntactically. The structural relationships of these
first four lines of this stanza are summarized in the following
diagram.

war images   ואני אמרתי חנו עלי גבורים   Pronoun marks
           סבבים בכל כלי מלחמותם   new stanza
           ויפרו חצים לאין מרפא
           ולהוב חנית באש אוכלת עצים }

The imagery of this stanza now changes. The poet is still
assailed by overwhelming forces, but these are now compared to
destructive waters. In the first line of this tricolon they
are like the מים רבים, the chaotic waters of the sea. In the
next line they become the נפיץ וזרם, which should be understood
as a hendiadys--the floods of rain. In the final line, the
cresting waves are the symbol of destruction. Water as a repre-
sentation of the forces of chaos has a long history in the OT
(see, for example, Psalms 93, 107, 29, as well as the creation
and flood stories in Genesis). Psalm 69 offers an especially

good comparison to this poem; although it is not quoted here,
it too compares the affliction by enemies to the overwhelming
forces of flood waters.

It is easy enough to pick out the chief images employed in
these lines, but their setting is less clear. No lines in this
psalm are more disputed or confusing. Poetic analysis can contribute to a resolution of some of these difficulties, at least.
Two words are obscure in this passage: למזורות, column line 27,
and אפעה, at the beginning of line 28. In addition, the syntax
of these final lines of Stanza C can be difficult.

Two observations seem to be critical to understanding
these lines. First, למזורות יבקעו אפעה is probably an allusion
to Isa 59:5: והזורה תבקע אפעה ("And from one which is crushed
[an egg] a viper is hatched"). Secondly, אפעה ושוא is a hendiadys like that in the previous line, נפץ וזרם. Analyzed in
this fashion, this second half of Stanza C must have three
lines rather than four, and the final line is quite dispropor-
tionately long: eighteen syllables rather than the ten to
twelve syllables of the other lines. Yet the allusion and the
grammatical structure support this arrangement. The apparent
anomaly and awkwardness are partially mitigated by the recognition of extremely long lines in other Hodayot. This extra-long
line is used strategically; it appears at the end of key stanzas
in a poem (5:5-19, 3:19-36), and once in the opening line of a
stanza containing another biblical allusion (14:8-22). This
type of line can be described as a "double line," the length of
a normal bicolon in the Hodayot, which serves in an emphatic or
climactic role.[14] Its use in Stanza C climaxes a list of seven
apocalyptic images of destructive forces fighting against God's
elect.

The problem of meaning and translation remains, however.
Comparison of the allusory phrase with Isa 59:5 shows considerable divergence in the forms used; and indeed, there is such a
great difference that many scholars have not been convinced
that the phrase למזורות יבקעו אפעה is drawn entirely from
Isaiah. The context here is completely different from the
Isaiah passage as well. Some scholars, while deriving a possible meaning for אפעה from Isa 59:5, have linked למזורות to

Job 38:32, where a constellation *mazuroth* is mentioned.[15]   The
resulting translation of the Hodayot phrase in this case has
been less than satisfying: "Up to the stars wickedness and evil
break forth in the cresting of their waves." This strange
phrase is then interpreted as a metaphor for excessive wickedness.

The alternative is to derive למזורות from one of the three
roots זור, including that used in Isa 59:5. It is at this
point that the meaning of אפעה must be considered. A similar
word occurs in Hodayot 3:3-18, derived from פעה, "groan."[16]
Burrows has also suggested that the word might be taken as אפע,
"breath, nothingness."[17] אפעה occurs only once in the OT, in
Isa 59:5, where it has the meaning "viper." Since למזורות and
אפעה occur in Hodayot 2:27-28 in a three-word phrase whose roots
can be drawn from a similar phrase in Isa 59:5 in the same sequence, it seems most probable that the root meaning of these
obscure words is intended to be that used in the Isaiah
passage.[18]

The difficulty of understanding the introduction of אפעה
(viper) into this Qumran psalm is resolved by the recognition
of the hendiadys אפעה ושוא. It is not necessary to extend אפעה
to mean evil in general,[19] since the hendiadys itself introduces a term for evil with which אפעה is to be understood:
"viperous evil." The change from הזורה to למזורות was necessi-
tated by the context of the psalm, and the linking of the allusion to the image of the waves in the second half of the line.

The poet has now given an extended, vivid description of
the overwhelming battle in which he is engaged. Seven images
of destruction have been evoked: four from the battlefield of
men, three from the world of chaotic waters. The poem turns to
a resolution of the stress in the closing stanza. Once again
the independent pronoun appears as the signal of a new stanza.
Since this is the summary stanza, however, both ואני and והם
make their appearance, one in each bicolon of the closing unit.

In the opening line of this stanza, the author plays on the
imagery of water once more. It has been remarked that the expected simile would be that the heart melts like wax.[20] There
is no need to label the expression here as peculiar, or to look

for biblical phrases to justify the "change" in the simile. It
is a continuation and contrast to the imagery of the destructive waters of the previous stanza. The second line of this
bicolon returns the thought to the introduction in the reference to salvation through the covenant. The final bicolon expresses the resolution of the battle: "they" are caught in the
traps laid for the author. The parallelism and more formal
structure of this last stanza contrasts with the rather fluid
and vivid lines of the preceding section, and returns not only
to the theme of the first lines, but to the style of those
lines as well. This contrast will be seen frequently in the
Hodayot: a rather conventional beginning, perhaps with standard
parallelism continuing throughout the following stanza, then a
"freer" more vivid or apocalyptic section, followed in some
cases by a more formal closing.

The final lines can be considered a coda rounding off the
psalm, and comparable to the opening formula. The words עמדה
במישור were added in the margin by a later hand. With their
addition, this coda corresponds almost exactly to Ps 26:12.
The only difference is that in Ps 26:12 the word is במקהלים
rather than מקהלם. (For further remarks on this quotation,
see the Excursus.)

Rhythmical Balancing

Although standard methods of determining meter do not work
well with the Hodayot,[21] there can be little doubt that this
psalm is well balanced. The opening and closing stanzas each
consist of four lines and are of the same length. The body of
the poem has two halves counterbalancing each other, both
structurally and rhythmatically. Stanzas A and B, which form
the "they" half of the poem each have four lines, providing a
further, inner balance in this section. Against them is poised
Stanza C, the "I" section, with seven slightly longer lines.
The preciseness of this balance is even more apparent if the
syllables of the stanzas, as vocalized in any of the various
editions, are counted. The opening stanza has 37-42 syllables,
while the closing stanza has 40-45. Each half of the body of
the poem has 80-90 syllables; and stanzas A and B have 39-44

and 41-47 syllables respectively, mirroring their structural
parallelism.

The individual lines of the psalm can be further classified into one of three patterns. There is a standard line of
9-13 syllables, and there is a shorter line of 7-9 syllables.
In this psalm, these are combined in three ways: two standard
lines form a bicolon (20-26 syllables); two short lines form a
bicolon (about 16 syllables); and twice a stanza is composed of
three standard lines with a short line summary (Stanzas A and
B). The concluding tricolon of Stanza C shows a third line
pattern, a double line of 18 syllables; and this double line
gives the stanza the additional syllables needed to balance it
against Stanzas A and B, as well as forming an effective conclusion to Stanza C. While the difference between these three
line patterns may not seem great, it will be seen in further
studies that almost all of the lines in the Hodayot fall within
these three patterns, and that regular rules of combination
seem to have been followed.

The following diagram summarizes the rhythmic patterns of
this psalm.

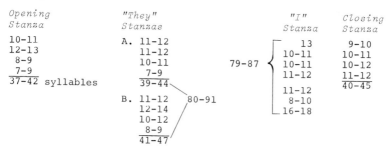

Opening
Stanza

10-11
12-13
8-9
7-9
‾‾‾‾
37-42 syllables

"They"
Stanzas

A. 11-12
   11-12
   10-11
   7-9
   ‾‾‾‾
   39-44

B. 11-12   80-91
   12-14
   10-12
   8-9
   ‾‾‾‾
   41-47

79-87

"I"
Stanza

13
10-11
10-11
11-12

11-12
8-10
16-18

Closing
Stanza

9-10
10-11
10-12
11-12
‾‾‾‾
40-45

Imagery and Theology

Within the carefully developed structure just explored,
the poet has unfolded his thanksgiving for deliverance, using
this structure to accentuate his theme. This is a poem of
contrasts--between death and life, between the evil ones and
those who belong to the covenant, between "they" and "I." The
heroic battle the righteous must fight is highlighted by these

extreme contrasts. This psalm presents in vivid, dramatic
language a basic tenet of the Qumran sectarians, their view of
themselves as a beleaguered but purified rampart surrounded by
evil in the last times.

Carmignac and Delcor insist that the language and imagery
of this hymn apply to the Teacher of Righteousness and his
persecutions. Specific, technical terminology that would prove
the case is found by the extension of meaning of certain terms.

1. מעמדי line 22 Delcor believes that the term must be
translated as in 1QM 16:5 where it is used to refer
to a military position. It then becomes a technical
term for the religious position the Teacher feels
he holds, which his opponents will not recognize.[22]

2. אפעה line 28 Carmignac believes this is a reference to religious rivals, understanding its meaning
literally as "viper."[23]

3. מקהלם line 30 Delcor translates "far from their
assembly," with the meaning "far from the assembly
of enemies," that is, the Jerusalem temple.[24]

It is noteworthy that these men who suggest a biographical
basis for this poem cite different terms as evidence of the
Teacher's authorship. The last two terms are somewhat obscure
as written, and can be understood in several ways. מעמד is
used in 1QS in reference to the place or position in rank of
each of the members of the community.

These terms cannot in any way prove the assumption that
the author of this psalm is the Teacher of Righteousness, and
that the psalm was not intended, therefore, for cultic use. To
come to such a conclusion on such evidence actually deprives
the poem of its power and theological insight. This is not a
biographical poem but an apocalyptic poem; the author's personal experiences have been viewed in apocalyptic terms that have
raised personal experience to a more universal level, so that
all the members of the community can identify with the "I" of
the poem. The military terminology is not reflective of actual
persecution but of the theological outlook of a community who
saw themselves as the army of God. Of course, to say that the
outlook of the poem is apocalyptic rather than biographical
does not solve the problem of the Sitz im Leben of this particular psalm: it may be simply the result of a personal experience

or experiences, or it may have been intended for community use
from the beginning.

What is far more significant than the argument over the
author and the Sitz im Leben is the masterly contrast between
the beleaguered poet and his enemies, emphasized constantly by
the pronouns "I--They." There is universal appeal in this
theme; pity and indignation are almost instantly evoked for the
author, who surely must be overcome. The multitude of enemies
is so great that at the height of the battle they can be compared to the "*mayim rabbim*" in strength. No more powerful
imagery of chaos and destructiveness and mindless elemental
force could have been invoked from Semitic mythology. This
ancient mythological motif is transformed by the poet of an
apocalyptic age, who combines with it his view of evil forces.
The apocalyptic imagery of this stanza fuses the poet's battle
with that of God. The battle of the poet against evil was the
battle of Yahweh against the sea dragon and the forces of
primeval chaos--the two battles are knit together in the preordained plan of the cosmos.

Again through the contrast of "they" and "I," which is the
key structural feature of the poem, the poet relates how he has
overcome the incredible odds in the battle with God's help. In
the "they" stanzas, while describing the evil intent of his
enemies, he repeatedly emphasizes the support he has from God
(my steps, my position are with you). But at the climax of the
poem, in the rush of the great battle that is described, this
reassurance is momentarily forgotten, so great is the anguish
of battle. When it is over, the poet realizes that even as he
weakened (my heart dissolved like water), he received the
strength he needed from God, by belonging to the covenant, and
he is saved. Although the theme of life versus death, introduced in the first bicolon of the psalm is never again explicitly mentioned, the language of the final stanza, recalling the
covenant, reminds the reader of its earlier mention and the
opening lines. In this way all the themes of the poem--death
and life, the wicked and the righteous, the "they" against the
"I"--are intertwined and brought to completion in the final
confident statement.

2. Excursus: The Problems of Biblical Language

The carefully balanced structure in 2:20-30 has just been
outlined, and its affinities with biblical poetry, as well as
some of its differences, have been observed. The fact that
biblical Hebrew has been employed has obscured for some the
creativity of the poet, however. Holm-Nielsen, for example,
says that the poem "consists almost exclusively of expressions
and phrases from the Old Testament to such a degree that it may
be justified to speak of a mosaic of Old Testament quotations."[25]
The chart on pages 53-55 lists all the words and expressions
which Holm-Nielsen and Carmignac (who is also interested in this
matter) cite as quotations. They comprise about sixty percent
of the psalm. If indeed these expressions are quotations, it
would appear that the psalm is not really poetry but chunks of
earlier poems cut away from the original and strung together
like beads on a string. This matter is of some importance, for
it would mean, if Holm-Nielsen's comment is taken at face value,
that the Hodayot do not indicate the nature of real poetry in
Palestine in this period. They would not be of aid in tracing
the evolution of poetry from the OT to the NT; they would be a
backwater, a deadend. In fact, no one holds this extreme view,
least of all Holm-Nielsen, who finds "remarkable" the way the
expressions have been built into a coherent whole.

The argument here turns on the definition of the term
"quotation." Holm-Nielsen does not define the term, and uses
it with such phrases as "allusion to," "derived from," and
"inspired by," to describe the language of each psalm. Often
the phrases appear to be interchangeable in his work. Holm-
Nielsen has done masterly work compiling the OT background of
almost every phrase in the Hodayot, but he leaves the impression that these psalms are indeed "mosaics of Old Testament
quotations." There are many scholars who apparently agree with
Holm-Nielsen, and an analysis of poetic technique is hemmed in
on every side by the low view of the creativity and originality
of the poet who modelled his work so clearly after biblical
compositions.

The problem stems from the rigorous limits in vocabulary and idiom apparently set by the author(s) of these psalms. There can be no doubt that imitation of biblical style and idiom was intended. On the other hand, stylistic differences from biblical poetry are no less apparent--it is the detailing of these differences that forms a large part of the present work. Just as in the analysis of the style and techniques of these poems certain methods for describing the poems must be followed, so in the study of the vocabulary itself certain standards must be made plain. It is to this problem that this excursus is devoted.

An examination of the phrases which Holm-Nielsen and Carmignac term quotations reveals the following.

1. Many of the quotations consist of only one or two words, and frequently the two words used in the Hodayot come from different parts of the biblical verse cited.

2. Both Carmignac and Holm-Nielsen frequently admit that in the case of these one- and two-word "quotations" the context and meaning of the words employed in the Hodayot has changed considerably.

3. In a number of cases, a "quotation" is actually an idiom occurring several times in the OT. Holm-Nielsen frequently has trouble deciding which passage is "quoted" by the poet in these cases-- a sure sign that no passage is quoted at all.

4. In most cases, the Hodayot passage considered a quotation employs different forms of the verb, and different pronominal suffixes, and stand in syntactical relationships quite different from the biblical passage.

Since a quotation is generally understood to be the repetition of a passage verbatim, it seems inappropriate in light of the above observations to call all these phrases quotations. Nor is it appropriate even to say they were "inspired by" specific passages without applying a consistent standard. There is obviously a great difference between a "quotation" of two lines of a psalm, differing only in the ending of a single word, and a "quotation" of a two-word idiom used several times in the OT. Surely more accurate descriptions can be made to differentiate such uses of OT expressions. An analysis of the biblical idioms in 2:20-30 shows at least four different types of borrowing from OT vocabulary.

1. Quotation or allusion is used to recall a *specific* passage to the reader/listener's mind.

2. Biblical literary forms are imitated by the use of standardized phrases in appropriate places.

3. Biblical imagery and metaphor characteristic of certain types of literature or certain theological ideas can be identified.

4. Many thoughts are expressed simply in a manner consistent with biblical langauge and terminology.

The second and third categories may be termed "deliberate use of biblical expressions." In both cases the poet has borrowed biblical expressions and used them as a kind of "common stock," authenticating his style, theology, and language. The fourth category includes verbal idioms occurring in several biblical passages, which are nondistinctive, normal expressions of action; unusual words used without reference to the context of the biblical passage in which they occur; and combinations of, or changes in more distinctive biblical idioms. The last category may be termed "free use of biblical idiom and vocabulary" to emphasize the creative part the Hodayot's poet has played in using these expressions.[26]

Although there are problems in assigning every phrase of a poem to one of these four categories, there are enough clearcut examples to support the contention that such classification is more appropriate than a simple division between "quotation" and "original material." The chart analyzing the relevant phrases of 2:20-30 shows the kind of evidence that can be cited in determining the usage.

Where there are problems in deciding which classification is most accurate, certain guidelines from the poetic text can be of help. An expression can be considered a "deliberate" rather than "free" use of biblical expression if any of the following qualifications is met.

1. The context of the Hodayot expression is the same as in OT usage and it is not a frequently employed idiom in the OT (נפץ וזרם, line 27).

2. The meaning of the expression is the same as in the OT, and it is not frequently employed there (בצרור החיים, line 20).

3. It marks a literary form (אודכה אדוני, line 20).

4. It is an OT metaphor or simile characteristic of
a certain type of imagery (ולהוב חנית באש, line 26).

There are several examples in 2:20-30 which do not meet
any of the above qualifications. חנו עלי גבורים, line 25, actually employs a frequently used idiom and is not confined to
any particular literary form. בוסדיכה תושיע נפשי, line 23, not
only employs a verb used rather often in the OT, but joins it
with נפש, which is not done in the OT, indicating a development
of the older idiom. These last two examples fit the criteria
of the fourth category: "free use of biblical idiom."

A quotation, by definition, must consist of several words
and appear with only the slightest variations from the original.
An allusion is a broader category. In popular usage it may refer to everything from an extremely loose quotation to the most
veiled hint. It can be said, however, that to be an allusion,
a phrase must refer to a single passage. In regard to the Hodayot, idioms occurring several times in the OT are suspect;
they are allusive to biblical Hebrew in general rather than to
a specific passage. In this study, a further limitation is
suggested: to be classified as an allusion, the context, meaning, and the idiom itself must converge on one text, or must
have incomplete convergence reinforced by surrounding references to the same passage.

Two examples illustrate these principles. The first is an
expression in Hodayot 2:21: ותשוך בעדי, an expression which
also occurs in Job 1:10. The idiom occurs three times in the
OT, once with the by-form סוך. The verb סוך/שוך means "hedge
up" and is generally used to indicate the obstructing of something. Only once in the OT is the verb used in the sense of
protecting something--in Job 1:10, where Satan complains that
God has hedged up Job from evil (שוך בעד). The meaning is
therefore quite distinctive in this case. The context of the
Hodayot passage is similar, though not identical: the author is
thanking God for protecting him (שוך בעד) from death (which is
later tied to the evil forces at work in the world). The same
distinctive meaning has been employed for the idiom, though the
pronominal elements are different, as the situation demands.
This may indeed be an allusion to the Job passage, since an

idiom is used with the same distinctive meaning and in a similar context.

A second example of allusion can be seen in Hodayot 7:6-
25 (see Chapter V), where a number of expressions in the hymn
point to Zechariah 3, a passage concerning Joshua the High
Priest. Here there is incomplete convergence: some idioms are
changed slightly, or used with other meanings than in the OT
passage. The expressions are scattered throughout the psalm,
which leaves the context in some doubt. However, there are
enough references, and enough contextual indications to show
that Zechariah 3 is certainly in the background of the poet's
thought.

If the descriptions of the chart on pages 53-55 are combined with the intensive work on OT background done by Holm-
Nielsen, a more accurate picture of the use of OT vocabulary
can be obtained. The following observations summarize the
main points.

1. The author of the Hodayot composed his work almost
   entirely with biblical vocabulary.

2. The vocabulary of some biblical books is used
   more extensively than others: Psalms, Isaiah,
   Job, and Deuteronomy were particular favorites.
   From these preferences a good deal can be learned
   of the author's theology. (It is in this area
   that Holm-Nielsen has made his greatest contri-
   bution.)

3. The poet's "biblical sound" is achieved by combining biblical metaphors or standardized phrases
   with his own free use of biblical langauge, with
   sparing use of quotations and allusions for
   special effect.

4. While the poet obviously knew the OT well enough
   to use its most unusual words and idioms, these
   are usually employed in contexts or with meanings
   slightly different from the OT. This indicates
   some facility to compose poetry in Hebrew, rather
   than mere awkward combination of biblical expressions. This conclusion is further reinforced
   by the intricate structures of the poems, which
   are not copied directly from the OT.

TABLE 1

ALLEGED QUOTATIONS IN HODAYOT 2:20-30

Hodayot phrase	Source[a]	Analysis
שמחה נפשי בצרור החיים	1 Sam 25:29:* והיתה נפש אדני צרורה בצרור החיים	Different verbs used, suffix added to נפש; the idea is the same, but context changed from human conversation to divine act. Deliberate use of biblical idiom.
ותשוך בעדי	Job 1:10:* הלא-את שכת בעדו	Expression used three times in OT. Only in Job 1:10 is verb used with sense of protecting rather than obstructing. Context of two passages close but not exact. Pronominal elements different. Allusion to Job 1:10.
מוקשי שחת	Ps 18:6:[H] קדמוני מוקשי מות	Same biblical idiom is used in Prov 13:14, 14:27. Context *generally* similar in all uses; none is exact match of Hodayot. Use of מות rather than שוח in keeping with vocabulary pattern of Hodayot author. Combination of biblical imagery with free expression.
עריצים בקשו נפשי	Ps 86:14:* עדת עריצים בקשו נפשי Ps 54:5:* ועריצים בקשו נפשי	Correspondence indicates quotation, but double occurrence in Psalms suggests more. In both psalms it is part of a longer verse repeat, and each time is set in context of thanksgiving for salvation. It does not mark a form, but is a phrase used in literary form Hodayot imitated.
בחסדיכה תושיע נפשי	Ps 6:5:[C] הושיעני למען חסדך Ps 31:17:[C] הושיעני בחסדך	Verb forms different; חסד plural in Hodayot; נפש is never used in OT with ישע. Certainly employs biblical idea, but a common one, and with different idiom. Free use of biblical language.

[a]Biblical source of Hodayot expression according to Holm-Nielsen and Carmignac; indicated by the following: H--according to Holm-Nielsen; C--according to Carmignac; *--according to both.

Hodayot phrase	Source	Analysis
מאתכה מצעדי	Ps 37:23:* (same as Prov 20:24): מיהוה מצעדי גבר	Suffix in place of construct form; divine name omitted (this is in keeping with practice of all Qumran writings). Idea is the same as Psalm 37, but expression also found in Ps 18:37, Job 31:4. Free use of biblical expression.
גרו עלי נפשי	Ps 94:21:* יגודו על-נפש צדיק	Verb is different (some wish to emend Psalm after Ps 59:4 which uses גור). Ps 59:4 has expression equally close to this one. Similar expressions with גור in Ps 56:7 and Ps 140:3, though these are not as close in wording. In view of frequent combination of נפש with other verbs in Hodayot and above evidence, free use of biblical language.
חנו עלי גבורים	Ps 27:3:[H] אם-תחנה עלי מחנה	חונה על, "encamp against," is a frequently used OT idiom (at least fourteen times). Psalm 27 is the only place where first singular suffix used, but no passages mention גבורים, and although idea of Psalm 27 is similar, it is not even loosely quoted here. Free use of biblical language.
סביב בכל כלי מלחמותם	Jer 21:4:[C] מסב את-כלי המלחמה	Meaning of סבב quite different in Jeremiah 21, due to difference in conjugation. Context completely different from Hodayot. Expressions using סבב with similar meanings in Pss 18:6, 109:3; neither uses כלי המלחמה. Free use of biblical expressions.
ולהוב חנית באש אוכלת	Isa 29:6, also 30:30:* ולהב אש אוכלת Job 39:23:* להב חנית וכידון	Besides passages cited, להב אש is found also in Isa 66:15, and להב חרב is parallel to חנית in Nah 3:3; cf. also Ps 29:7, 2 Sam 23:7. Frequent appearance and connection with wrath, destruction indicates this expression part of common stock, deliberately borrowed in Hodayot.

Hodayot phrase	Source	Analysis
וכהמון מים רבים שאון קולם	Jer 51:55:* והמו גליהם כמים רבים נתן שאון קולם	Hodayot line is very close to Jeremiah verse, but all terms have been placed in a single line instead of in parallel lines. This is the only place in OT where מים רבים and שאון קולם both appear, but both expressions common in OT. המון appears with water imagery (not with מים רבים) and with קולם. Context of Jeremiah close to that of entire Hodayot stanza (note later use of גליהם). A broad allusion to Jeremiah verse.
נפץ וזרם	Isa 30:30:* נפץ וזרם ואבן ברד	נפץ occurs only in Isa 30:30. Since this phrase succeeds reference to להב אש (cf. above), it is reasonable to assume some use of Isaiah verse. But here it is reworked as part of hendiadys, not part of a list.
למזורות יבקעו אפעה	Isa 59:5:* והזורה תבקע אפעה	An application of Isa 59:5, as noted by Holm-Nielsen, Gaster.
בהתרומם גליהם	Ps 107:25:* ותרומם גליו Ps 89:10:C בשוא גליו אתה תשבחם	Despite closeness to Psalm 107, the context fits Jer 51:55 (cf. above) rather than Psalm 107. Waves usually connected in OT to sound; twice waves are "raised up"—once with נשא, Ps 89:10, and once with רום, 107:25. Hodayot author chose "correct" verb and used it freely.
במיס לבי כמים	Ps 22:15:C כמים נשפכתי	Not at all close to passage cited although idea is similar.
ותחזק נפשי בבריתך	Isa 56:4, 6:C ומחזיקים בבריתי	"To hold fast to covenant" found only in Isaiah 56, but idiom has been reworked with new vocabulary.
רשת פרשו לי תלכוד רגלם ופחים טמנו לנפשי נפלו בם	Ps 9:16:*- זו טמנו נלכדה Ps 35:8:* ורשתו-טמן תלכדו אשר-טמן תלכדו Ps 142:4:* טמנו פח לי	Examples given (see also Ps 140: 6) show that the idea and its vocabulary part of common stock in OT. No need to suppose a combination of texts by Hodayot author--he simply used the stock vocabulary.
ורגלי עמדה במישור מקהלט אברכה שמכה	Ps 26:12:* רגלי עמדה במישור במקהלים אברך יהוה	Almost exact correspondence--but becomes quotation only because a later hand filled in missing words in margin.

3. Hodayot 3:19-36 (Plate 37)

This second complete hymn also has a text relatively un-
marred by deterioration. The lacunae (in four lines) are all
small, from one to three letters; and there is little disagreement in the restoration of this text.[27] In three places
scribal additions have been made.

line 29: על added above the line (בליעל על כול,
          loss due to haplography.

line 32: פ above the line, to be inserted in רפש.

line 35: ב above the line, before קולם.

All of these are minor corrections which seem necessary, and
they can be accepted as part of the text.

The usual paragraphing technique is employed in the text
of this psalm, with the opening formula indented to the middle
of line 19. Line 36 concludes some distance from the left margin, and the opening formula of a new psalm can be seen in the
following line. Within this psalm there are no other paragraph
indications. In lines 23 and 26, near the end of the line,
spaces of two to three letters are found, but these seem to be
the copyist's efforts at marginal fitting, one of which is more
successful than the other.[28]

There are no indications by the copyist, then, of the
units of this psalm, other than those marking the beginning and
the end. Unlike the previous poem, there are no repeated independent pronouns to guide analysis, either. The strategic
use of ואני in line 23 is unique in this poem. The stanzas in
this poem are indicated in more subtle ways. As in most of the
Hodayot, the stanza which follows the opening formula appears
to consist of four lines, which have a structure similar to
other psalm openings. The division of the rest of the poem
into larger units must rest on the evidence drawn from the stylistic devices of the entire psalm. Parallelism, infinitive
clauses, and lists mark out many small units. Some of these
units are joined together by strategic words or phrases to form
larger stanzaic units. When the evidence offered by these stylistic and strategic devices has been sifted, it appears that
there are five stanzas in the psalm in addition to the opening

stanza. It can be argued successfully that some of the smaller
units in the longest stanza are actually stanzas themselves.
However, there are several indications that these subsections
in Stanza D are interrelated, and the present stanzaic arrangement has been chosen to highlight these interrelationships.

Hebrew Text of Hodayot 3:19-36

19	אודכה אדוני	
	כי פדיתה נפשי משחת	Opening
19-20	ומשאול אבדון העליתני לרום עולם	Stanza
	ואתהלכה במישור לאין חקר	
20-21	ואדעה כיא יש מקוה לאשר יצרתה מעפר לסוד עולם	
	ורוח נעוה טהרתה מפשע רב	Stanza
21-22	להתיצב במעמד עם צבא קדושים	A
	ולבוא ביחד עם עדת בני שמים	
22-23	ותפל לאיש גורל עולם עם רוחות דעת	
	להלל שמכה ביחד ר[נ]ה	
	ולספר נפלאותיכה לנגד כול מעשיכה	
23-24	[a]ואני יצר[a]החמר	Stanza
	מה אני מגבל במים	B
	ולמי נחשבתי	
	ומה כוח לי	
	כיא התיצבתי בגבול רשעה	
25	ועם חלכאים בגורל	
	ותגור נפש אביון עם מהומות רבה	
	והוות מדהבה עם מצעדי	
26	בהפתח כל פחי שחת	Stanza
	ויפרשו כול מצודות רשעה	C
	ומכמרת חלכאים על פני מים	
27	בהתעופף כול חצי שחת לאין השב	
	ויורו לאין תקוה	
	בנפול קו על משפט	
27-28	וגורל אף על נעזבים	
	ומתך חמה על נעלמים	
	וקץ חרון לכול בליעל	
	וחבלי מות אפפו לאין פלט	
29	וילכו נחלי בליעל על[b] כול אגפי רום	Stanza
	כאש אוכלת בכול שנאביהם	D
29-30	להתם כול עץ לח ויבש מפלגיהם	
	ותשוט בשביבי להוב עד אפס כול שותיהם	
30-31	באושי חמר תאוכל וברקוע יבשה	
	יסודי הרים לשרפה	
	ושורשי חלמיש לנחלי זפת	

---

[a]Larger than usual spacing with these words probably due
to marginal fitting.

[b]על written above the line by a later hand.

31-32   ותאוכל עד תהום רבה
                  ויבקעו לאבדון נחלי בליעל
                  ויהמו מחשבי תהום בהמון גורשי רפש‎ᶜ
32-33   וארץ תצרח על ההווה הנהיה בתבל
                  וכול מחשביה ירועו
                  ויתהוללו כול אשר עליה
34   ויתמוגגו בהווה ג[דו]לה

                  כיא ירעם אל בהמון כוחו   Stanza
34-35   ויהם זבול קודשו באמת כבודו   E
                  וצבא השמים יתנו בקולם‎ᵈ
                  [ו]יתמוגגו ויירעדו אושי עולם
35-36   ומלחמת גבורי שמים תשוט בתבל
         ולא תש[וב ע]ד כלה ונחרצה לעד ואפס כמוה

                  Translation of Hodayot 3:19-36

19   I thank you, O Lord,

         For you redeemed my life from the Pit,
19-20   And from Sheol Abaddon you raised me to
                 an eternal height,
             And I walk about on a plain without limit,
20-21   And I know that there is hope for that which you
                 formed from dust into an eternal community.

         And a perverted spirit you purified from great sin,
21-22   So that it might be stationed in rank with
                 the host of holy ones,
             And so that it might come together with the
                 congregation of the sons of heaven.
22-23   And you cast for man an eternal lot with the
                 spirits of knowledge
             So that he might praise your name together
                 in rejoicing,
             And so that he might recount your wonderful deeds
                 before all your works.

23-24   And I--a creature of clay,
             What am I?--kneaded with water!
             And how am I reckoned?
             And what is my strength?
             For I stand within evil bounds,
25   And with the lost[A] in lot.
             And the life of the poor one sojourns mid the
                 tumults of the great one,
             And the disasters of the raging one are with
                 my footsteps.[B]

---

[c]פ of this word written above the line by a later hand.

[d]ב of this word written above the line by a later hand.

[A]חלכאים occurs only in Ps 10:10, 14, and its meaning here
must be derived from context: both times in this psalm it is
parallel to רשעה. "Lost" is therefore suggested as a complementary counterpart to רשעה.

[B]See the discussion of this enigmatic bicolon on p. 68.

26   When all the snares of the Pit are opened,
         Then all the nets of evil are spread out,
         And the fishing net of the lost ones is upon
             the face of the waters.
27   When all the arrows of the Pit fly forth without return,
         Then they rend beyond hope.
         When falls the measuring line for judgment,
27-28   And the lot of anger against the abandoned,
         And the outpouring of wrath against the hypocrites,
         And the moment of wrath for all of Belial,
         And the cords of death encompass without escape.

29   Then the rivers of Belial flow over all the high banks,[C]
         Like a fire consuming all their watering places,[D]
29-30   To destroy every tree, green or dry, from
             their channels.
         And it rushes in tongues of flames until none of
             their drinkers are left.
30-31   The foundations of clay it consumes and the
             dry land surface,
         The foundations of the mountains by burning,
         And the roots of flint by the rivers of pitch.
31-32   And it devours as far as the great abyss,
         And the rivers of Belial break into the nether world,
         And the schemers of the abyss groan with the noise
             of the writhing mud.
32-33   And the earth cries out over the disaster which
             comes on the world,
         And all her schemers scream,
         And all who are upon her are destroyed,
34   And they are melted in the great disaster.

         But God thunders with the sound of his strength,
34-35   And his holy dwelling groans in this glorious truth,
         And the army of heaven sends forth their voice,
         And the eternal foundations are melted and shaken,
35-36   And the war of the mighty army of heaven rushes
             across the earth,
         And it does not draw back until it is complete,
             and its decision is forever, there is
             nothing like it.

Three Poetic Devices in This Poem

Before analyzing this psalm unit by unit, three poetic devices used extensively in this poem deserve some general comment. These devices are parallelism, infinitive clauses, and

---

[C]The meaning and derivation of this word is by no means
certain, but most translators feel that the context suggests
the bank or side of a river channel.

[D]In view of the parallel with מפלגיה, this strange word
may be derived from שאב, and refers either to watering places
or drawers of water.

lists. A survey of the extent and type of parallelism in this
psalm is instructive, for the bicola show wide variations in
the use of these devices.

As in the psalm previously investigated, the introductory
stanza has more complete parallelism than most of the poem, and
consists of two bicola.

כי פדיתה נפשי מֶשַׁחַת
וּמִשְׁאוֹל אֲבַדּוֹן הֶעֱלִיתַנִי לרום עולם
וְאֶתְהַלְּכָה – – – – –
ואדעה – – – – – – – -/לסוד עולם

In the second bicolon, both lines begin with the same construction, but there is no strict parallelism of the remainder, although the idea of God's graciousness to man seems to be carried through both lines. Other structural features account for
the divergence of these lines in form.

Stanza A has a different type of parallelism. Lines 2 and
3 are subordinate to line 1 and parallel to each other. Lines
4 through 6 are arranged similarly, except that the independent
clause (line 4) is a result of the action introduced in the
first set of subordinate clauses.

Stanza B presents a more complicated picture in regard to
parallelism. There seem to be two units within this section
structurally. The first section opens with the pronoun וְאָנִי,
followed by a set of rhetorical questions. This section is
well balanced and parallels two expressions not found in the OT.

ואני יצר הֶחֶמֶר
מה אני מְגֻבָּל במים
וּלְמִי נֶחְשַׁבְתִּי
וּמַה כוח לי

Particularly interesting in these lines is the rearrange-
ment of an expression which occurs in Hodayot 1:21: יצר החמר
וּמגבל המים. Here the expression has been split in half and
arranged with the halves as parallel terms. A similar device
is used in canonical poetry, where occasionally a short stereotyped expression is divided between the halves of a bicolon so
that complementary parallelism is achieved. This example from
the Hodayot is longer than the biblical expressions split in
this manner, but it appears to apply the same principle.

Recognition of this device clears up the awakwardness of many
translations at this point. מגבל במים has frequently been attached as a dependent clause to the following question: "knead-
ed with water, how shall I be reckoned?"[29] This destroys the
parallelism of this section, however. In the splitting of a
stereotyped expression, traditional grammar rules do not apply,
since the second half of the phrase simply completes the expression introduced in the first part of the bicolon.

> And I am a *creature of clay*--
> What am I?--*kneaded with water!*

The recognition of this device is further evidence of the
author's facility in poetic composition. The whole expression
is one characteristic of the author's theology and is founded
on Mishnaic rather than biblical Hebrew.[30] The use of this
device--the break-up of a stereotyped expression--can be no
accident achieved by recombining biblical expressions; it shows
instead that the author knew of and used some of the traditional poetic techniques.

Following the rhetorical questions are four lines of
rather standard parallelism.

> כיא התיצבתי בגבול רשעה }
> ועם הלכאים בגורל
> ותנור נפש אביון עם מהומות רבה }
> והוות מדחבה עם מצעדי

The next stanza, C, might be characterized as extended
alternating parallelism. Its arrangement will be discussed in
more detail shortly, for it involves three infinitive clauses
set in parallel construction.

With Stanza D there is a marked change in the use of parallelism. This large unit is a counterweight of Stanzas B and
C in bulk, and prominent subsections can be detected in it.
Although parallel terms are scattered throughout this stanza,
there are few strongly parallel lines. The first subsection of
this stanza is quite prosaic, despite the introduction of the
parallel terms, שנאביהם and מפלגיהם. The chief feature of the
second unit is a type of short list. Only in the third and
fourth subsections does real parallelism appear.

> ‏ריבקעו לאבדון גוזלי בליעל }
> ‏ריהמו מחשבי תהום בהמון גורשי רפש

> ‏ריתהוללו כול אשר עליה }
> ‏ריתמוגגו בהווה ג]דו[לה

Despite the lack of standard parallelism, Stanza D has a number
of strong structural features. These will be discussed under
"Stanza Analysis."

The parallelism of the last stanza, E, is rather loose.
Its three bicola employ alternating parallelism, but it is a
thematic rather than formal parallelism for the most part. This
is due primarily to the vocabulary of the stanza, which gathers
significant theme terms from the earlier stanzas in the poem to
describe God's final victory. It is these theme terms which
are set in the alternating parallel lines, effectively bringing
the poem to its climax.

A second device worthy of note in the composition of this
poem is the use of infinitive phrases. The infinitive construct appears in Qumran documents with far more frequency than
in the OT. Its frequency in the Manual of Discipline, for example, occasionally causes difficulty in translating and understanding syntax. The infinitive construct occurs frequently in
the Hodayot also, more frequently than this form occurs in
canonical poetry. In the Hodayot, the infinitive clause is
handled with some finesse and is not the prosaic element it is
sometimes supposed.

Two excellent examples of the use of the infinitive clause
are found in this psalm. In Stanza A, the infinitive phrase
makes its appearance as a key poetic device.

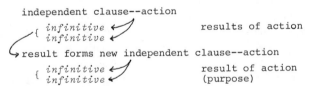

The diagram shows the four infinitival phrases used, arranged
in two sets of parallel pairs, each set subjoined to an independent clause stating an action. The stanza is in this way given
a symmetrical arrangement. There is also a more subtle aspect

to the arrangement. The first line states the action of God
(the cleansing of man's spirit); the two infinitive phrases
attached to this clause indicate the purpose or result of this
action. It is done *so that* (ל) man can take his place in the
assembly of the elect. The second independent clause of the
stanza begins with a restatement of that result--God places man
with the elect--and a new set of purposive or result clauses
are attached to this statement. The whole stanza, then, is
arranged not only with some attention to parallelism, but in an
interlocking fashion.

A second example of the use of infinitive clauses is found
in Stanza C. This unit consists of three infinitive clauses of
time (ב + the infinitive construct), each followed by a perfect
verb continuing the action of the phrase (when...then...). The
simplest of these is the second in the series.

בהתעופף כול הצי שחת לאין השב
ויפרו לאין תקוה

The first and third clauses are more prolix in style, but the
three all share this basic verbal construction, and stand out
as a unit. The question arises whether this unit belongs with
the preceding or the following material in the poem's organization. The choice here rests chiefly on the affinities in vocabulary between these clauses and the preceding matter.
Nevertheless, the final clause offers, thematically, a transition to the next section of the poem. The entire unit of infinitive clauses represents an expansion of the use of similar
phrases in canonical poetry. Its bulk, in comparison to similar indications of time in canonical poetry, appears awkward.
This awkwardness is somewhat mitigated by other formal considerations, and once the form is perceived, the crescendo effect
of this unit, building toward the fiery imagery which follows,
provides both suspense and transition nicely. The three
clauses are arranged in a kind of alternating parallelism.

| infinitive + perfect verb | first clause |
| infinitive + perfect verb | second clause |

The final clause, to provide the maximum of suspense, is
lengthened by a list between the infinitive and the perfect
verb. This device is the third of those reviewed in this general discussion. In this final infinitive clause, five judgment images are introduced.

קו על משפט	measuring line for judgment
גורל אף על נעזבים	the lot of anger against the abandoned
מתך זמה על נעלמים	the outpouring of wrath against the hypocrites
קץ חרון לכול בליעל	the moment of wrath for all of Belial
חבלי מות	the cords of death

The delicacy of balance used by the poet can be seen here;
the first and last members of the list depict the judgment by
the same symbolic object--rope/cord--while the three central
members of the list state that wrath will be visited upon the
wicked (Belial's adherents). The first member of the list is
tied to those that follow by the preposition על, which does not
appear in the last two links of the list. The complete effect
of the whole cannot be translated, even though the sense of the
passage is clear.

It is sometimes difficult to decide what constitutes a
list. When the terms occur without intervening material, as in
the passage just examined, there is no problem. Sometimes
three or more terms occur within a section employing other features. This more ambiguous case can be seen in Stanza D.

בֽאושי חמר תֽאוכל ובֽרקוע יבשה
יסודי הרים לשרפה
ושרשי חלמיש לנחלי זפת

These four terms are obviously synonymous, but the listing is
broken by an imperfect verb, and by the use of ב with only the
first two terms. The last two terms, set in parallel construction with each other, are synonymous with the first two terms,
but grammatically dependent on the first line. The final
prepositional phrase weaves in a reference to the fiery river.
The unit can hardly be considered a parallel bicolon, but seems
to be a blend of parallelism (two sets of parallel pairs) and
listing devices.

Stanza Analysis

The three devices just discussed--parallelism, the use of infinitive clauses, and lists--are the most important organizational devices employed in this poem, but they are by no means the only ones. Other devices, together with problems in understanding the text, must now be discussed.

The opening stanza has a pattern whose chief features are seen over and over again in these psalms. Characteristic of such an opening stanza is its "good" parallelism and generalized comment on the poet's situation. The most common statement is that the poet has been rescued by God from some distress or from the wicked. The language is of the type that could be applied to almost any conceivable difficulty. The most common opening line consists of כי followed by a second masculine singular perfect verb and either a first singular suffix or another reference to the poet (e.g., נפשי). The opening stanza of this psalm and the opening stanza of 2:20-30 are good examples of this standard form.

In this psalm, the opening stanza has other, more distinctive elements as well. The limits of this first stanza are marked by an inclusio: לסוד עולם recalls לרום עולם in the second line, and coming as it does at the end of a very long line, provides a rounding off of the initial theme. Other opening stanzas in the Hodayot, as it will be seen, often have an extra line or a long final line, which serves as a coda to the unit. The interpretation of these two terms used to set off this unit is somewhat of a problem, and involves the other distinctive phrase in the stanza as well: מישור לאין חקר. Do these terms refer to life after death or not? Paradoxically, both parties in this argument *translate* the terms almost identically: לסוד עולם = eternal council (of which the Qumran community is an earthly counterpart); לרום עולם = eternal height; מישור לאין חקר = plain without limits or level ground.[31]

Translation does not fully answer the question, however. One group argues that these terms refer simply to deliverance from death on this earth, and that "eternal" is figurative language to express the greatness of the deed.[32] A second

group of scholars takes "eternal" to be more literal--the
contrast is between death (שׁחת, שׁאול אבדון) and eternal life.[33]
This passage, and the lines that follow, form the longest and
best preserved passage on this topic in the Hodayot, and deserve some consideration. This, however, must await the full
delineation of the poem's structure.

Three rather important terms in this introductory stanza
are picked up in Stanza C: שׁחת, which is repeated twice in that
stanza; the construction using לאין, used three times in Stanza
C; and מקוה, recalled later by תקוה. לרום עולם is recalled in
the final stanza by the contrasting phrase אושׁי עולם--the single
tie of the latter half of the poem with the opening statements.
These repeated terms bear important weight in the poem's structure, for the language of rescue from distress, which is part
of the stock introduction of the psalm, does not reappear in
the poem.

Keeping in mind the good parallelism of the standard introduction, the inclusio, and the use of terms repeated later
in the poem for linking purposes, the intricate interweaving of
distinctive terms can be seen in this diagram.

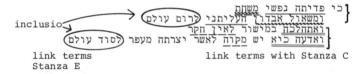

    link terms   link terms with Stanza C
    Stanza E

Some scholars consider the next section, Stanza A, to be of one
piece with the opening stanza, and there would then be no break
in the psalm before ואני.[34] No definitive answer perhaps can
be given in this matter, but indications in the structural development of the poem argue that ורוח נעוה begins a new unit.
לסוד עולם, and the long line which it completes, provide a coda
structurally for the opening statements. The lines that follow
are built around infinitive clauses. Since there are units
that employ several types of structure within them (for example,
Stanza D), this in itself does not mean these two sections are
separate stanzas. Other considerations play a part here as
well: all personal references are absent in the section labeled

Stanza A, in contrast to the opening lines; Stanza A balances E
in size and weight, while B and C also counterbalance D. And,
as a survey of the various psalms will show, the most common
length of an introductory stanza is four lines (two bicola) or
four lines with a coda. Such an introductory stanza frequently
stands alone, with no balancing unit at the end of the poem.

The chief features of Stanza A have already received comment in the discussion of the intricate infinitive clause construction of these lines. The interlocking nature of the two
sets of statements in this stanza, achieved by the use of parallel sets of infinitive clauses, is further enhanced by the
repetition of other terms: ביחד in the second infinitive phrase
of the first tricolon and in the first infinitive phrase of the
second tricolon. עם רוחות דעת in the second statement of God's
action recalls עם צבא קדושים and עם עדת בני שמים which close
the first two result clauses--emphasizing the way in which the
first result becomes the new statement of God's action.

ורוח נעוה טהרתה מפשע רב   → action

להתיצב במעמד עם צבא קדושים   result →
    leads
ולבוא ביחד עם עדת בני שמים   to

ותפל לאיש גורל עולם עם רוחות דעת   → action

להלל שמכה ביחד רנ[נ]ה   result →

ולספר נפלאותיכה לנגד כול מעשיכה

The following stanza, B, is the only unit outside of the
opening stanza with personal references. It opens with a series of rhetorical questions whose parallelism has already been
analyzed, and it concludes with two bicola which continue the
theme of the low estate of the author. Parallelism is the
chief device used in the stanza, and it is quite complete parallelism; but there are other devices used as well. The splitting of a stereotyped expression between halves of a bicolon
has already been discussed. Ballast variant is employed in a
later bicolon in which the poet speaks of his wretched condition (which nevertheless is ordained by God).

כיא התיצבתי בגבול רשעה   10 syllables

ועם חלכאים בגורל   8 syllables

There is an interesting parallel of גבול (territory) with גורל
(lot), which are similar in sound and complement each other in

meaning. גורל is also one of the key integrative terms of the psalm, appearing in Stanzas A, B, and C.

The final bicolon of the stanza repeats the idea of the previous statement, but carries it further by a device that can be called "reversal of object." Before this device can be delineated, however, another problem in these two lines must be resolved. Up to this point in the poem there is no serious disagreement on the basic translation of the terms employed, although there are numerous interpretations of the theology involved. In this bicolon there are two expressions which are troublesome, both in lexical meaning and syntactic relationship. Recognition of the parallel constructions in this bicolon at least points the direction for resolution of the problem.

ותגור נפש אביון עט מהומות רבה

והרות מדהבה עם מצעדי

As the diagram indicates, this bicolon employs chiastic parallelism. The enigmatic expressions each employ a feminine plural noun followed immediately by what appears to be a feminine singular noun or adjective. The situation is further complicated by מדהבה, a word known only from Isa 14:4, where it is usually emended after the Greek to מרהבה (root: רהב = rage).[35] Such emendation finds support from the Qumran Isaiah Scroll, which reads מרהבה.[36] Since the author of the Hodayot used מדהבה both here and in 12:18, it seems likely that variant traditions were alive even within the Qumran community. And since the word is used twice in the Hodayot it must be considered intentional, and should be understood in a way consistent with the single usage in Isaiah. Whether it is correct in Isaiah or not, the idea of rage or fury seems indicated there by the context, and most translators of the Hodayot have been content to accept that meaning here.[37]

To solve the syntactical problems of the bicolon, several translators have suggested that רבה be understood as an adverb or adjective and the second phrase, as a construct chain.[38] This suggestion violates the parallelism of the bicolon, and

the translation of רבה as an adverb in the first line gives
little sense. The syntactic relationship of the two phrases
ought to be the same, since they are parallel in both construction and use. The possibilities would seem to be: (1) the
feminine plural noun is used for intensification and should be
understood as a singular noun, followed by a singular adjective;
(2) the feminine plural noun is used with an adverb; (3) the
expressions are construct chains. The first solution is sometimes suggested rather tentatively with Gesenius as support,[39]
but there is no comparable example from either the Bible or the
Hodayot. The difficulty of rendering the second word of each
expression in an adverbial sense argues against the second
solution. The third solution is often used for the second expression alone, but could also be used with the first phrase,
if רבה is understood as a noun epithet for Belial.

> The life of the poor one sojourns among the tumults
>   of the great one,
> And the destructions of wrath (or, raging one)
>   with my footsteps.

Such an understanding would accord well with the synonymous
parallelism of the bicolon, and suggests a compound epithet for
Belial--the great raging one, or the great one of wrath. Once
again, this might be an example of the splitting of a stereotyped phrase in the bicolon.

The possibility of such a sophisticated interweaving of
themes is indirectly supported by another device which is used
here as well as in many other places in the Hodayot. This device can be called the "reversal of object." While the chief
terms in this bicolon are inverted to achieve chiastic parallelism, עם occupies the same position in both lines, so that the
object of the preposition changes. In the first line its object
is the tumult (parallel in the next line, "disaster"), while in
the second line the object of עם is the author. The bicolon is
thus a set of interlocking statements: the poet stands in the
midst of disaster and disaster encompasses the poet. This
double entanglement of good (represented by the author) and
evil (the disaster) is reminiscent of the essay on the two
spirits in man in the Manual of Discipline. It represents one

of the basic insights of the community, that in this world good
and evil are inextricably interwoven. Statements of this entanglement of good and evil in the Hodayot frequently employ
this simple but subtle device of reversing the subject and object nouns in a bicolon. This device is used rarely, if at all,
in canonical poetry.

The following diagram summarizes all the structural features of this stanza.

breakup of stereotyped phrase	וראני יצר החמר מה אני מגבל במים ולמי נחשבתי ומה כוח לי	questions
rev. ⤢ of ✗ object	כיא התיצבתי בגבול רשעה ועם חלכאים בגורל ותגור נפש אביון עם התנמות רבה ורהות מדהבה עם מצעדי	statements

Most of the structural features of Stanza C have already
been discussed in connection with infinitive clauses and lists.
Its place in the context of the poem is worthy of comment, however. Canonical poetry, although it uses infinitive clauses of
time ("when--then"), uses them sparingly and as single bicola
in poems. The size of this unit presents a great contrast to
canonical standards, and its size raises some questions. Is it
to be considered an independent unit in the poem or is it an
appendage to the preceding or following material? It has been
treated in a variety of ways in translations, and has even been
divided between the preceding and following units, but it has
not been recognized as an independent unit in and of itself.[40]
There are several indications that it should be so regarded.

Thematically, this unit brings the reader/listener close
to the description of the eschatological war; it is, in fact, a
transition and introduction to that war which appears full-scale
in Stanza D. On the other hand, its affinity in vocabulary is
with the Opening Stanza, not with Stanza D: שחת, לאין + a noun,
and תקוה all recall the Opening Stanza while not a single distinctive term from Stanza D appears. These observations confirm
both the extent of the unit, and its function as a transition
unit. Its differences from Stanza B suggest that it is an independent unit as well. All personal references have disappeared,

and except for the link term גורל, used in Stanzas A, B, and C,
there are no vocabulary affinities with B. Thematically, its
orientation is quite different from B.

As a transition unit, Stanza C is admirably constructed.
The three infinitive clauses, alternating with finite verbs,
spin out the suspense of the early stages of heavenly warfare.
The suspense is further heightened by the insertion of the list
of judgment symbols in the final clause. Throughout the whole
there is a persistent beat, a kind of *basso ostinato*, provided
by the word לכול שחת פחי כל, כול מצודות, כול חצי שחת, כול חצי, כול בליעל.

בהפתח כל פוזי שחת	infinitive clause
ויפרשו כול מצודרות רשעה	
ומכמרת חלכאים על פני מים	
בהתעורף כול חצי שחת לאין השב	infinitive clause
ויפרו לאין תקוה	
בנפול קו על משפט	infinitive clause
רגורל אף על נעזבים	
ומתך חמה על נעלמים	list
ורקץ חרון לכול בליעל	
וחבלי מות אפפו לאין פלט	

link terms with Opening

With Stanza D it is almost as if a new poem has begun.
A completely different vocabulary is introduced; in all of
Stanza D only one distinctive term (הורה) is used from the
earlier part of the poem. There are no references to the author again in the poem, either in the first or third person.
Despite the independence in word and structure of this stanza
from earlier stanzas, there are signs that the poem is a single
composition. The long infinitive clause section of Stanza C
demands a climax which is not contained within it. Nor can the
fiery judgment section, D, stand alone as a poem; it lacks a
satisfactory introduction without the preceding material. Furthermore, Stanzas D and E balance Stanzas A, B, and C rather
exactly in weight. As it now stands, the poem is intended as a
single composition.

Stanza D as a unit is strongly interwoven with the themes
and terms of destruction, but subsections can also be detected.
There appear to be four of these sections, with structural features corresponding to the themes introduced. In the first

line, the distinctive idiom for the eschatological forces of
evil is introduced, נחלי בליעל. Two lines describing its
course follow, suggesting a tricolon, although the arrangement
of the lines is rather prosaic. The second and third sections
are introduced by third feminine singular imperfect verbs, both
describing the fiery river. The second section, of four lines,
describes the destruction of the firmament and its foundation,
the mountains. The third section provides a balancing tricolon describing the destruction of the abyss. The final four
lines bring the destruction to a climax--the whole earth and
its inhabitants shriek in agony as the destruction reaches
them. Chronologically, this section is out of place, since the
earth's inhabitants could logically be expected to be destroyed
before the firmament. This is a climactic statement, however,
not subject to rules of logic or chronology. The entire picture of destruction is both magnificently graphic and frightening in scope. If it depends on biblical language for its terminology, the picture is the author's own, not a simple (or
even complex) weaving of OT passages. It matches or surpasses
in its conception of far-reaching destruction any eschatological description in either the Old or New Testaments.[41]

A diagram of this long stanza is the best summary of its
many structural and stylistic elements.

The entire stanza is drawn together not only by its theme
of destruction by the fiery river, but by various repetitions
as well. Once again there is the insistent beat of כול, empha-
sizing the extreme and ultimate nature of the catastrophe:

בכול שנאביהם, כול אגפי רום, כול אשר עליה, וכול מחשביה
כול שותיהם, כול עץ לח. The fiery river appears in three of
the four subsections. In such a long section it is not surprising that so many devices are employed to draw the unit together: parallelism, a list, matched sections, strategic repetitions, including the emphasis on כול, and the reversal of
object in the third subsection (see the diagram above).

The final stanza, E, is somewhat strange at a first reading. The heavenly war is also the subject of this stanza, but
the focus has shifted from the destructiveness of the evil
powers to the army of God. The six lines of the stanza bring
the poem to a rather abrupt end with the statement that

> The war of the heavenly army sweeps across the world,
> And it does not turn back before completion--
> What is decided is forever,
> There is nothing like it.

The poet's personal problem is not referred to again.
Nevertheless, an answer to his problem is given, when the poem
is contemplated in its entirety. The clues lie in the repetition and variation of key phrases throughout the poem, which are
are summed up in this final stanza. Almost half of the words
and phrases of this stanza are what might be called "gathering
words," drawing the themes of the poem together (see the following section on theology). Because of this, the parallelism of
this final stanza is rather loose, more thematic than structural
or syntactical. There are three bicola employing alternating
parallelism; in the first line of each of the bicola a heavenly
figure is mentioned (God, the heavenly army), and the following
line completes the description of his action. Many of the
terms used in the description of the rivers of Belial (Stanza
D) are picked up in the description of the ultimately triumphant
heavenly army: המון, מגג, שוט, אפס--emphasizing the relationship
of the two stanzas and the change of victors midway in the battle. The climax of the poem contrasts sharply with the personal
opening statement of the poem. The psalm has shifted completely
from contemplation of personal deliverance to the final outcome
of history. The transition, accomplished in the gradual build-
up of the infinitive clauses of Stanza C leads to the vivid,
terrible world vision of the second half of the poem.

Rhythmical Balance

This psalm, like that in 2:20-30, appears to be without a regular pattern when analyzed by canonical metrical standards, but it can be seen that the units are well balanced against each other in syllable weight. As in the previous psalm, the body of the poem appears to be composed of two halves with equal weight. Stanzas A and E, the outer units, balance each other rather exactly (having 72-81 syllables and 76-82 syllables respectively). Stanzas B and C balance the long unit D (156-167 syllables compared to 161-177 syllables). It should be noted that there is no stanza at the close to balance the opening unit. This is frequently the case in the Hodayot, as will be seen in other poems as well. The poem ends quite abruptly in Stanza E, without a coda, the final statement of God's triumph ending the psalm on a high note.

Each stanza has its own rhythmical arrangement, and although the stanzas are balanced against each other, there is considerable variety in the internal arrangement. Stanzas A and E, balanced against each other, illustrate the simplest of these rhythmical patterns, with six fairly even lines each. Stanza A is composed of two tricola and Stanza E of three bicola, a simple but effective contrast in itself.

Stanza A		*Stanza E*	
10-12	syllables	9	syllables
13		13	
12-14			
		12-13	syllables
13-14	syllables	12-13	
9-11			
15-17		13-15	syllables
72-81	total	17-19	
		76-82	

Once again, as in 2:20-30, the line of nine to fourteen syllables syllables appears as the standard.

Other units show some of the patterns noted in 2:20-30. Stanza B has two parts structurally and the length of the lines reflects these differences.

```
rhetorical    ⎡7-8  syllables    10   ⎤   syllables
questions     ⎢8-9               8    ⎥
              ⎢                  12-13⎥
              ⎢5-6               10   ⎦   statements
              ⎣4
```

                   total for stanza: 64-68 syllables

The first part of the stanza is composed exclusively of the
short line noted in 2:20-30 (five to nine syllables) for three
lines and has one short line. Both of these patterns were
found in 2:20-30, although in the second case the short line
came at the end of the unit rather than in the middle.

     In Stanza C the neat structural balance of the first two
infinitive clause constructions against the third, expanded by
a list, is reflected in the rhythmical balance, although it is
not exact.

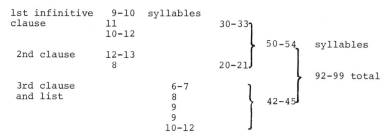

As might be expected, the lines of the list use the "short
line," but a short line is also used in the second clause.

     Stanza D, the longest stanza, has the most intricate and
well-balanced structure of all. It will be recalled that
structurally four units can be detected within this stanza, the
inner two with parallel features.

Unit 1	Unit 2	Unit 3	Unit 4
14-16 syllables	14-16	8	14-15
10-11	13-14	14-15	8-9
13	8-9	14-17	10-11
37-40	10-12	36-40	11
	45-51		43-46

              └─ parallel units ─┘

The units alternate between three and four lines each. If
the parallel units (2 and 3) are combined, they consist of seven
lines and eighty-one to ninety-one syllables, while the outer
units consist of seven lines and eighty to eighty-six syllables.
Alternatively, each *half* of the stanza has the same arrangement:
seven lines each, with eighty-two to ninety-one and seventy-nine
to eighty-six syllables respectively. Such balance could never
be achieved by chance, but is certainly part of the metrical
design of the poem.

A summary of the entire poem showing the balance of the
syllable weights follows. Included in this summary is the plan
of the opening unit which has no counterpart in the poem.

Opening Stanza	*Stanza A*		*Stanza D*		
8-9	Tricolon	35-39	Unit 1	37-40	
14-16	Tricolon	37-42	Unit 2	45-51	(82-91)
11-12		72-81	Unit 3	36-40	
20 (actually			Unit 4	43-46	(79-86)
two lines	*Stanza B*			161-177	
10+10)	Questions	24-27			
53-57 syllables	Statements	40-41			
		64-68		*Stanza E*	
	Stanza C			Bicolon	22
	Clauses 1 & 2	50-54	156-167	Bicolon	24-26
	Clause 3	42-45		Bicolon	30-34
		92-99			76-82

Theology and Imagery

Although the structure of this poem is now clear, there
are unanswered questions about the meaning and theology. Unlike the psalm in 2:20-30, there is no single theme running un-
mistakably through the poem, highlighted by strategic phrases.
This poem seems to be composed of chunks; it seems choppy, even
awkward in thematic development, quite in contrast to the
sophisticated structure. The psalm moves from first person
narrative to impersonal description with little attempt to re-
late the sections in terms of the sequence of action. This
choppiness is apparent even in the summaries of the psalm provided by Mansoor and Holm-Nielsen. Yet Holm-Nielsen insists
that the psalm is simply a mixture of thanksgiving, complaint,
and confidence elements, with the note of thanksgiving predomi-
nating. As evidence for this statement he cites the motivated

thanksgiving with which the poem begins, and וארי, which occurs exactly where the narrative motive appears in OT thanksgiving psalms.[42]

These statements are somewhat misleading; וארי can be considered to occur in the same place as the narrative motive of the OT prototype only if all the material preceding it is considered a single opening stanza, part of the opening thanksgiving itself. At the very least, this would have to be considered an expansion of the OT form, due to the intervening material of Stanza A. Moreover, it is difficult to fit the eschatological descriptions of this poem into the categories of complaint and confidence. Although some of the key terms seem to be drawn from Psalm 18 (חבלי מות, נחלי בליעל), the descriptions which utilize these phrases are more cosmological in scope than those of the Psalms. Holm-Nielsen himself realizes this, for he comments that the vocabulary and background of this poem are those of the prophets rather than the Psalms.[43]

In fact, there are only two sections of this poem which are written in the style of the thanksgiving psalm--the Opening Stanza and Stanza B, both employing first person references. The intervening stanza, A, is not unlike other parts of the Hodayot and the OT Psalms, but it is noteworthy for its impersonal language in the description of cleansing by God. The rest of the poem deals with heavenly warfare. The problem of the relationship of these somewhat disparate units is rarely faced by commentators; either its themes are dealt with line-by-line, or else it is given an overall description like that of Holm-Nielsen, which fits only at certain points. Discussion of the psalm's theology is thus determined by the approach taken.

Structural analysis cannot hope to resolve all the controversial questions in regard to this psalm, but it can mitigate some of the difficulty. Since the various sections of the poem are not explicitly related by a single theme, it is logical to look for implicit relationships drawn out by the repetition or recapitulation of certain words. When the entire poem is examined with this in mind, it is seen that a few key words are found throughout the poem, or introduced at the opening and recapitulated at the end. These thematic words draw the poem

together and supply the single thread of action that is missing
in the change from personal to impersonal language, from individual plight to eschatological warfare.

While no section of the poem is devoid of such key terms,
the bulk of these phrases are found at the opening (Opening
Stanza, Stanza A), and at the close (Stanza E). The Opening
Stanza also shares related terms with C (שחת, לאין + a noun,
מקוה), and a common pronoun with B (the first person singular).
Stanzas A, B, and C are linked by the term גורל, and Stanzas D
and E are linked by several words (see diagram below). In the
latter connection, it is worth noting that A, B, and C are
balanced rhythmically by D and E.

Stanza E:	כיא ירעם אל בהמון כוחו	Opening
	ויהם זבול קודשו באמת כבודו	Stanza
	וצבא השמים יתנו בקולם	Stanza A
	ויתמרגגו וירעדו אושי עולם	Stanza D
	ומלחמת גבורי שמים תשוט בתבל
ולא תשוב עד כלה ונחרצה לעד ואפס כמוה

It is clear that Stanza E is meant to draw the poem together structurally and thematically in its gathering of terms
from throughout the poem. The distress of the author introduced in the Opening Stanza is to be resolved by the statement
of the final lines, which mirror or repeat several of the opening phrases: the author is to see his own problem in the light
of the final ultimate victory of God's army. The struggle of
the individual against evil is the same struggle of God against
Belial. The rescue of the poet from evil, declared in the
Opening Stanza, has as its balance the judgment of evildoers,
matched term for term (Stanza C).

The psalm can indeed be described as one of thanksgiving,
complaint, and confidence, but the identification of the individual's (or community's) salvation with a universal battle
goes far beyond the OT development of these forms.

It is also clear that the question of the author's belief
in immortality must be seen from the standpoint of the psalm as
a whole. Although the scholars who have examined this problem,
and related questions, have all recognized the necessity of
examining other passages in the Hodayot employing the same key
words, none have considered the literary unit as a whole of

importance in this matter. In this case, at least, the psalm
as a whole has much bearing on the question. The extreme positions on the question of immortality in the Hodayot are represented on the one hand by van der Ploeg and Delcor,[44] and on
the other by Laurin.[45] The former maintain that the reference
to eternity in this psalm, as well as the statement of community with the angels, are evidence of a belief in resurrection of
the dead or immortality of the soul or both. With this viewpoint, Laurin has taken issue and maintains that all such references are merely figurative, and actually refer metaphorically
to rescue from vicissitudes in this life. A subsidiary point
is raised by Murphy, who has tried to show that references to
šaḥat in this psalm and others does not refer so much to the
nether world as to moral corruption.[46] These scholars have
done a great deal of work compiling lists of phrases from
throughout the Hodayot as evidence for their opinions. Here
the focus will be on the evidence of a single psalm, taken as
a unit.

Just as the key words of the poem provided the thread of
unity for the theme, so do they illustrate the scope of meaning
for the various terms employed. לרום עולם and לסוד עולם in the
Opening Stanza are thus balanced by אושי עולם in the final
stanza, and the references to the angelic companies of Stanza A
by the terms for the heavenly armies in Stanza E. In contrast
to these "eternal" images and groups into which the author is
inducted, are the references to šaḥat and Belial, from which he
is delivered. The artistic form of the poem clearly sets these
terms into contrasting relationships; none can be considered
separately. At the extremes are the eternal heights and the
eternal depths (foundations). It is quite clear from a consideration of the poem as a whole that these terms are eschatological images drawn from a full-blown dynamic mythology, not simply
ancient metaphors designed to provide superlative language for
rescue in the present life.

The warfare described in this psalm, in which the author
had a part, extends to the whole creation--from the heaven
above where God dwelt to the nether world where the foundations
of the earth were located. This psalm deals with the ultimate.

Thus the community God establishes on earth is eternal, and it can have communion with the heavenly army;[47] thus the heavenly war is one to which no other can be compared. The imagery employed in reference both to God and his heavenly army and to Belial and šaḥat is concrete and dynamic, and is not simply a reminiscence of OT metaphors. This cosmological scheme is indeed borrowed from the OT, but its completeness and its vividness testify to the continuing development and use of the OT scheme in this period. Neither a doctrine of resurrection nor of the immortality of the soul is delineated in this psalm. Nevertheless, in view of the ultimate nature of the war described, and the author's identification of his deliverance with God's final victory, the psalm's theology is consonant with a belief in resurrection and reward for the righteous. There is no support for belief in the immortality of the soul as separate from the body, and there is no reason to insist that the language of the psalm is metaphorical rather than literal.

4. Hodayot 5:5-19 (Plate 39)

Of the three poems investigated in this chapter, this is the most complicated. A cursory reading does not suggest this, for this psalm, unlike the others studied, has a central image carried throughout the poem, unifying it. Other imagery is clearly subordinated to the ravening lions from whom God has rescued the poet. The story of Daniel comes immediately to mind, offering comparisons in both symbolism and language. But despite the familiarity of the theme, poetic analysis is difficult. There are large lacunae in the opening and closing lines of the psalm which hamper the determination of the exact shape of the first and last stanzas. Certain patterning features within the body of the poem are easily detected, but which of them mark off the larger units of the poem can be disputed.

The Text

Since unlike the previous two psalms there are very large lacunae in 5:5-19, it is appropriate to comment at this point

on the methods of restoring the text. The first and most important test which any suggested restoration must pass is
whether it fits the size of the hole in the text. Restorations
which pass this first test can then be criticized on other
grounds: the vocabulary, theology, and syntax employed must be
weighed against the evidence of the whole document, and the
restoration must also be in harmony with the poem's organization. For example, in line 5, there is a gap of twenty-five to
twenty-seven spaces. Generally it is assumed that the end of
the first line of the initial bicolon, the second line of the
bicolon, and the word ולא at the beginning of the third line
are missing. Licht suggests instead a restoration in which no
complete line has fallen out, but in which three words are
missing at the end of the first line and two words at the beginning of a second line before כאשׂמחי.[48] Both solutions take
into account the number of missing letters, and so both are
possible; but it can be argued that Licht's restoration is less
likely on poetic grounds.

In some instances in this psalm, the consideration of the
size of the gap in the text appears to have played little part
in the restorations offered by scholars. In the lacuna of line
6, suggested restorations range from four to fourteen spaces,
and obviously the size of the gap precludes some of these solutions. Ironically, those restorations which are too short to
fill the gap fit the context better than do those which are of
the right length. A suggested solution in this particular case
is deferred to the section on stanza analysis.

Of course, even when suggested restorations fit the size
of the lacunae, they are often not accepted by all scholars.
Generally, the larger the gap is, the less the agreement. Those
restorations in this psalm which are almost universally agreed
upon--usually two to four spaces in length--are shown in the
following transcription and translation of the poem without
notes. The other lacunae are shown schematically by lines enclosed with brackets, and possible restorations are discussed
in the pages that follow. Almost without exception, the gaps
in lines 7, 11, and 16 are restored as shown. The gap of ten

spaces in line 18, at the end of the psalm, like the two lacunae in lines 5 and 6, is difficult to restore.

In line 15, there is a small hole about four spaces long.
Immediately preceding the hole are the letters בלו and the
upper right tip of a fourth letter. Sukenik has transcribed
the word בלי, implying that a new word begins where the leather
has rotted away.[49] The missing word is undoubtedly a verb,
since חה- can be seen at the left edge of the hole, and the
syntax of the line demands a verb. It seems highly unlikely
that בלי is the preceding word, however, because the space between the ל and the י/ו is larger than that between the י/ו and
the tip of the fourth letter. Since the copyist of this portion of the scroll was a careful scribe with clear handwriting
who invariably left longer spaces between words than between
the letters of a single word, it would seem likely that the
word here is בלוא. בלוא with a perfect verb is found several
times in the Hodayot,[50] although it is an infrequent construction in biblical Hebrew. The reconstruction of the missing
verb is considered under "Stanza Analysis."

Once again, there are a variety of scribal corrections in
the text. In line 14, לשורנו was erased and replaced by שניהם,
and י was erased at the end of נפשי. In line 15, בי was added
above the line after the verb הגבירכה. In the final full line
of the hymn, the word נפשי, written after חשוב, has been dotted
above and below to indicate deletion. The first and last of
these corrections seem to tighten the poetic structure--the
original readings made sense grammatically, but were perhaps
less pleasing structurally.

One other comment on the text of this psalm is perhaps
appropriate. Mowinckel's arrangement of this poem shows the
coda ברוך אתה, balancing the opening formula.[51] Examination of
the photographic plate of this column reveals clearly that this
is actually the opening formula of the next psalm. The final
word of the hymn in 5:5-19, אריות, appears at the right-hand
margin on line 19. The rest of the line is blank, indicating
the end of the hymn. The new psalm in line 20, which begins at
the right-hand margin, originally had the formula אודכה אדוני.
The first word was dotted above and below by the corrector--the

usual indication of a deletion--and ברוך אתה was written above
the dots and just below the word אריות.

Both of the psalms appearing in this column begin with the
opening formula at the right-hand margin, with the previous
psalm ending so that a blank half line clearly separates the
poems. Within this psalm there is a single long space indicating a major break in the poem; line 17 ends with a blank space
a quarter line in length and line 18 begins ואתה אלי, almost
certainly a new unit. Interestingly enough, אתה אלי appears
two other times in the psalm, but these are not set apart by
any spacing.

Hebrew Text of Hodayot 5:5-19

5	אודכה אדוני	
	[---] בעם בגורי עזבתני לא כי[a]	Opening
	[--------------------]	Stanza
5-6	[ולא]כאשמחי שפטתני	
	ולא עזבתני בזמות יצרי	
	ותעזור משחת חיי	
6-7	ותתן [-----------][b] בתוך לביאים	Stanza
	מועדים לבני אשמה	A
	אריות שוברי עצם אדירים	
	ושותי ד[ם] גבורים	
7-8	ותשמני במגור עם דיגים רבים	Stanza
	פורשי מכמרת על פני מים	B
	וצידים לבני עולה	
8-9	ושם למשפט יסדתני	
	וסוד אמת אמצתה בלבבי	
	ומיה ברית לדורשיה	
9-10	ותסגור פי כפירים אשר כוזרב שניהם	Stanza
	ומתלעותם כחנית חדה	C
	חמת תנינים כול מזמותם לזותוף	
10-11	וירבו ולא פצו עלי פיהם	
11	כי אתה אלי סתרתני נגד בני אדם	Stanza
	ותרתכה חבתה [בי]	D
11-12	[ע]ד קץ הגלות ישעכה לי	
	כי בצרת נפשי לא עזבתני	
	ושועתי שמעתה במרורי נפשי	
13	ודנת יגוני הכרתה באנחתי	
	ותצל נפש עני במעון אריות אשר שננו כחרב לשונם	

---

[a]Lacuna of twenty-five to twenty-seven spaces; most scholars are agreed that ולא appeared before כאשמחי. For comments
on restoration, see p. 81.

[b]Lacuna of twelve to fourteen spaces; see p. 89 for
discussion.

14	ראתה אלי סגרתה בעד שניהם^c	Stanza
	פן יטרפו נפש^d עני ורש	E
14-15	ותוסף לשונם כחרב אל תערה	
	בלוא [---]חה^e נפש עבדכה	
	ולמען הגבירכה בי^f לנגד בני אדם	
15-16	הפלתה באביון	
	ותביאהו במצ[רף כזה]ב במעשי אש	
	וככסף מזוקק בכור נופחים לטהר שבעתים	
17	רימהרו עלי רשעי עזים במצוקותם	
	וכול היום ידכאו נפשי	
18	ראתה אלי תשיב^g סערה לדממה	Stanza
18-19	ונפש אביון פלטתה כ[------]	F
	[---]טרף מכח אריות	

Translation of Hodayot 5:5-19

5   I thank you, O Lord,

For you did not abandon me when I wandered among
    a [foreign]^A people,
[   ]

5-6   [And not] according to my guilt did you judge me,
Nor did you abandon me to my wicked nature,
But you helped my life out of the Pit.

6-7   And you placed [me]^B in the midst of lions,
Those appointed for the sons of guilt,
Lions who shatter the bones of the noble,
And who drink the blood of the mighty.

---

^cCorrected by a later hand; originally read לשונם.

^dOriginally read נפשי; י erased by corrector.

^eAlthough the א is conjectural, the plate clearly shows that the word had four letters, rather than the three shown in Sukenik's transcription.

^fבי added above the line by the corrector.

^gנפשי is written in the original but has been dotted above and below by corrector to indicate deletion.

^Aנכר, "foreign," is a plausible restoration here, but not necessarily the correct one (see p. 88). It is supplied here for the convenience of the reader, to round out the general sense of the opening line.

^BThis lacuna is considerably larger than a single word, but undoubtedly contained a reference to the poet which the simple pronoun can convey. See p. 89 for a discussion of this restoration.

7-8   And you set me a camp with many fishermen,
       Those who spread a net upon the face of the waters,
       The hunters for the sons of unrighteousness.

8-9   And there for judgment you established me,
       And a foundation of truth you fortified in my heart,
       And from it^C a covenant for those who seek it.

9-10   And you shut the mouth of the young lions,
         whose teeth are like a sword,
       And whose fangs are like a sharp spear,
       And like the poison of dragons, whose whole evil
         plan is to rip apart.
       And they strove^D but they did not open their
         mouths against me.

       For you, O my God, you concealed me in the sight
         of the sons of men,
       And your torah you hid in me
11-12 Until the time of revealing your salvation for me,
       For in the distress of my life you did not abandon me,
       But my cry you heard in the bitterness of my being,
13   And the strife of my grief you acknowledged in my
         groan.
       And you rescued the life of the afflicted in the
         den of lions, whose tongue is sharpened
         like a sword.

14   And you, O my God, you shut their teeth,
       Lest they tear apart the life of the poor afflicted;
14-15 And their tongue was drawn back^E like
         a sword to its sheath,
       Lest it [smite]^F the life of your servant;
       So that you might be reckoned mighty through me
         before the sons of men,
15-16 You did wonderful works^G with the poor one,
       And you brought him for refining like gold
         in the work of the fire,
       And like silver refined in the furnace of the smith
         to sevenfold purity.
17   But the strong and wicked rushed against me with
         their oppressions,
       And all the day they trampled my life.

18   And you, O my God, you turn a storm to stillness;
       And the life of the poor one you rescued like [_____]
       [_____] tearing apart from the
18-19   power of the lions.

---

^{C}This is a difficult phrase to interpret. See p. 90.

^{D}The verb here might be either ארב or ריב; see p. 91.

^{E}ותוסף is probably a third feminine singular verb rather than second masculine singular; see p. 195 n. 52.

^{F}נכה is the most probable verb for this gap; see p. 94.

^{G}The verb here might be פלא or פלה; see p. 93.

Stanza Analysis

The variety of stanzaic arrangements shown in translations of this psalm suggests that the poem lacks clear indications of its total structure. Actually, the repetition of certain words and forms makes it relatively easy to establish the larger units of the poem. Two forms in particular stand out: אתה אלי, occurring three times in the poem; and the recurrent second person imperfect form of the verb. The latter is noteworthy because, of seven occurrences of this verb form in the psalm, six occur with the vav conversive and begin new lines in the poem.[52] In the first half of the psalm, where אתה אלי does not appear, these verb forms (four of them) are spaced at more or less regular intervals. In the latter half of the poem, one of these imperfects begins the poetic line immediately before the second אתה אלי, and the final one occurs between the second and third appearances of אתה אלי. The particle כי appears in its customary place at the opening of the first unit and also stands before the first אתה אלי.

No other phrases or verb forms show this repetition at the beginning of the psalm's lines, and it would seem quite certain that the above phrases are meant to indicate the larger units of the poem. Two questions remain in the determination of the stanza units. Following the opening lines, second person imperfect verbs begin two consecutive lines: do both belong to the same unit? And secondly, what is the strategic usage of the second person imperfect in the latter half of the poem where אתה אלי clearly marks the units? In both these cases it will be shown later that these second person verbs are not indicators of new stanzas, but fulfill another strategic purpose: they mark the end of a unit or the opening of a sub-stanza.

With this preliminary analysis accomplished, it can be seen that there are seven stanzas in the psalm, as diagrammed below.

וכי ⎤
ותעזור ⎦   opening phrase
           closing phrase

ותתן ⎤
ותשמני ⎥
ותסגור ⎦

וכי אתה אלי ⎤   opening phrase
ותצל ⎦   closing phrase
ואתה אלי ⎤   opening phrase
ותביאהו ⎥   substanza opening
ואתה אלי ⎤

The opening stanza has the usual beginning formula, and is
followed by three stanzas which open with the second person imperfect. The final three stanzas open with divine address. It
is no accident that the first of the stanzas in the latter half
of the poem has כי preceding the divine address; it will be
seen later that this stanza marks the turning point of the poem
and has certain relationships structurally and metrically with
the opening stanza.

The most difficult aspect of the Opening Stanza is the
large lacuna of twenty-five to twenty-seven spaces at the end
of line 5. The majority of scholars agree that לא can be restored immediately before כאשמתי, on the basis of sense;[53] the
rest of the lost text is problematic. Except for Licht, all
those scholars who have concerned themselves with poetic arrangements agree that one word is missing at the end of the
first line after עם, as well as the second half of the initial
bicolon. Licht believes that no complete poetic line has fallen out, but that three words follow עם to round out the first
line and that two words precede כאשמתי in the second half of a
bicolon.[54] Such an arrangement would yield an initial bicolon
of approximately thirty-two syllablves (seventeen + fifteen)--
a length not substantiated by a single psalm opening in the

rest of the scroll.[55] The line arrangement suggested by the
majority of scholars on the other hand would yield a four-line
stanza, with an initial bicolon of about twenty-six syllables
(thirteen + ten)--the standard line and bicolon length in the
Hodayot.

It can be further guessed that the missing line contained
a negative statement, since לא is used in the surrounding lines.
Dupont-Sommer believed he could restore נכרי after עם on the
basis of the remnants of three letters which can be seen on
Plate 39.[56] Carmignac, Delcor, and Gaster[57] have followed this
lead, although other scholars have been reluctant to do so. An
examination of the plate weighs in Dupont-Sommer's favor; although only the ligatures at the bottom of the three letters
can be seen, the first two are more likely to be נ and כ than
any other letters.

The repetition of לא עזבתני in the fourth line of the poem
is significant. It suggests that the first four lines of the
poem had an "envelope" structure, with the first and fourth
lines forming the envelope around parallel second and third
lines. לא עזבתני is repeated in Stanza D, tying that stanza,
which is the turning point of the poem, to the opening unit.

The fifth line of the poem, ותעזור משחת חיי, has been
thought by some to mark a new unit; indeed, since it begins
with the second person imperfect verb, which is a strategically
used form in this poem, such an arrangement can be considered.
However, further reflection suggests that it is rather the
"coda" of the opening unit. It will be seen shortly that there
are certain similarities in structure shared by Stanzas A and B.
This patterning breaks down if ותעזור is regarded as the opening of Stanza A. The clinching evidence comes from the words
of the line itself. שחת and חיי are paired elsewhere in the
Hodayot,[58] and there is no doubt that שחת is a reference to the
underworld, not simply the noun "destruction," as Holm-Nielsen
suggests.[59] The statement this line makes is that salvation is
accomplished; such a statement does not belong to the beginning
of the narrative motif, if the thanksgiving form is considered;
nor can it logically be attached to the following statements in
which the poet recalls his ordeal. Moreover, עזב and עזר would

seem to be deliberate word play by the author to further reinforce his statements of divine help. The fifth line of this
stanza forms a "coda" for the opening stanza quite similar in
length and weight to the extremely long line ("double line") at
the close of the first stanza in 3:19-36.

With Stanza A, the image of the ravening lions is introduced. Once again, the stanza is marred slightly by a gap, but
this one is much shorter and less troublesome than the first.
The context definitely requires a reference to the author.
Various restorations involving נפש, a favorite term for personal reference, have been suggested; the problem with most is
that they are too short--only nine to ten spaces rather than
the eleven to fourteen needed.[60] Both Dupont-Sommer and Licht
have suggested restorations ending with the letter ט, which can
be seen at the left edge of the hole.[61] Both of these restorations are to be criticized, however, for introducing material
extraneous at this point in the poem, and Dupont-Sommer's restoration is a bit short as well. If, however, the final letter
of the phrase was ט, perhaps the original was עבדכה למשפט. This
phrase is the requisite length, avoids the use of את, and the
reference to judgment can be justified as a balance for the same
word in Stanza B. The final letter of the phrase is smudged and
the scroll is slightly decayed; it seems possible that it may
have been ש rather than ט. If so, such a phrase as נפש עני ורש,
used later in the poem, may have been the personal designation
here.

The structure of the four lines of Stanza A (diagrammed on
p. 90) is echoed in the opening of Stanza B. Both stanzas begin with second person imperfect verbs whose meanings are
quite similar, both mention the evildoers who are sought out
for destruction, and both describe action with a participle in
the construct state. The order of these elements has been
changed in Stanza B, however: the construct participle is used
in the second line rather than the third, exchanging places
with the reference to the evildoers. Stanza B is also longer
than Stanza A, and the remaining lines diverge from the structure of A, just as the imagery of the stanza does; here the
instruments for judgment are fishers and hunters rather than

lions. Stanza B consists of two tricola. The first is
modelled on the structure of Stanza A. The second opens a
statement complementing that of the opening tricolon: first
tricolon: "And you set me a camp with many fishermen"; second
tricolon: "And there for judgment you established me."

Only the final line of Stanza B is difficult. The interpretations of ומיהברית outnumber the commentators, and all
involve either emendation of the text or recognition of some
orthographical variation. Mansoor and Bardtke believe ומיה
should be emended to מהזה, which equals מָזֶה and thus they turn
the final statement into a question.[62] Rhetorical or not, a
question scarcely fits the context here. Wallenstein suggests
an interpretation of מיה from מים, "water."[63] Again this suggestion does not fit well in the context and is not supported
by the style or vocabulary elsewhere in the Hodayot. Others,
by either emendation or orthographical variation have read some
form of מיהא or מזה, "from this."[64] Although the usual combinations of מן with a pronoun suggest some orthographical peculiarity here, the spelling is not impossible. Such an interpretation of מיה is still enigmatic, since it is difficult then
to determine to what the demonstrative pronoun refers--to the
heart? to the foundation of truth? At the present, however, it
seems to be the best solution offered.

The following diagram summarizes the structural features
of Stanzas A and B.

With Stanza C, the imagery of the poem returns to the
lions. The structure of this stanza is a type already seen in
the Hodayot, an envelope pattern in which the first and fourth
lines complement each other, while the inner lines are parallel.

Once again the stanza opens with the second person imperfect
verb. The one feature of this stanza which has disturbed commentators is the verb וירבו. Wallenstein sets it on a poetic
line by itself, a rather improbable solution.[65] Holm-Nielsen
concludes that it should have stood before the preceding infinitive, where it would then reproduce a phrase from Ps 10:9
which refers to lion's prey.[66]

A large part of the problem is the ambiguity of the verb;
it is taken by some translators as a form of רבה,[67] by others
as a form of ארב.[68] It might also be from ריב. The latter two
verbs offer better sense than does רבה, and despite those who
feel the word is misplaced or awkward, both offer adequate
sense and syntax for the final line of the stanza. It is unusual in the Hodayot to find both an imperfect verb with a vav
conversive and a perfect verb in the same line, but this is the
only arrangement which yields both sense and balance in the
stanza. Although a form of ארב, in which the א has become
quiescent is certainly possible here, ריב would seem to fit the
context equally well or better. It offers a more effective
contrast to ולא פצו, which the syntax seems to require; and it
has as well a legal and judgmental significance which is in
keeping with the focus of the poem (see below, "Theology and
Imagery"). The ambiguity of the word may be deliberate, with
both ארב and ריב intended; one of the lines in Stanza E, a key
line, has a similar ambiguity.

Stanza D is the turning point of the poem. The symbolic
judgment of the author is resolved here in the profession of
God's support through the test. Once again the strategic particle כי appears, opening each of the two tricola that form the
body of this stanza. Following the first כי is the phrase of
divine address which opens the stanzas in this second half of
the poem. Both כי and the phrase לא עזבתני at the opening of
the second tricolon link this stanza to the Opening Stanza.

There is an interesting and difficult problem in the second tricolon of this stanza. ודנת יגוני has been interpreted
in a variety of ways, but none has been satisfactory in all
respects. Unfortunately what should be the best clue here--the
parallel structure--is not of great help. Ironically it can be

seen that the final two lines of this tricolon have exact and
complete parallelism. However, it seems that the author has
once again employed reversal of the prepositional object, and
this complicates matters.

וישועתי שמעתה במרורי נפשי
ודנח יגוני הכרתה באנוזתי

It would seem that שועתי and אנוזתי are parallel terms, and
that דנח יגוני is paralleled by מרורי נפשי; but ב is employed
with one term from each of these pairs, so that these parallel
terms play different syntactical roles in each line. This phenomenon was also seen in 3:19-36, and there too, traditional
analysis of parallelism is complicated by this feature. It is
possible as well that, in each case, ב is meant to be construed
as a double-duty preposition, but even in this case, the interpretation of דנח is not much clearer. The two construct chains
seem intended to be synonymous in meaning. Wallenstein suggests that the word is from Aramaic, meaning "pitcher" or "jar,"
which is extended to mean "cup" as well ("cup of affliction").[69]
A jar is not the same kind of container as a cup, however, and
this interpretation seems a bit strained. It has been suggested
that דנח might be a copyist's mistake for רנה,[70] but elsewhere
in the Hodayot רנה is used only in a positive sense. Although
there is no other use of דנח in the OT or the Hodayot, דנח might
be related to מָדוֹן, "strife, contention." Such a derivation
offers the requisite meaning demanded by the parallel phrase.[71]

     To close Stanza D, there is a rather prosaic and lengthy
line, opening with a second person imperfect verb. As it will
be seen in the discussion of meter presently, this line is
about twice the length of the usual poetic line in the poem,
but cannot be set in the usual bicolon arrangement, due to the
grammar employed. It might be called a "double line." Such an
arrangement has already been observed in the Opening Stanza of
3:19-36, where very similar syntax is used, and it will be seen
elsewhere in the Hodayot. This "double line" is shown in diagrams as a single long line to emphasize its difference from a
normal bicolon. Here, as in 3:19-36 this "double line" provides a coda for the stanza.

At the extremes of Stanza D are two phrases which link the
stanza forward and backward to the neighboring stanzas. נגד
בני אדם at the end of the first line of the stanza reappears
in the middle of Stanza E, while the final phrase of Stanza D,
אשר שננו כחרב לשונם, is only a slightly different version of
אשר כחרב שניהם in Stanza C. These phrases produce an interlocking effect.

Stanza C   אשר כחרב שניהם
Stanza D   נגד בני ארם
                אשר שננו כחרב לשונם
Stanza E   לנגד בני אדם

Stanza E is rather long in comparison to the preceding
stanzas of the poem, and this is offset by a very short Stanza
F. Both the lion imagery and a subsidiary metaphor appear in
Stanza E. Four lines of alternating parallelism dealing with
the lions open the stanza. A rather oddly unbalanced bicolon
follows restating the purpose of God's testing. This bicolon
is the center of the stanza metrically (see below), and relates
equally well to the lion imagery which precedes it and to the
depiction of gold refinement which follows. Interestingly
enough, due to the spelling conventions at Qumran, the verb in
this short line can be derived from either פלא, "to work won-
drously," or from פלה, "to set apart." The former verb has
been used in the translation in this paper, but once again, the
ambiguity may be intentional, so that both meanings are kept in
the reader's mind. A single bicolon introduces the final image
of the poem, of the author as gold to be refined by fire. The
last bicolon of the stanza contains a generalized statement of
persecution by the wicked.

The parallelism of Stanza E is, on the whole, quite regular. It is of some help in restoring the small gap in column
line 15. Here, it may be recalled, the gap is preceded by the
word בלוא, with only the tip of the א visible, but with the
placement of the letters virtually assuring this reading (page
82). A close guess at the verb which followed בלוא can be
made if the alternating parallelism of the first four lines of
Stanza E is noted. The lines beginning פן and בלוא are parallel

to each other; the only divergence is the use of the third
person verb in the former and a second person verb in the latter. The missing verb was most likely נכה.[72]

The final stanza, F, is greatly marred by a gap towards
the end of column line 18, but the general sense is clear. In
structure, this closing stanza or coda is a tricolon which
opens with a divine address similar to the previous two stanzas.
From the phrases that can be read and a consideration of the
size of the gap, it seems almost certain that a single word is
missing from the second line and one word from the beginning of
the third line.[73] It is generally agreed that מכה in the third
line is a variant of מכוח, rather than a mistake for מפי, as
Bardtke suggests.[74]

Rhythmical Balancing

Like the psalm in 3:19-36 and unlike the psalm in 2:20-30,
this poem at first glance seems to be metrical chaos. Not only
are the lines of quite varied lengths, but the stanza units are
uneven in length. However, once again it can be determined
that syllabically the majority of the lines fall within the
nine to thirteen syllable pattern that seems standard in the
Hodayot. The shorter and longer lines seem to be placed for
strategic effect. Syllabically, the stanzas are quite uneven,
but those units sharing the same strategic opening at the beginning of the poem balance the units of the second half of the
psalm. Stanza D, which shares thematic and vocabulary terms
with the Opening Stanza appears to be the pivot point of the
poem's balance.

It is obvious that the syllabic length of the opening and
closing stanzas is a guess, because of the large lacunae. However, a fairly accurate guess can be made if the length of the
space and the parallel character of the lines is taken into
account. As was shown earlier, the missing lines in the Opening Stanza could not be longer than twenty-five to twenty-seven
spaces. This would be room enough for six words at the most,
and probably not fewer than four. The opening line has six
words (counting the missing word at the end of the line), and

even if the parallelism were exactly complete, כי would not be
reduplicated. Syllabically a line of four or five words could
range from eight to fifteen syllables, and in view of the
"standard" length of the other lines in the stanzas, it is
likely that the missing line was nine to thirteen syllables in
length. In the final stanza, where there is a ten-space gap,
the last two lines are each lacking a word, and there is most
likely a letter missing before טרף. The syllable count here
ranges from eleven to twelve and nine to eleven for these final
lines. The counts for these stanzas appear in the diagram below with a question mark to indicate the guesswork involved.

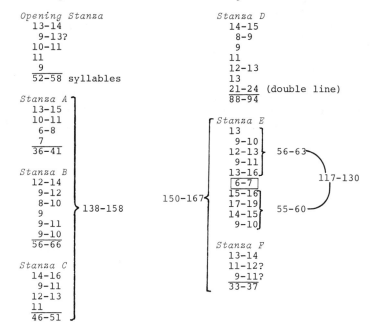

Opening Stanza
13-14
9-13?
10-11
11
9
52-58 syllables

Stanza A
13-15
10-11
6-8
7
36-41

Stanza B
12-14
9-12
8-10
9
9-11
9-10
56-66

Stanza C
14-16
9-11
12-13
11
46-51

138-158

Stanza D
14-15
8-9
9
11
12-13
13
21-24 (double line)
88-94

Stanza E
13
9-10
12-13   56-63
9-11
13-16
6-7   117-130
15-16
17-19
14-15   55-60
9-10

Stanza F
13-14
11-12?
9-11?
33-37

150-167

It will be noted that the pivot stanza, D, is one-third
shorter than the larger units on either side; the Opening Stanza
with which it shares several phrases corresponds exactly to this
one-third weight, so that there are three well-balanced units in
the poem metrically.

Interesting also are the occurrences of the long lines and
the very short line in Stanza E. This short line occurs exactly halfway through Stanza E, the longest stanza in the poem.
The longer lines of the poem fall into two groups. In the
first group belong the long line at the beginning of Stanza C,
the long line at the beginning of Stanza D, the "double line"
coda of D, and the fifth line of Stanza E. These lines were
analyzed on page 93, where their function as interlocking
phrases, tying Stanzas C, D, and E together was discussed. The
repeated phrases which produce the interlocking effect also
lengthen the lines. The second group of long lines are those
in the latter half of Stanza E, where three long lines with a
standard line of nine must balance five lines in the first half
of the stanza.

Theology and Imagery

All commentators have noted the similarity between this
poem and the stories in Daniel. Intriguing also is the observation that this imagery is employed in each case by writers
immersed in apocalyptic thought and expectations. Poetic analysis of this psalm suggests some additional nuances in the
author's thinking that are usually missed.

The major imagery of the poem centers about the lions, but
this is not the only imagery involved. The poet also speaks of
the hunters and fishers with nets--a theme found in Jeremiah
and Habakkuk--and of purifying gold and silver through refinement in fire, as in Malachi.[75] These subsidiary images are
neatly enclosed, one in the first half of the poem and one in
the second half, by the imagery of the lions. All three images
are judgment images, and it is important to remember this. Many
scholars comment that the psalm focuses on the rescue of the
poet from dire distress, represented by the ravening lions.
Poetic analysis, and the careful sequence of three judgment
images suggests that an additional focus is the ordeal of judgment through which all those declared righteous must pass.
This ordeal is depicted by each of the three images, by the
lion imagery as well as the other two. The poet's thanksgiving

is not for rescue as such, but for God's support by which he
achieves salvation. The verb in the opening phrase is not פדה,
or נצל--verbs used elsewhere in the Hodayot--but לא עזב.

Once the true thrust of the psalm is seen in the sequence
of judgment motifs, the theological insight of the author is
even more interesting. The poet's theological statement is one
of salvation by grace alone, not due to any righteous works on
the part of the poet.

The lions are appointed to ravage the evil; the hunters
and fishers with nets are intended to seek out the evil ones
also. In each case, the poet recognizes that his survival is
due to God's work, and that he is declared innocent because God
places his salvation within him. (A counsel of truth you for-
tified in my heart; "You hid your Torah within me.") This
would seem to be the thrust of the Daniel story as well; the
lions do not harm him because he is blameless before God (Dan
6:22). In view of the focus on judgment in this psalm, it
seems likely that the verb in the last line of Stanza C is ריב,
rather than ארב, because of its connection with legal judgment.
The lions attempt to destroy the poet, but cannot because of
God's salvific work in the poet. The final stage in the judgment process is like the refining of precious metal, in which
the dross is washed away, and the poet's salvation is complete.
The lions cannot conquer because of God's declaration of inno-
cence and salvation.[76]

CHAPTER IV

TWO HYMNS

1. Hodayot 7:26-33 (Plate 41)

This psalm has frequently been analyzed; its brief length, the relatively good condition of the text, and the brief repetitious lines have been conducive to scholarly study. Despite this attention, many of the most important structural features have gone unnoticed.

There are a number of small holes in the text, as well as some scribal corrections. As usual, the psalm begins on a fresh line of the manuscript (line 26), indented halfway across the column; the previous psalm closed at the middle of line 25. The opening formula on line 26 is missing except for the initial two letters, אז; this is due to the longitudinal tear which mars much of the previous psalm (see Chapter V). Immediately below, in line 27, there is also a gap of 4-5 letters, and the tear tails off below this in line 28 with a space of one missing letter. This tear, then, is responsible for three lacunae in the psalm:

line 26: where אוֹ[דכה אדוני] can certainly be restored
line 27: where there is a more problematical gap
line 28: where ד can certainly be restored in יצ[ד]ק.

There are four other small gaps in the psalm: in line 30, three letters are missing in the fifth word, but the tops of two of these can be seen; and at the end of the line, ה can certainly be restored in ר[ה]מיכה. At the beginning of line 32, the smeared word is undoubtedly נצחים, closing the idiom begun in line 31. In line 33 the last word or words of the psalm are smeared past all recognition. It can also be added that in the photographs of this column, the beginning of line 28 is so smeared that reliance on Sukenik's transcription is now necessary.[1]

The poem has been corrected by a later hand in three places. In line 29, the letters צבו/י stand over the word רוה. The insertion of this word in the text causes vexing problems,

99

and will be commented upon later. In the following line (30),
חביא has been added above the line to be inserted before
בסליחות. In line 29, a כ has been erased in הכמתכה to achieve
the reading המתכה.[2] It can easily be seen on reading the psalm
that none of these changes were absolutely essential grammatically or syntactically. These changes, then, must be weighed
on other grounds.

   Besides the usual paragraphing conventions at the beginning and end of the psalm, there is a long space left before
כי אל עולם in line 31; and in view of this highly strategic
phrase, involving divine address, this is most likely a paragraph marking.

Hebrew Text of Hodayot 7:26-33

Line		Stanza
26	או[דכה אדוני][a]	Opening Stanza
27	כי השכלתני באמתכה וברזי פלאכה הודעתני ובחסדיכה לאיש][----][b] ברוב רוזמיכה לנעוי לב	
28	מי כמוכה באלים אדוני ומי כאמתכה ומי יצ[ד]ק לפניכה בהשפטו	Stanza A
28-29	ואין להשיב על תוכחתכה כול רוז][c] ולא יוכל כול להתיצב לפני זהמתרה[d]	Stanza B
29-30	וכול בני אמתכה תביא[e] בסליחות לפניכה	Stanza C
30-31	]למה]רם מפשעיהם ברוב טובכה ובהמון ר[ח]מיכה להעמידם לפניכה לעולמי עד	
31-32	כי אל עולם אתה וכול דרכיכה יכונו לנצו[נ]צח][ים] ואין זולתכה	Stanza B'
32-33	ומה הוא איש תהו ובעל הבל להתבונן במעשי פלאך][---------][g]	Stanza A'

---

[a]Only the first two letters of the opening formula can be
seen, but the spacing indicates that this restoration is almost
certain.

[b]Discussion of restoration on p. 102 and p. 199 n. 3.

[c]Over רוז, three letters have been written: צבו (the third
is disputed). Because the expression with this addition makes
little sense, and because the word does not occur elsewhere,
some scholars delete it. See pp. 104-105.

Translation of Hodayot 7:26-33

26   I thank you, O Lord,

        For you gave me insight into your truth,
27   And your wonderful secrets you made me know,
            And your steadfast love to [sinful] man,[A]
            And your great compassion to the perverted heart.

28   Who is like you among the gods, O Lord?
        And what is like your truth?
        And who is declared innocent before you when he
            is judged?

28-29   There is no spirit who can answer against your judgment;[B]
        And no one can stand before your wisdom.

29-30   But all the sons of your truth you will bring
            in forgiveness before you,
        To cleanse them from their sins in your
            great goodness,
30-31   And in the abundance of your compassion to make
            them stand before you forever and ever.

        For you are an eternal God,
31-32   And all your ways are established forever and ever;
        There is none but you.

        And what is the man of chaos and the master
            of nothingness,
32-33   That he should understand your wonderful deeds?

Stanza Analysis

One of the major units of the psalm is marked for the
reader by spacing and the phrase כי אל עולם. The other units
of this poem are rather easy to recognize. There are the usual
four lines of introduction, followed by three questions beginning מי. This marks the separation of the introductory unit

---

[d]Copyist A originally wrote חכמתך, and the כ was erased
by a later corrector.

[e]This word was written above the line by a later hand.

[f]This restoration is not universally agreed upon; some
suggest it should be תמהרט. The verb סהר is not disputed,
however.

[g]One or more words missing from the text.

[A]This restoration approximates the sense of the original;
see p. 199 n. 3.

[B]This line is translated to reflect the textual discussion
on pp. 104-105.

from the body of the poem. Towards the end of the poem is
another question, beginning with מה. This suggests a new unit,
one intended to balance the first section. Further analysis
will substantiate this. The remaining section of the poem, ly-
ing between the מי section and that beginning כי אל עולם, can
be analyzed into stanzas by terms linking it with and balancing
it against the other units of the poem. What emerges is a
well-balanced, chiastically-arranged psalm, contrasting God
and man and focusing at its central point on the community God
has established.

The opening stanza pattern is by now immediately recognizable. The major distinction of this stanza from other openings is its brevity, both in number of lines and length of bicola. In fact, the second bicolon does not even have a verb,
and the prepositional phrases which compose it must be connected in some way to the first bicolon.[3] This has caused
translators problems--are all four *beths* to be translated in
the same way or not, and how is the final bicolon to be linked
with the poem? Burrows and Sanders are undoubtedly correct in
maintaining that this final bicolon is to be loosely attached
to the whole.[4] As Sanders points out, the first bicolon employs very complete chiastic parallelism, and the objects of ב
in the second bicolon are not synonymous with the objects in
the first bicolon, but extend the list.[5] Since the connection
is loose, however, it is not necessary that all four *beths* play
the same syntactical role. It is sometimes an assumption that
nuances of meaning and syntax are not allowed when the expression employs the same word. This is not substantiated in the
OT literature, where such nuances are often deliberately used.
Because in English the use of the preposition indicating object
is considered to be substantially different from an adverbial
use of the preposition does not mean that such distinction was
made in Hebrew. The translator, however, must show the structural relationship of these phrases in the translation, so far
as possible, and the easiest way to show this in this case is
with the same translation for the preposition each time.[6]

Although once again the Opening Stanza is quite general in
language, certain terms from it serve as link words to the rest

of the poem (just as in 3:19-36 and 5:5-19). Here the major
link word is אמתכה, which reappears in Stanzas A and C. A second term from the Opening is also employed in Stanza C, but in
a rearranged fashion: ברוב רחמיכה. It is interesting that both
these link terms come from the extreme limits of the Opening
Stanza, and it is significant that both are employed in Stanza
C, which is the center of this chiastic poem. פלאכה, in the
first bicolon, is also repeated, in the final line of the poem.

The body of the poem is arranged in five stanzas on a
chiastic pattern. B. Thiering has also arranged this poem in a
chiastic pattern, but her analyses of chiasm in the Hodayot
fail to take into account the fact that the Opening Stanzas are
rarely balanced by closing stanzas. She bases her analyses
strictly on repetition of words and pays little attention to
structural analysis. This leads to the ironic situation in
which she correctly perceives that there is chiastic movement
in this poem, but because of her assumption that the entire
poem, including the Opening Stanza, must fit the chiastic
structure, the structure is skewed so that she must see Stanza
B as the center of the poem. The repetition of terms which she
points out fits far better in the present analysis than in her
own.[7]

The first stanza in the body of the poem is composed of
three rhetorical questions, each beginning מי. In each case
the answer to the question "Who is like God?" is obvious. It
is curious that Holm-Nielsen, who has assigned almost every
word or phrase of other Hodayot to OT passages, is reluctant to
state that מי כמוכה באלים has a specific biblical locus. He
points out that the phrase appears several places in the OT.[8]
But surely it must be said that it is precisely because the
statement from Exodus 15 is a rallying cry that it is used
elsewhere and that it is picked up here. The antiquity of the
question, both as a battle cry and a creedal statement, is exactly why a poet imitating canonical poetry would choose such a
statement. The same type of phenomenon can be seen in the
psalms where "stock" phrases such as כי לעולם חסדו are similarly employed.

To this ancient question, reaching back to the roots of
his tradition, the poet has appended further questions to
demonstrate God's greatness in contrast to man, ending with the
question of who can stand blameless before him in judgment.
The focus is thus shifted for the second stanza of the poem to
man, who is sinful.

The two lines which form Stanza B are the most difficult
of the poem syntactically and textually. Its existence as a
separate unit can be deduced not from a strong internal arrangement but from the structure of the rest of the poem. Its corresponding unit, B', is of the same length, and B' closes with
the phrase זולתכה ואין. This matches the opening word here:
ואין. Both units also employ כול, although it is used elsewhere in the poem as well. The bicolon which forms B does
utilize parallelism, and this is of help in solving the knotty
textual problem of column line 28. At the end of the first
line of the bicolon, the middle of line 28, the word צב- is
written directly above רוח. The first problem is the reading
of the word itself. It is generally taken to be צבי ("glory,
beauty").[9] However, if the final letter is י/ו, it is written
in a rather strange fashion, separated from the rest of the
word. The photograph of column 7, line 28, shows the situation
to be this: רוח צב ו.

The "correction" is identified by Martin as the work of
Scribe C, a "clumsy" scribe. Martin says that each of the letters of the correction corresponds to C's script, including the
final י/ו.[10] However, there are faint traces showing in the
photograph which suggest that the final letter may have been a
ה: ◥. Not only can the outlines of the first half of the ה be
made out in the plate (although this could be the trick of
photography), but the hook of the supposed ו is fat and straight
rather than downward curved, as ו is usually written in this
scroll by both the original scribe and the corrector.

It would seem then that the reading may be either צבי ו/ו or
צבה. Neither of these words appears elsewhere in the Sectarian
scrolls. The standard translation of צבי as "beauty" or "glory"
does not yield much sense. Usually it is inserted before רוח,
and in this case the whole phrase, כול צבי רוח, is read

separately as an aside in the poem.[11] Licht has suggested that
the correction may have been made by someone who did not ap-
prove of the original theology of the psalm and "corrected" it
accordingly. He suggests that the corrector substituted the
Aramaic צבו, "word," for רוח and read כול צבו as the object of
the infinitive: "no one returns a word concerning your
reproof."[12] If this theory is accepted, it must be at least
provisionally assumed that the other changes in the psalm have
the same intent, especially the change of וכמתכה to חמתכה in
the following line. A case could be made for this. Against
Licht's theory is the fact that elsewhere in this scroll the
corrector either erased or dotted the word to be deleted, and
that the use of Aramaic words in the Hodayot can rarely be
verified.

Another possible textual solution might be the translation
of צבה as equivalent to צבא, "company, host," a word frequently
employed in the Hodayot and other Qumran texts. Such a translation can be justified by the orthography at Qumran, in which
final א was sometimes replaced by a ה. צבא is found several
times in conjunction with רוח in the Hodayot (usually in the
construct).[13] If used with רוח here, the placement of צבה
would seem to indicate a reading as the absolute, and this
would be highly unusual. However, it may have been intended,
as in Licht's suggestion, as a replacement or substitute for
רוח. The failure to delete רוח may have been due to the
strength of the original text tradition.

Whatever the textual reading used, it seems unlikely that
the end of the first line is to be detached as an aside. This
would be the only awkward phrase in an otherwise tightly constructed hymn. Moreover, the arrangement of the following line
lends support to the syntactical analysis of כול רוח as the
continuation of ואין. It seems likely in view of the parallelism, that the negative particle at the beginning of each line
is to be construed with כול:

ואין להשיב על תוכחתכה כול רוח
ולא יוכל כול להתיצב לפני חמתכה

It is curious that the original reading, חכמתכה, in the
second line gives both excellent sense and is perhaps more in
keeping with the theology of the psalm. The parallel of תכוזת
and חכם is found in Prov 15:31; the emphasis of the present
verse would then be that man is unable to stand before the wise
judgments of God, rather than before his wrathful judgments.
The correction made by the scribe also has biblical precedent
and is characteristic of the Qumran theology, but the tone of
the psalm suggests that it is God's truth before which man goes
down in sin, rather than a failure to keep the law being the
reason for estrangement. In this case, חכמה rather than חמה
would seem a more likely parallel.

Despite these textual problems, Stanza B clearly offers
the contrast required by Stanza A: man is unable to stand before God. Once again, man's sinful situation is to the fore.
Stanza C, the center of the poem, deals with this problem, and
again the author's central affirmation is made. Man receives
salvation, God's grace, only within the community. This central unit of the poem lacks any strategic opening or close, and
can be separated from the surrounding material only because of
the chiastic patterning and the return of key terms from the
psalm's opening. אמתכה appears in the first line of the unit,
this time identifying the members of the community. The second
key term, ברוב רחמיכה, has been rearranged to allow expansion
of the list of divine attributes. ברוב is now connected with
טובכה in the second line of the stanza, and רוזמיכה receives a
new qualifying phrase, בהמון, in the third line. The theological thrust of this central unit of the poem is that an eternal
community is established by God in which man can be forgiven
and cleansed of sin.

The central point of the poem has been reached; the
balancing of the earlier stanzas must now take place. B' opens
with divine address, and continues with the extolling of God's
greatness. As previously noted, it closes with the strategically located ואין. The lines of this stanza--or phrases might
be a better term--are quite uneven. This phenomenon in the
Hodayot is denied by Mowinckel, who insists that such short
lines are not possible.[14] In this case, there is little choice.

The syntax is not ambiguous and the limits of the stanza are
rather well defined. Such an arrangement may not have been
permissible in canonical poetry, but here the apparent uneven-
ness of the lines is resolved by a look at the stanza as a
whole. It is almost exactly the length of its counterpart
B, and has simply split the weight of a single line over two
very short lines, with the standard line separating them.

The final stanza, A', like its counterpart A, begins with
a question. A's question was, "Who is like God?" A' counters
with, "What is the man of chaos?" (ומה הוא איש תהו). The exact
shape of this stanza is marred by the gap where the final word
or words would be, but it can certainly be seen that the unit
is intended to balance A. The infinitive opening the final
line is to be understood instrumentally: "that he should
understand...." Presumably the final word was an adjective or
a prepositional phrase modifying the construct chain.

Rhythmical Balancing

The chiastic arrangement of this psalm has been delineated
using strategic indicators, but a count of the syllable weight
of the lines gives added support to the analysis. The Opening
Stanza is rather short compared to other opening stanzas: only
38-42 syllables. In the remainder of the poem, the balancing
of the units can be seen.

Opening Stanza	Stanza A	Stanza B	Stanza C	Stanza B'	Stanza A'
10	10	12-15	16	6	11
10-11	6-7	15	12	13-15	15?
9-10	12-13	27-30	21	6	26?
9-11	28-30		49	25-27	
38-42					

The poem has one extra-long line, that closing Stanza C, the
center of the poem. Each stanza, except B, employs at least
one shorter-than-standard line. Stanza B' and Stanza A' have
two short lines; in B' this represents the splitting of a standard line.

Theology and Imagery

The theology of the psalm is enhanced by the recognition
of the chiastic arrangement. If the psalm is diagrammed, the
thematic approach is even more apparent.

```
Stanza A:    God          (rhetorical questions)
Stanza B:    Man
Stanza C:    Community (center of poem)
Stanza B':   God
Stanza A':   Man          (rhetorical questions)
```

Thus, God's attributes are each time contrasted to man's estate
in the following stanza, and at the same time contrasted to man
in the balancing section later or earlier in the poem. In the
center are the statements about the community God establishes.
In this poem, the resolution of all the questions raised in the
"man" sections is found in this central section.

As Holm-Nielsen and others have noted, the absence of a
complaint motive and the first person pronoun suggest that this
is a hymn. The central figure is certainly God, not man, and
the focus is on God's attributes. If all the nouns to which
the suffix ‑כה is added are diagrammed by occurrence, the force
of the poem can be seen.

	Opening Stanza:	אמתכה	
		פלאכה	
		חסדיכה	
		רוזמיכה	
3	Stanza A:	אמתכה	(link to opening)
terms	Stanza B:	תוכזחתכה	
		ח]כ[מתכה	
3	Stanza C:	אמתכה	
terms		טובכה	(link to opening)
		רוזמיכה	
	Stanza B':	דרכיכה	
3		זולתכה	
terms	Stanza A':	פלאך	(link to opening)

The relation of the terms in the central stanza, C, to the
Opening has already been observed. The first two terms of the
Opening also mark the limits of the body of the poem, with
אמתכה coming in the first line of Stanza A, and פלאכה in the

final line of A'. The attributes of Stanza B and Stanza B' are
introduced fresh into the poem. Once again it can be seen that
הוכמתכה fits better in the psalm than הממתכה. All of the other
divine attributes of the poem have positive connotations--even
תוכחתכה, "reproof, judgment."

The intricacy and delicacy of the organization of this
psalm and the necessity for proper delineation of its structure
for understanding its theology will also be seen in the following psalm analysis.

2. Hodayot 11:3-14 (Plate 45)

The text of this psalm is marred by only two holes, one
near the beginning of the poem and the other in the final three
lines. The usual devices were used to set off the hymn; the
previous psalm closes with a blank half line (column line 2),
and the opening formula for this psalm is set at the right-hand
margin of column line 3. This practice is again followed at
the close of this psalm and the opening of the next at column
line 15.

The first gap in the text is a small horizontal tear which
has destroyed three or four letters at the beginning of line 4
and three letters at the beginning of line 5. The first of
these lines is almost universally restored as הודע]חני;[15] the
gap in line 5 is more problematic, and two or three nouns have
been suggested, although all have roughly similar connotations.[16]

Restoration of the missing letters in the second gap, in
column lines 11, 12, and 13, has no consensus, although the
understanding of the phrases is not seriously disturbed since
the hole is small. Some of the restorations seem more likely
than others on structural grounds, and these are shown in the
transcription of the text. In addition to these gaps, there is
a smudge in the text at the close of lines 11 and 12. The letters here, blurred but readable, are not bracketed in the
transcription.

There is a single, enigmatic correction in the psalm in
column line 3, where מודה is written above the line. It is
evidently to be inserted before the word ואני, and would then

be a repetition of the previous word. The meaning of this word
is uncertain, and the repetition of it with the same spelling
is doubly troublesome.

It would seem that there is a single paragraphing space
left in the psalm, preceding ולמען, at the middle of column
line 10. In line 3 there is a space longer than is usual before the final word, כיא, and this may be significant or it
may be marginal fitting.

Hebrew Text of Hodayot 11:3-14

3	אודכה אלי	
	כי הפלתה עם עפר	Opening
	וביצר חמר הגברתה מודה מודה[a]	Stanza
3-4	ואני מה	Stanza A
	כיא [הודע]תני בסוד אמתכה	
	ותשכילני במעשי פלאכה	Refrain
4-5	ותתן בפי הודות	
	ובלשוני [תהל]ה[b]	
	ומול שפתי במכון רנה	
	ואזמרה בחסדיכה	
5-6	ובגברותכה אשוחחה	
	כול היום תמיד אברכה שמכה	
6-7	ואספרה כבודכה בתוך בני אדם	
	וברוב טובכה תשתעשע נפשי	
	ואני ידעתי	Stanza B
	כי אמת פיכה	
	ובידכה צדקה	
7-8	ובמחשבתכה כול דעה	
	ובכוחכה כול גבורה	
	וכול כבוד אתכה הוא	
9	באפכה כול משפטי נגע	
	ובטובכה רוב סליחות	
	ורחמיכה לכול בני רצונכה	
	כי הודעתם בסוד אמתכה	Refrain
10	וברזי פלאכה השכלתם	
10-11	ולמען כבודכה טהרתה אנוש מפשע	Stanza C
	להתקדש לכה מכול תועבות נדה	
	ואשמת מעל	
11-12	להוחד [עם] בני אמתך	
	ובגורל עם קדושיכה	
	להרים מעפר תולעת מתים לסוד [עולם]	
13	ומרוח נעוה לבינה[כה]	
	ולהתיצב במעמד לפניכה עם צבא עד	
14	ורוחי [עולם]	
	ולתחודש עם כול נהיה	
	ועם ידעים ביחד רנה	

Translation of Hodayot 11:3-14

3   I thank you, my God,

For you have done mighty things for Dust,
And the creature of clay you have strengthened
   exceedingly.

     And what am I?
3-4   For you made me [know] the counsel of your truth,
         And you enlightened me with your wonderful deeds.

     And you set in my mouth praises,
4-5   And on my tongue a [psalm],
         And my circumcised lips in a place of rejoicing.
         And I will sing of your steadfast love,
         And on your strength I will meditate.
5-6   All the day continually I will bless your name,
         And I will recount your glory among the sons of men,
6-7   And in the greatness of your goodness my life
            delights itself.

     And I know
         That truth is in your mouth,
         And in your hand is righteousness,
7-8   And in your reckoning is all knowledge,
         And in your strength is all might,
         And all glory is with you,
         And in your wrath are all punishing judgments,
9   And in your goodness is great forgiveness,
         And your compassion is for all the sons of
            your good will.

     For you made them know your truthful counsel,
10   And with your wonderful secrets you enlightened them.

     For the purpose of your glory you cleansed man from sin,
10-11   That he might sanctify himself[A] for you out of
              all the wicked abominations and great shame;
           To bring him together [with] the sons of your truth
11-12   and in lot with your holy ones.
           To raise up from dust the worms of men to an
              [eternal] company and from a perverse spirit
              to your understanding;
13   And to station him in a place before you with an
              eternal host and the spirits of [eternity];
13-14   To renew him with all that is and with those who
              know in a community of rejoicing.

---

[a]Second מודה was written above the line between the first
מודה and ואני. For meaning and use, see pp. 112-113.

[b]The noun used here is not certain; see pp. 109 and 200 n. 16.

[A]The third person pronoun seems to be understood in each
of these clauses--אנוש being the antecedent.

Stanza Analysis

Once again the major units of the poem are relatively easy
to ascertain, and there is only one slight irregularity. (The
irregularity is in the opening of the poem which is a mere two
lines in length. However, despite its brevity it has the customary opening formula intact, substituting אלי for אדוני.)
The independent pronoun ואני occurs twice in the hymn (column
lines 3 and 7), and further analysis confirms its strategic
position at the opening of two stanza units. In each case, it
is part of a short statement (two words) followed by כי, also
a strategic particle. And in each case the units are further
marked off by a refrain bicolon which is set at the opening of
Stanza A and at the close of Stanza B. Immediately following
the second occurrence of the refrain is a paragraph spacing
mark and a phrase beginning ולמען. Subordinated to this phrase
are five infinitive clauses. There seem to be, then, three
major units or stanzas in this poem.[17] This psalm shares some
attributes with that in 7:26-33. The focus in Stanzas A and B
is on the attributes of God, again used with the suffix כה-.
The vocabulary is largely the same, and once again scholars are
agreed that there is little dependence on OT passages. Although
personal references are more frequent in this psalm than in 7:
26-33, the common attributes of both are taken as the mark of
the hymn type.

The opening formula is followed as is customary by כי and
a second person verb form, but there is no reference to the
first person in this opening bicolon. The parallelsim is good,
and the only textual problem is the placement and understanding
of מודה מודה. These two words must almost certainly belong
with this opening bicolon. No matter how they are translated
they make little sense when construed with ואני מה which follows. Furthermore, ואני מה is almost certainly paralleled by
ואני ידעתי and both mark the opening of stanza units. Even if
different openings are hypothesized for the stanzas, and the
phrase מודה מודה אני מה is considered as a line, the sense is
awkward and unlike anything else in the Hodayot. On the other
hand, although there are still difficulties if the phrase is

attached at the end of the opening bicolon, following the
strategic stanza indicators, there is little or no syntactical
awkwardness involved.

There would seem to be two possible root meanings for
מודה. It might be derived from either ידה, "to thank," or
from מאד. The participial form or a derived noun from ידה
yields little sense, whether attached to the opening bicolon
or to ואני מה.[18] In the latter case, the syntactical arrangement would be hopelessly awkward. Holm-Nielsen objects to deriving מודה from מאד, but this type of spelling is found in the
Hodayot; a quiescent א may be dropped from a word, and the
lengthened ה ending is frequently used. Furthermore, the sense
and syntax of such a word work well in the opening bicolon, and
the doubling of מאד is found in canonical Hebrew.[19] מודה also
appears elsewhere in the Qumran documents, and there, too, a
derivation from מאד offers the best sense and syntax.[20]

The structures of the first two stanzas of the body of
this psalm, A and B, are quite similar and are interwoven with
each other. Each begins with ואני in a short, two-word phrase
followed by כי. In addition, there is a refrain bicolon following ואני מה in Stanza A and closing Stanza B. The outline
of these two stanzas is thus quite clear.

ואני מה	Stanza A
כיא הודעתני בסוד אמתכה } ותשכילני במעשי פלאכה }	Refrain
]	Body of Stanza A
ואני ידעתי	Stanza B
כי- - -]	
כי הודעתם בסוד אמתכה } וברזי פלאכה השלכתם }	Refrain

It will be noticed that the refrain is not repeated exactly.
The pronoun suffix is changed, the word order is different in
the second line, there is a different form of שכל, and the word
in construct with פלאכה is different. Nevertheless, the refrain quality is unmistakable.

The main sections of both Stanzas A and B present ornate
lists of divine attributes. In Stanza A five attributes are

listed, and in Stanza B there are seven. In Stanza A the list
is compounded with references to parts of the author's body.
Stanza B actually presents two matched lists of seven divine
attributes, one of which is set in a framework of references
to the divine personality.[21]

The body of Stanza A begins with references to the poet:
his mouth, tongue, lips. This forms a short tricolon.[22]

ותתן בפי הודות
ובלשוני תהלה
ומול שפתי במכון רנה

A list of five divine attributes follows these references to
the poet, set in parallel bicola.

ואזמרה בחסדיכה
ובגורתכה אשוחחה
כול היום תמיד אברכה שמכה
ואספרה כבודכה בתוך בני אדם
וברוב טובכה תשתעשע נפשי

Several minor features are of interest here. Each of the
first four lines of this section contains a first person cohor-
tative with the object of the verb a divine attribute. The
first two lines contain only these two elements. The third and
fourth lines each have an additional phrase. כול היום תמיד is
balanced by בתוך בני אדם in the following line. (It should be
noted that although the length of these four lines vary, all
fall within the pattern most commonly found in the Hodayot--
9 to 14 syllables.) Both bicola have a chiastic structure; in
the first bicolon the two elements are simply reversed, while
in the second bicolon the verb and object form a unit in the
chiastic patterning. The final line of the stanza is a summary
line. It begins with the fifth divine attribute and closes by
combining the list with the earlier personal references.

The double list in Stanza B begins immediately after the
strategic phrase ואני ידעתי. In Stanza A the suffix -כה was
attached to each member in the list of attributes. In Stanza B,
the same suffix is attached to features of the divine personality and to each of these terms an attribute is matched. Sig-
nificantly, the list begins with פיכה, the part of the author's
body first mentioned in Stanza A.

It will be noted that the main section of Stanza B, without the opening and the refrain, consists of eight lines. The
final line does not contain an attribute, although it does contain a reference to the divine personality (the list with כה-
attached). The fifth line of the section, on the other hand,
lists an attribute, but in the place of the reference to the
divine personality there is only the nonspecific אתכה. The
double list of seven contained in this stanza is not, therefore, simply one-to-one matching, but is a more complicated
affair. This complication may simply be due to a love of the
ornate, but a longer examination of the stanza suggests that
theological and literary considerations were uppermost. That
attribute which stands in a statement independent of the divine
personality list is כבוד, the only divine attribute which appears in all three stanzas. The poet has further placed this
statement as close as possible to the middle of the stanza (the
fifth line of ten), and at almost the exact midpoint of the
poem (see "Rhythmical Balance"). Its independence from the
attribute list of the stanza further marks it out. The balancing member of the attribute list closes the final line of this
section.

כי אמת פיכה
ובידכה צדקה
ובמחשבתכה כול דעה
ובכרוחכה כול גבורה
נגול כבוד אתכה הוא
באפכה כול משפטי נגע
ובטורבכה רוב סליחות
ורחומיכה לכול בני רצונכה

attributes →   ← divine personality
list   list

A number of small niceties mark the construction of the
stanza. In the divine personality list the intermediate members
are prefaced by ב, while the first and last members are independent prepositions. In the attributes list the third through
sixth members begin with כול. Also of interest is the fact that
טובכה, a part of the attributes list in Stanza A is instead part
of the divine personality list in Stanza B, and that רוב, which
prefaced טובכה in A has been transferred to סליחות, the attribute matched to טובכה in B. This shifting of vocabulary emphasizes both the intertwined structure of the lists in Stanza B,

and also reflects the intent of the author in introducing a second list, qualities of the divine personality, into the poem (see "Imagery and Theology").

Stanza C, in contrast to the ornate patterns of Stanzas A and B, seems a trifle plodding and prosaic. However, here too, there is evidence of tight organization. The introductory line again mentions כבודכה, the link word of the poem. Following this statement of man's cleansing for God's glory are five infinitive clauses outlining the purposes and results of the cleansing. The structure of these lines is completely unlike anything else in the poem. Though the lines vary slightly in length, each is basically a "double line" in weight: the syntactical structure does not allow separation into halves of a bicolon, but the length (18-20 syllables) would normally dictate such a separation. This phenomenon has been seen before in the Hodayot, but has always marked a strategic point in the poem, usually the close of a key stanza. This is the only instance in the eight psalms analyzed in this paper where a stanza employs "double lines" throughout. Each of the five clauses begins with an infinitive, and each employs parallelism toward the end of the line. In the case of the third and fifth clauses, the paralleled terms are almost long enough to support the more normal division of the line into halves of a bicolon. In the other three lines, the paralleled terms are quite short and would yield extremely uneven lines when divided. It therefore seems best to describe all five as essentially "double lines" in weight and organization.

Rhythmical Balance

The three stanzas of this hymn are not of equal length, although certain sections show great regularity in the length of the lines employed.

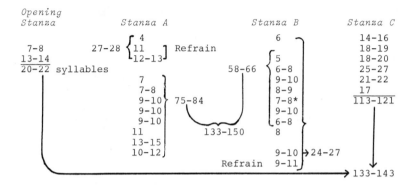

Both A and B, though not of equal length, show similar rhythmical development: a very short introductory phrase, followed by
the lists whose lines vary from short (6-8 syllables) to standard length. Stanza C has lines, as previously noted, of
double the standard length, and is rather regular throughout.
The longest line in the stanza is approximately in the middle
so that the stanza appears tapered on both ends. The line
marked with an asterisk in Stanza B in the diagram is the key
line which mentions כבוד and is approximately in the middle of
the stanza and the middle of the psalm. It can be observed
that the bodies of Stanzas A and B are equal in their combined
weight to Stanza C combined with the Opening, and that the two
refrain sections balance each other.

Imagery and Theology

Holm-Nielsen believes that there is little use of scripture
in this hymn.[23] However, the vocabulary and phrases of Stanzas
A and B are not at all remote from OT thought and expression.
In fact, Stanzas A and B, for all their uniqueness in organization, bear many similarities to Psalm 145, which also stresses
divine attributes. In fact, of the 48 different words used in
Stanzas A and B, 25 also appear in Psalm 145, a higher proportion of vocabulary than this hymn shares with other psalms.
Moreover, although there are no real quotations from Psalm 145,
the two share a number of phrases and forms: בני אדם, אברכה שמך,

the hiphil of ידע, the ך suffix attached to attributes. Many
of the attributes (and the divine personality attributes) of
Stanzas A and B are shared by the two psalms: אמת, יד, רחמים,
אף, צדקה, רוב טוב, כבוד, שם, גבורה, חסד.

In view of the shared ideas, vocabulary, and expressions
of these two poems, their differences are all the more striking. Psalm 145 is an alphabet acrostic, a form never used in
the Hodayot. The organization of the two poems is entirely
different. Psalm 145 employs rather well-balanced parallel
bicola; Hodayot 11:3-14 is formed of lists, set within refrains
and uses little standard parallelism.

The focus of the psalm is upon God's attributes, brought
out by the several lists delineated earlier. The attributes
are the standard ones mentioned at Qumran: truth, righteousness,
knowledge, glory, forgiveness. Many of the same expressions
were found in the psalm previously analyzed, 7:26-33. Here,
however, the attributes have been intertwined with a second
list, qualities of the divine personality.

In Stanza A, five divine attributes appear: חסד, גבורה, שם,
רוב טוב, כבודך. These attributes follow a tricolon describing
the author's praise and recognition of God: with his mouth, his
tongue, his lips. The two lists are separate. In Stanza B,
the poet's personality does not appear; there is a list of
seven divine attributes, and here they are matched with the
divine personality. This list of qualities of the divine personality employs several designations for parts of the body:
mouth, hand, nose. What is intended is not anthropomorphism,
however, but the psychical functions customarily connected with
these designations.

The divine personality list suggests both the concrete
understanding of the terms and an abstract attribute. Mouth
and hand which begin this list, are the most concrete of the
terms used to depict God's word and God's power. The other
members of this list would not separately remind a reader of a
relationship to the body or personality, but within the total
setting of this list point to an author mindful of their ori-
gins. אף and רחמים certainly suggest their counterparts--the
nose and the womb (רֶחֶם). מחשבה and כוח might be classified as

products of a person: the one of the mind and the other of
muscle. Elsewhere they appear as attributes, but their relationship to the personality is obvious enough within the present list. The one surprise of this list is טוב, which appeared
in Stanza A as a divine attribute. Though in the OT, and in
the Hodayot, it is usually a reference to good things or goodness, it is used in Exod 33:19 of Yahweh's beauty or fairness.
Like כוח and מחשבה, it is in a category between personal quality and attribute, apparently with enough qualities to fit it
to either list.

The matching of attributes to the divine personality list
is quite natural.[24] Knowledge is matched with planning, might
with strength, punishing judgments with wrath, truth with mouth
(word), righteousness with the strength of the hand. All have
OT counterparts in thought, and are more generally understandable as well. Glory, as has been previously noted, stands
alone in the list, for emphasis and thematic linkage. Wrath
and judgment are followed in the list by goodness (beauty),
linked to forgiveness and compassion. Once again, the author's
emphasis on God's graciousness to the chosen is revealed by the
careful structuring.

CHAPTER V

THREE PSALMS WITH POOR TEXT

The three psalms described in this chapter, though rather
different from each other in theme, have in common a severe deterioration of their text. Unlike the other poems of the Hodayot whose text has suffered the same fate, the limits of
these three poems are not in doubt, and thus they fall within
the purview of this analysis. The question is whether poetic
analysis can be undertaken with such poor texts, and whether it
will add anything to what is known of these psalms. The answer
to both questions is yes. In all three poems, the major organizational features can be detected, and in each case, poetic
analysis yields new information about the psalm or strengthens
conjectures made on other grounds.

The first of the psalms explored in this chapter is quite
long, taking up almost two-thirds of column 7. It is the longest of the psalms investigated in this study, but it is by no
means the longest in the scroll, if Licht and Dupont-Sommer are
correct in their delineations of the psalms. Its text is marred
throughout by large holes. Nevertheless, it sheds some light
on the features of the longer psalms. The second psalm discussed in this chapter began at the bottom of column 9 and con-
tinued into column 10; it is now missing about one-third of its
text, chiefly the lines from the poem's beginning. The third
poem, from column 14, is rather short, and some of its gaps can
be restored with a fair amount of certainty. All three poems
are interesting in themselves. The long psalm in column 7 seems
to draw in a unique way on Isaiah and Zechariah for its imagery;
the short psalm in column 14 suggests definite cultic usage in
its theme. The hymn from column 10 shares certain similarities
in vocabulary and style with 7:26-33, with a stronger rhetorical
note.

1. Hodayot 7:6-25 (Plate 41)

The opening lines (6-14) of this poem have only a few small
gaps; with the exception of the eight-space gap in line 10,

121

there is almost universal agreement on restorations in this
section of the poem. Beginning with line 15, however, a verti-
cal tear in the scroll has left a hole varying from 6-16 spaces
in each of the remaining lines of the poem. In addition, there
has been deterioration of the scroll at the right-hand margin
in lines 14, 15, 17, 18, and 19, and at the left-hand margin in
lines 16 and 17. A small hole, about two spaces wide, disrupts
lines 24 and 25 at the middle of each line.

The textual damage is worst in column lines 18-20 (in
Stanza D). Here the amount of text lost is so great that the
structural pattern remains in doubt except for its demarcation
from the surrounding material. There are numerous places in
the psalm where Sukenik's transcription must be trusted, due to
smeared letters and rotted material. A number of scribal corrections were made in this psalm.

line 9: ז is substituted for ד as the second letter
          in חזעזע

line 15: י added above the line to לשבילי

line 15: וחיים has been erased after כבוד

line 21: י added above the line to בוזיק

There is also a dittography which the corrector missed: שפתי
which ends line 11 is repeated inadvertently at the beginning
of line 12.

Although the usual paragraph indentations mark off this
psalm as well as the others in this column, there are no internal paragraph markings visible in this psalm. However,
strategic phrases employing אתה occur four times at the right-
hand margin (lines 10, 13, 16, and 25). In two cases (lines 16
and 25), there is some indication that this is deliberately
done, for lines 15 and 24 end some distance from the left-hand
margin.

Hebrew Text of Hodayot 7:6-25

66	אודכה אדוני	
	כי סמכתני בעוזכה	Opening
6-7	ורוח קודשכה הניפותה בי בל אמוט	Stanza
	ותחזקני לפני מלחמות רשעה	
7-8	ובכול הוותם ל[וא] הזתתה מבריתכה	
	ותשימני כמגדל עוז כחומה נשגבה	Refrain
8-9	ותכן על סלע מבניתי ואושי עולם לסודי	
	וכול קירותי לזומת בזן ללוא תזעזעᵃ	
10	[ו]אתה אלי נתתניᵇ לעפיט לעצת קודש	Stanza A
	רת [-------] בריתכה	
	ולשרוני כלמודיך	
11	ואין פה לרוח הוות	
	ולא מענה לשון לכול [ב]ני אשמה	
11-12	כי תאלמנה שפתיᶜ שקר	
	כי כול גרי למשפט תרשיע	
	[ל]הבדיל בי בין צדיק לרשע	
13	כי אתה ידעתה כול יצר מעשה	Stanza B
	וכול מענה לשון הכרתה	
13-14	ותכן לבי [כל]מודיכה	
	ובאמתכה לישר פעמי	
	לנתיבות צדקה	
14-15	להתהלך לפניך בגבול [החיי]ם	
	לשביליᵈ כבודᵉ ושלום לאין [----]	
	[ללוא] להשבת לנצח	
16	ואתה ידעתה יצר עבדכה	Stanza C
	כי לא [----------נש]עני	
16-17	להרים ל[בי] [ו][ל]העיז בכוח	
	ומחסי בשר אין לי	
	[--------]אין צדקות	
17-18	להנצל מפ[שע] [בל]ראᶠ סליחה	

ᵃו was written above the line to replace ר as the second letter in this word.

ᵇReading the text as נתתי rather than נתתו, and emending this to נתתני. See discussion on p. 129.

ᶜשפתי appears twice in the text due to dittography.

ᵈThe final י is written above the line.

ᵉוהייס, originally written at this point, as been crossed out.

ᶠThis reconstruction of the text is discussed on p. 132.

	ואני נשענתי ב]----------[	Stanza D
18-19	]-----[חסדכה אוחיל	
	להציץ [בי]שׁע ולגדל נצר	
	להעיז בכוח ו]--------[	
19-20	]----------[צדקתכה	
	העמדתני לבריתכה	
	ואתמוכה באמתכה	
	ואת]--------[	

	ותשימני אב לבני חסד	Refrain
21	וכאומן לאנשי מופת	
	ויפצו פה כירנ[ק -----[	
22	וכשעשע עולול בחיקᵍ אומניו	

	ותרם קרני על כול מנאצי	Stanza E
	ויתח]------[ארות אנשי מלחמתי	
22-23	ובעלי רבי כמוץ לפני רוח	
	וממשלתי על ב]--------[	
23-24	]-------[לי עזרתה נפשי	
	ותרם קרני למעלה	
	והופעתי בא[ור] שבעתים	
	ᵇ[אור אשר הכינ]ותה לכבודכה	

25	כי אתה לי למאור [עו]לם	Coda
	ותכן רגלי ב]מישור -----[	

Translation of Hodayot 7:6-25

6	I thank you, O Lord,
	For you supported me with your strength,
6-7	And your holy spirit you waved over me lest I slip.
	And you strengthened me for the wars of wickedness,
	And in all their disasters you did [not]
	frighten \<me\> from your covenant.ᴬ
	And you set me like a tower of strength,
	like a high rampart.
8-9	And you established my building on a crag,
	and eternal foundations for my grounding;
	And all my walls for a tested rampart,
	which is not shaken.

ᵍי written above the line.

ʰThis reconstruction does not have universal agreement, but most scholars do restore the verb כון here.

ᴬA double-duty suffix from the previous line supplies the pronoun for the hiphil verb. The meaning here seems to be related to that of Jer 1:17, where the same verb appears. See discussion on pp. 127-128.

10   And you, my God, you gave me to the weary,
            to the holy council;
        And you [set me]B in your covenant
        And <made> my tongue like those whom you teach.
11   But no speech is allowed for the spirit
            of destruction,
        And no answer of the tongue for any of the
            sons of guilt,
11-12   For the lips of deceit are dumb;
        For all my attackers you declare guilty in
            judgment,
        To separate in me between the righteous and
            the evil.

13   For you, you know every creature made,
        And every answer of the tongue you observe.
13-14   And you established my heart among those whom
            you taught,
        And in your truth, to make straight my footsteps
        For paths of righteousness,
14-15   In which to walk about before you in the
            borders of [life];
        For paths of glory and peace without [_____]
        [Which will not] ever cease.

16   And you, you know the intention of your servant,
        That I have not [leaned _____]
16-17   To lift [my heart] and to seek refuge in strength,
        And the defenses of the flesh I do not have.
        [_____] there is no righteousness,
17-18   To be saved from [sin except] by forgiveness.

        And I lean upon [_____]
        [_____] your steadfast love I await,
18-19   For the blossoming of salvation, and for the
            maturing of the shoot;
        To seek refuge in strength,
        And [_____] your righteousness;
19-20   You make me stand in your covenant,
        And I hold firmly to your truth,
        And I [_____]

        And you set me as a father to the sons of
            loving-kindness,
21   And like a nurse to the men of portent
21-22   And they open their mouths like a nursing child, [___]
        And like the delight of the child in the bosom of
            his nurses.

_____

    BExact reconstruction is uncertain, but the sense supplies
these words.

```
            And you exalted my horn over all who condemn me,
                And the men warring against me [                  ]
22-23       And the lords of my strife are as chaff
                before the wind,
                And those ruling over me [                ]
                [                ] you save my life.
23-24   And you exalted my horn on high,
            And I shine in a sevenfold light,
            In a [light which you] prepared for your glory.
25      For you are an eternal light to me,
            And you established my feet in an even place...
```

Stanza Analysis

Independent pronouns are very prominent in this poem, particularly in conjunction with other strategic terms. Once
again, these pronouns indicate most of the major divisions of
the poem. The opening phrases of the psalm have the standard
form, כי plus a second person verb with a first-person suffix.
The parallelism of the first two bicola is quite standard and
complete, and there can be little doubt that this formed the
introductory stanza of the poem. These four lines are followed
by a tricolon which begins ותשימני, after which the independent
pronoun makes its first appearance. This slight peculiarity in
structure is resolved in the recognition of a similar unit beginning ותשימני towards the end of the poem (column line 20).
It can be tentatively determined that here, as in 11:3-14, there
is a refrain; as in 11:3-14, the main stanzas of the poem appear between the refrains.

Following this first refrain, the independent pronoun אתה
can be seen three times: ואתה ידעתה אלי (line 10), כי אתה ידעתה (line
13), and ואתה ידעתה (line 16). In view of the frequency of
these words and phrases as stanza indicators in other poems,
there seems little doubt of their function here. In line 18,
ואני נשענתי marks the next stanza unit, but from here to the
last line of the poem there are no more independent pronouns.
However, in line 20, the "refrain" unit appears. Following this
refrain is a unit which contains a definite inclusio, beginning
and ending ותרם קרני. The final line of the poem returns once
again to the כי אתה formula. Although the gaps in the text are
grievous, particularly in the unit from ואני נשענתי onwards, it
seems unlikely that any stanza indicator phrases are missing,

and context does not indicate that any new units began with any
gap. From ואני to the second refrain little can be determined
of poetic structure, but the context suggests that no new theme
is taken up in the missing material.

The stanza organization pattern can thus be diagrammed as
follows.

כי סמכתני בעוזכה}	Opening Stanza
ותשימני}	Refrain
ואתה אלי}	Stanza A
כי אתה ידעתה}	Stanza B
ואתה ידעתה}	Stanza C
ואני בשענתי}	Stanza D
ותשימני}	Refrain
ותרום קרני}	Stanza E
ותרם קרני}	(use of inclusio)
כי אתה}	Coda

The pattern of stanza development employing strategic independent pronouns, is thus similar to patterns in the other poems
analyzed except for one feature: the unit beginning ותרום. Its
placement after the refrain suggests that it is a closing unit,
yet following it is a definite and separate coda. None of the
other shorter and complete poems, except possibly 2:20-30 which
closes with a scripture quotation, has both a closing stanza
and a coda. Frequently, as we have seen, the final stanza of
the poem, rather than balancing the opening stanza, is part of
the body of the poem itself. The development of this psalm can
be compared instead to 11:3-14, where the first two stanzas are
enclosed by the refrain bicolon, and the third and final stanza
is quite different stylistically, and introduces new thoughts
as well.

The Opening Stanza is of the standard pattern of the Hodayot. It is noteworthy that a double-duty suffix is employed
in the second bicolon. This device appears infrequently in the
Hodayot, but there are several definite examples (see Chapter
VI, Section 3).

וַתְּחַזְּקֵ(נִי) לִפְנֵי מִלְחֲמוֹת רֶשַׁע
וּבְכֹל הַוּוֹתָם לֹא הֶחְתַּתָּ מִבְּרִיתְכָה

The recognition of the double-duty suffix in this bicolon
is of some importance, because it helps to solve the problem
of how הֶחְתַּתָּה is to be understood. Holm-Nielsen notes that some
confusion has been caused by the "missing suffix," and that
most translations of this line involve circumlocutions to ar-
rive at a text that makes sense.[1] Once the double-duty suffix
and the parallelism of the bicolon is recognized, translation
is less of a problem. However, the meaning intended by the
poet is still somewhat unclear. A similar usage of חתת is
found in Jer 1:17, and it seems quite likely that the Qumran
poet was deliberately alluding to this passage. Yahweh com-
mands Jeremiah to carry his word to the people whatever their
threats; the verb חתת is used twice, once in the qal and then
in the hiphil: אַל תֵּחַת מִפְּנֵיהֶם פֶּן אֲחִתְּךָ לִפְנֵיהֶם ("Do not be dis-
mayed by them, lest I dismay you before them"). Interestingly
enough, מן, used with the qal in Jeremiah is used here in the
Hodayot with the hiphil. The meaning suggested by this bicolon,
then, by both its own parallelism and a similar usage in Jeremiah, is that the poet has been held fast in the covenant bond
despite frightening experiences with the wicked. That some allusion to Jeremiah 1 is intended by the Hodayot poet can be
seen not only from the usage of חתת from Jer 1:17, but in the
verses which follow in Jeremiah, where Yahweh compares his
prophet to a strong city and an iron pillar. Although different vocabulary is used, similar metaphors are employed for the
Hodayot poet in the lines immediately following the Opening
Stanza.

Following the Opening Stanza is a unit that has been tentatively labeled a "refrain." This description is chosen for
want of a better term. This tricolon is matched by a four-line
section towards the end of the poem. Both begin וַתְּשִׂימֵנִי and
both continue with a series of comparisons employing כ. The
first "refrain" section compares the author's position to strong
walls and buildings; the second refrain compares him to a parent
or nurse. Like the more standard refrain in 11:3-14, these sections enclose the major body of the poem. Here the poem's

organization is more elaborate since both a closing stanza and
a coda follow the second refrain, but the parallel to the pattern of 11:3-14 is quite clear.

Although shown in the transcription as a tricolon with
long lines, it can be argued that a different arrangement would
be more accurate for this refrain. The first two lines of this
"tricolon" can be broken into rather equal and parallel halves.
The third line is more uneven, and confuses the situation. The
second refrain quite clearly consists of four lines, all of
standard length.[2] Two arrangements of the first refrain thus
seem possible: that of a tricolon employing long lines, or the
following five-line arrangement.

ותשימני כמגדל עוז
כוומה נשגבה
ותכן על סלע מבניתי
ואושי עולם לסודי
וכול קירותי לחומת בחן ללוא תזעזע

The long final line in this arrangement would be similar to
that employed at the end of the second refrain, which may have
been a few syllables longer than the other lines. There can
be no objection to such a five-line arrangement except that
elsewhere in the Hodayot the author has balanced a long three-
line section against a more standard four-line section (in 2:
20-30); and here, as there, the balanced sections are approximately equal in weight (first refrain: forty-five to forty-eight
syllables; second refrain: thirty-seven to forty-four syllables).

The opening of Stanza A is quite clear: ואתה אלי; but some
of the phrases that follow are enigmatic, and the lines appear
to be somewhat uneven. In fact, understanding the first line
of the stanza as it stands appears somewhat hopeless. נחתו,
with its apparent reference to the third person is problem
enough, and the following word, לעפים, however interpreted,
remains somewhat problematic. Some scholars have retained
נחתו, and have explained the suffix pronoun as due to modesty
on the part of the author, or as a reference generally to the
similes employed in the preceding unit.[3] Both explanations and
translations seem less than satisfactory, and emendation to
נחתני (actually involving the addition of a single letter)
seems well warranted.[4]

The word לעפים must be examined in relationship to the
whole line. God has given the author some distinctive place--
this is clear from the line's opening. Scholars seem to be
rather evenly divided on interpreting עפים as a form of עָאפִים,
"the weary ones," or as the Aramaic loanword "branches" (which
appears in Psalm 104). Those who argue for the latter meaning
can point to the later reference in the psalm to the shoot
blossoming, and to the frequent references at Qumran to the
community as an eternal planting. The branches, in this case,
would be the community, and the best translation would approximate that of Vermes: "Thou hast placed me, O my God, among the
branches of the Council of Holiness."[5]

Unfortunately, if this line is so interpreted, it is difficult to see any connection with the surrounding lines in
theme, and the later reference to the shoot sprouting is somewhat difficult to tie to such an unelucidated statement early
in the poem.

On the other hand, a derivation of עפים from עָאפִים fits
the context well.[6] The following line almost certainly alludes
to Isa 50:4, where the weary are mentioned in almost the same
way.

אדוני יהוה נתן לי לשון למודים
לדעת לעות את יעף
דבר יעיר בבקר בבקר
יעיר לי אזן לשמע כלמודים

The use of such a passage from the Servant Songs accords well
with the tenor of the whole psalm, which draws heavily on Messianic imagery (in much the same way that 3:3-18 does).

The restoration of the lacuna in the second line of Stanza
A is not universally agreed upon, but the sense of the line is
not seriously in question. All agree that the verb is parallel
in meaning to נתן in the first line, and that a personal reference (נו, בי, פי, לבי) is missing.[7] Interestingly enough,
these first two lines of the stanza in which all the interpre-
tive difficulties lie, are long lines (sixteen to seventeen
syllables each), while the remaining tricolon and bicolon fall
within the standard line length for the Hodayot and are easily
understood. A possible explanation for both differences perhaps
lies in the allusive character of the two opening lines.

Stanza B again employs the pronoun אתה in its opening
phrase. With this stanza it becomes apparent that the author
is employing a technique seen elsewhere in the Hodayot (5:5-19),
linking his stanzas backwards and forwards. The opening phrase
of Stanza B is repeated in Stanza C, while the second line of B
recalls Stanza A with the reference to מענה לשון. In a hymn
which uses a wide variety of metaphors and imagery, this linkage of phrases is an important unifying feature. Although link
phrases to Stanzas A and C are provided in this opening bicolon
of B, the parallelism of the bicolon is retained as well. The
third line of the stanza also provides a link to Stanza A, if,
as is generally supposed, the restored text read בלמודיכה or
כלמודיכה.[8]

The remaining lines of the stanza are not difficult to
understand, but initially appear a bit ragged in structure,
even prosaic. Here is one place where a knowledge of the syllabic length of most cola in the Hodayot may be of some aid.
Long lines (fourteen or more syllables) occur almost invariably
at the close of a stanza, or can be determined to be strategic
lines for other reasons. Lines shorter than nine syllables
seem to be more randomly placed, but most lines have nine to
thirteen syllables. The opening bicolon of this stanza has
eleven/twelve syllables; line 3 has ten. Standard lines therefore can be expected, at least up to the close of the stanza.
Only one division of the phrases in the latter half of this
stanza yields standard line lengths, and this division is further supported by indications of alternating parallelism, as
shown in the diagram below.

10 syllables	ובאמתכה לישר פעמי	
6-7	לנתיבות צדקה	path reference
12-13	להתהלך לפניך בגבול הזיים	infinitive clause
12	לשבילי כבוד ושלום לאין - - - -	path reference
7-8	ללוא להשבת לנצח	infinitive clause

Several scholars agree that היים can be restored in the gap in
the first infinitive clause;[9] the noun or nouns which followed
לאין are more problematic. The negative particle seems to be
required in the final line to achieve sense, and most scholars
have restored ולוא.[10] However, in keeping with the opening of

the previous three lines, and also parallel with the other
infinitive clauses, ללוא would seem more likely.

    With Stanza C the deterioration of the text becomes pro-
nounced. The thrust of the stanza is still clear, but certain
structural matters are more difficult to discern because of the
lacunae. The opening line of the stanza links it with Stanza
B. Other terms link it with Stanza D: להעיז בכוח and, if the
restoration is correct, [נש]ענחי.[11] The long gap in the second
line of the stanza cannot be restored with certainty aside from
the last word. But in the line which follows, לבי can almost
certainly be restored. This gap occurs at the end of column
line 17, and can hardly be more than two or three letters.[12]
Moreover, the phrase in which the gap occurs is parallel to
להעיז בכוח and probably approximated that phrase in length. In
the final lines of the stanza it is again difficult to find
consensus on restoration, but it seems clear that the author is
stating that he possesses no righteousness of his own that can
bring him to salvation. Of the restorations suggested,
מפ[שע בל]וא סליחה seems very close to the original, if it is
not completely accurate.[13] The stanza would seem to consist
then of two closely related tricola.

ואתה ידעתה יצר עבדכה ⎫
כי לא [--------] נשענתי ⎬   infinitive line
להרים לבי ולהעיז בכוח ⎭

ומחסי בשר אין לי ⎫
[---------] אין צדקות ⎬   infinitive line
להנצל מפשע בלוא סליחה ⎭

    So little remains of the text of Stanza D that it is im-
possible to restore its exact configuration. Terms linking it
with Stanza C have already been noted, and the linking terms
in these two stanzas seem to be set in contrast: no trust in
human means, but trust in God's righteousness and salvation.
As to the structure of this stanza, two conjectures seem possible: either six lines as in Licht, or eight lines. Licht's
arrangement, with his restorations, is as follows.[14]

ואני נשענתי ב[רוב רחמיכה]
[לגדול] חסדכה אוחיל
להציץ [בי]שע ולגדל נצר   12 syllables
להעיז בכוח ול[הפריח פרח]   12 syllables
[כיא ב]צדקתך העמדתני לבריחתכה   16 syllables
ואתמוכה באמתכה ואת[יסד בחוקיכה]   16 syllables

The basic problem with this restoration and structure is
that the lines are a bit too long and too regularly matched for
the general stanza pattern of the Hodayot. The extra-long
lines could be the important summary lines for the stanza, but
their syntax in this reconstruction is a bit awkward. Two כ-
suffixes in a single line of poetry (outside a list) would be
quite rare in the Hodayot; and two verbs in the final line,
both parallel to the verb in the previous line, would be rare
too. Licht has undoubtedly patterned his structure in its number of lines after that of Stanza C, where the link terms occur; however, Stanza C is about one quarter shorter than the
other three stanzas in the body of the poem. Stanza A has
seven lines, Stanza B has eight lines; it seems more likely in
view of the awkwardness of cramming the text of D into six
lines, that there were eight lines.

```
ואני נשענתי ב[--------]          }
            [----------]חסדכה אוחיל
להציץ [בי]שע ולגדל נצר          }
         להעיד בכוח [------]
               צדקתכה[--------]           }
               העמדתני לבריתכה
           ואתמוכה באמתכה          }
               ואת[--------]
```

The sixth line in this arrangement may have contained a verb
parallel to העמדתני, in which case there would be four bicola;
possibly this line contained another infinitive clause. In the
latter case, there would be two tricola ending the stanza.

Following Stanza D is the refrain already noted and discussed, and finally, Stanza E. This stanza is marked by an
inclusio: ותרום קרני. Again there are holes in the text, but
the structure is fairly clear.

```
ותרום קרני על כול מנאצי          ⌐
ויתפ[--------]ארות אנשי מלחמתי   │
ובעלי רבי כמוץ לפני רוח          │  }    inclusio
      וממשלתי על ב[---------]      │
         לי עזרתה נפשי[------------]│
ותרט קרני למעלה                  └
והופעתי באור שבעתים
ב[אור אשר הכין]ותה לכבודכה
```

The coda draws together two images from the poem--the
light image of Stanza E and the earlier reference to the

author's footsteps (from Stanza B). In view of the earlier
references to righteous paths, the restoration of במישור at the
end of line 25 is the most probable of the conjectured endings.[15]

Rhythmical Balance

Although it is somewhat difficult to give exact syllable
counts in a poem whose text has so badly deteriorated, it is
possible to estimate these counts and to use several controls
on this counting. A rough estimate of the missing syllables
can be obtained by counting the missing spaces and dividing by
two. Better estimates can be made by analyzing the lines and
text so that the number and approximate size of the missing
words can be determined. In several lines quite accurate
guesses can be made: where there is enough of the context given,
all the restorations suggested are within one or two syllables
of each other. Even when the missing phrases are quite lengthy
and quite divergent restorations are suggested, these are usually surprisingly close to each other and to the rough estimate
in syllable length. Of the stanzas in this psalm, only the
count of Stanza D can remain much in doubt, and even here, it
would be difficult to reduce it below seventy syllables or
increase it above eighty-five.

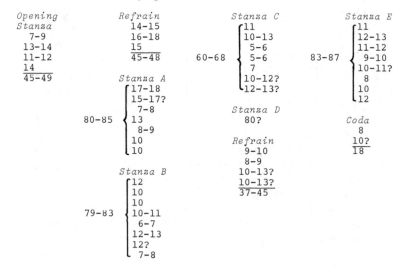

The mathematical relationships and evenness of the stanzas
seems fairly well established. The two refrains, when taken
together, are approximately equal to the lengths used in three
of the four stanzas. Stanza C is one-fourth shorter than the
other stanzas.

Theology and Imagery

This psalm is not an easy poem to understand when taken
as a whole. It is full of ideas and imagery found throughout
the Hodayot, but as in 3:19-36, the sequence and structuring of
the images is rather confusing. Some of the confusion is due
to the missing text, but much more is due to the rapid succession of images and metaphors--walls and towers, the tongues of
good and evil men, footsteps in righteous paths, the blossoming
of salvation, foster-parents, the horn, a sevenfold light--all
of these and other images appear in this psalm.

It must be remembered first of all that the poet has
linked his stanzas forwards and backwards, and matched the refrain sections. The recognition of these units gives a sequence
and flow to the imagery. In the refrains the author compares
his role to the protective force of walls and towers, and to
that of a father or nurse. Though quite different images, both
illustrate the poet's place as a protector of the community,
increasing its safety and security. In the stanzas, the lines
dealing with tongues of men, good and evil, overlap with
another bodily reference, to the footsteps. The footsteps are
linked also with the יצר or impulse of the author, and this in
turn is linked to the first of two contrasting stanzas in which
the poet declares his trust in God and his expectation of a
special shoot or blossom, surely a messianic reference. In the
final stanza of the hymn the poet returns to military terminology used in the first refrain; this time he declares that his
horn will be exalted. This reference is drawn from several
canonical psalms with military imagery, employing this expression to indicate victory over enemies (Pss 18:3, 75:11, 89:18,
92:11). The linking phrases and refrains bear the weight of
the changing flow of imagery, so that the psalm does not break
down into chaos.

Holm-Nielsen comments that this psalm draws quite heavily
on the language of Isaiah;[16] his chief interest is in finding
"quotations" of scripture and not all of his comments are pertinent here. However, he does point to a very important quality of this psalm. The OT passages he cites, as well as a number of others which seem to be used in this psalm, are drawn
from passages in Isaiah and Zechariah which are immediately
recognizable as messianic passages or which speak of the restoration of Israel. The passages which provide the background
for this psalm include Isa 50:4 (a Servant Song), Isaiah 11
(reference to the shoot from Jesse), 27:6 (the shoot marks the
restoration of Israel), 30:26 (the sevenfold light marks Israel's restoration), 60:21 (Israel is God's shoot), 66:12
(Israel is a child safe in its play). Holm-Nielsen mentions a
number of other Isaianic passages he feels are important for
various phrases, but the above passages, none of which are
quoted, nevertheless have undoubtedly shaped the theology of
the Hodayot's author here. Mention must also be made of Zechariah 3, in which Joshua the High Priest is designated the
Branch. The expression "men of portent" (column line 21) is
drawn from this passage, Holm-Nielsen feels. When this pattern
of scriptural influence is outlined, and 7:6-25 is read with
these passages in mind, it seems likely that this psalm, like
3:3-18, ought to be seen as chiefly a testimony of belief in
the coming messianic age. In view of some of the textual difficulties and of the author's strong emphasis here on his place
in the community, this "messianic" background deserves further
investigation.

2. Hodayot 9:37-10:12 (Plates 43-44)

The first lines of this hymn are almost entirely missing,
but the last half of the poem is relatively intact. This psalm
is one of two in the Hodayot scroll whose limits were indicated
by blank spaces. In this case, an entire line was left blank
before the first line of the poem (9:37), and a similar space
was left at the end (after 10:12). Similar blank spacing sets
off the psalm in column 17:17-25.

Of the beginning of the psalm in column 9, only a few
words at the ends of lines 37-40 remain. The top line of
column 10, as shown in the transcription, has only two readable
words, but the situation improves in line 2. In lines 2 and 3,
only the first and last words are missing, and in line 4, only
the final word is gone. The remaining lines are in good condition, except for a small hole in line 12, about two to three
letters in length.[17]

An examination of the scroll photographs suggests that
column 10 originally had at least two more lines at the top of
the column. Column 9, part of the same sheet as column 10,
shows fragments of two lines higher up than what now remains of
the first line of column 10. Even in column 9, the top margin
is not visible, however, so it is possible that column 10 is
missing more than two lines at the top. Column 9, even in its
present condition, has parts of forty lines; only column 4 has
as many lines, and in column 4 the top and bottom margins can
be seen. Column 9 could not have had more than one or two
lines missing at the top, if any. It is also possible that
column 9 may be missing one or more lines at the bottom of the
column. The implication for the psalm under consideration is
that one to four column lines are most probably missing, in
addition to the poorly preserved lines of 9:37-40 and 10:1.

Interestingly enough, there are no scribal corrections in
this psalm except for the dotting of a single letter in the
word אכשיל in 10:6. Sukenik has suggested that the word intended was אשכיל,[18] with the dot indicating the metathesis.
This emendation is commonly accepted.

Hebrew Text of Hodayot 9:37-10:12

9:37	[-----] הגברתה עד אין מס [--------------a]
38	[-------] שמכה בהפלא מ[-] [---------------]
39	[---------] ך השבח[-] [----------------]
40	[------] כלו וחלל[-][----------------]

---

[a]The first four lines are simply shown with Sukenik's
transcription without poetic form.

10:1-2   ל [------------] זמה לבכה [---------] [---------b]   End of
10:2   ובלוא רצונכה לא יהיה   Stanza B
2-3   ולא יתבונן כול בהו[-----]
          [-----]יכה לא יביט כול

          רמה אפהו אדם ואדמה חוא   Stanza C
3-4   [-----] קורץ ולעפר תשובתו c
          כי תשכילנו בנפלאות כאלה
4-5   ובסוד א[מתכה] תודיענו

          ואני עפר ואפר   Stanza D
          מה אזום בלוא וזפצתה
5-6   רמה אתחשב באין רצונכה
          מה אתחזק בלא העמדתני
6-7   ואיכה אשכיל d בלא יצרתה לי
          ומה אדבר בלא פתחתה פי
          ואיכה אשיב בלוא השכלתני

8   הנה אתה שר אלים   Stanza E
          ומלך נכבדים
          ואדון לכול רוח
          ומושל בכל מעשה
9   ומבלעדיכה לא יעשה כול
          ולוא יודע בלוא רצונכה
          ואין זולתך
10   ואין עמכה בכוח
          ואין לנגד כבודכה
          ולגבורתכה אין מחיר

10-11   ומי בכול מעשי פלאכה הגדולים   Stanza F
          יעצור כוח להתיצב לפני כבודכה
12   ומה אפהוא שב לעפרו כי יעצור [כוח]
          רק לכבודכה עשיתה כול אלה

Translation of Hodayot 9:37-10:12

9:37   ...you increased beyond number
9:38   ...your name in working wonders

10:1   [_____] plan of your heart [_____]
10:2   And without your will it will not be;
2-3   And no one understands all [_____]
          And all of your [_____] no one sees.

          And what then is man? He is but earth.
3-4   [From clay] he is pinched off, and to dust
              is his return.
          Yet you make him wise in wonderful deeds like these,
4-5   And a council of truth you make him know.

---

bFor the labelling of stanza material, see pp.

cThe scroll photograph indicates that there is a word
missing at the end of line 3; either מחזר or מעפר is possible.

dThe כ of this word was dotted, apparently to indicate
metathesis of the כ and the ש; אשכיל was undoubtedly meant.

And I am dust and ashes,
    What can I devise unless you desire it?
5-6   And what can I plan without your will?
    What strength have I unless you make me stand?
6-7   And how shall I have insight unless you so
        intend for me?
    And what shall I say unless you open my mouth?
    And how shall I return answer unless you give
        me insight?

8   Behold, you are the prince of gods,
    And king of the honored ones,
    And lord of every spirit,
    And ruler of every created thing.
9   And apart from you nothing is made,
    And nothing is known except by your will,
    And there is none but you,
10   And none comparable in strength,
    And none before you in glory,
    And for your strength there is no price.

10-11   And who among all your great wonderful works
        Has strength enough to stand before your glory?
12   And what then is he who returns to his dust
        that he should have [strength]?
    Only for your glory you made all this.

Stanza Analysis

Since the opening lines, and presumably one stanza at
least, are missing, the analysis has to begin *in medias res*,
with the evidence that remains. Most striking is the large
number of rhetorical questions, beginning with מה, מי, and איכה.
The pronoun אני also appears to open one stanza, and הנה אתה
undoubtedly marks the beginning of an important unit of the poem.
The rhetorical questions are ranged on either side of the pronoun statements. Preceding the first rhetorical question are
several lines with no interrogatives, but with a resemblance in
vocabulary to the הנה אתה unit. In a departure from the usual
procedure in this section, the complete units of this poem will
be analyzed first, and then the fragmentary beginning will be
discussed.

The first complete unit of the poem begins in 10:3: ומה
אפהו אדם. A complete bicolon comes before this point in the
column, but as noted above, it has definite affinities with a
later section of the poem. Since it is provisionally assumed
that at least one stanza of the poem is missing, this first

complete stanza cannot be labeled A. Based on material to be
discussed later, its designation is C. The rhetorical question
which begins this stanza is not unlike the questions of the
hymn in 7:26-33. The first bicolon, of which the question is a
part, employs internal parallelism in each half of the bicolon.
The second bicolon, which is a kind of "answer" to the question, employs more standard parallelism. In each bicolon there
is a small gap which can more or less certainly be restored.[19]

ומה אפהו אדם ואדמה הוא

internal parallelism

[מחמר] קרוץ ולעפר תשובתו
כי תשכילנו בנפלאות כאלה
ובסוד א[מתכה] תודיענו

A new unit begins with the pronoun ואני (Stanza D). Six
rhetorical questions follow the initial statement of the poet's
lowly position, forming a seven-line stanza. The structural
relationships of these six questions are varied. Four begin
with מה, two with איכה. All are followed by a first person
imperfect, but two of these verbs are hithpael (questions two
and three), two are hiphil (four and six), one piel (question
five) and one qal (question one). The third element in each
question is a negative particle (בלא in all questions except
the second, which uses באין). The final element is a second
person imperfect verb, augmented by a first singular object
pronoun in questions three through six. The opening patterns
in these six lines match questions one and five, two and three,
and four and six, while the closing of the lines matches one
and two and three through six.

מה אזרע בלוא ופצתה
ומה אתחושב באין רצונכה
מה אתחזק בלא העמדתני
ואיכה אשכיל בלא יצרתה לי
ומה אדבר בלא פתחתה פי
ואיכה אשיב בלוא השכלתני

The third complete unit of the poem (Stanza E) contains
two lists, welded together by an opening statement and a single
bicolon situated between the two lists. The opening of the

stanza is a phrase unmistakable in its strategic function: הנה אתה שר אלים. Three synonyms of שר אלים, expanding the kingly imagery of God, follow. At the end of this first list is a bicolon employing complementary parallelism which greatly resembles in vocabulary the last bicolon before Stanza C (see the next section). The bicolon ends with the statement that "[nothing] is known unless it is your will." Four additional phrases expand this statement in list form, all employing ואין. In the final phrase אין appears at the end of the list, changing the syntactical relationships seen in the previous phrases. This reversal in relationships is somewhat similar to the device of reversal of prepositional object noted in 3:19-36.

> ואין זולתך
> ואין עמכה בכוח
> ואין לנגד כבודכה
> ולגבורתכה אין מחיר ← Reversing of Syntax

The rhetorical question in the following line signals the opening of the final unit of the poem (Stanza F). The earlier structure of the psalm is recalled in these final two units beginning מי and מה. These bicola seem rather prosaic in syntax, but the repetition of the verb עצר and כוח, and the earlier question about man's nature, save the quality of the poem. The final statement of God's power and glory forms a simple but effective close.

The Shape and Rhythmical Balance of the Poem

The question now is, apart from the delineation of these four complete units in this poem, can more be said? A few clues come from the repetition of certain words and structures in the psalm. The lines immediately preceding Stanza C are echoed in Stanza E, and the rhetorical questions about man in Stanza D are recapitulated in Stanza F. The sequence of these elements is shown in the following diagram.

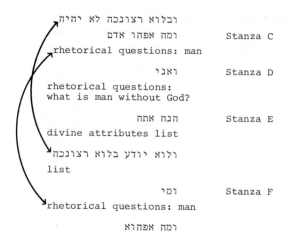

ובלוא רצונכה לא יהיה

רמה אפהו אדם   Stanza C

rhetorical questions: man

ואני   Stanza D

rhetorical questions:
what is man without God?

הנה אתה   Stanza E

divine attributes list

ולוא יודע בלוא רצונכה

list

רמי   Stanza F

rhetorical questions: man

רמה אפהוא

The sequence of the repeated elements suggests quite strongly
that the poem is not chiastically arranged; this is supported
by the character of the final stanza, which seems to be a summary of the poem's themes and which has an effective closing
line (in contrast to the chiastic poem in 7:26-33).

If we turn back now to the scanty evidence of the beginning of the poem, two constructions stand out in relation to
the rest of the poem: --- מ אין in 9:37, and בהפלא in 9:38.
The first recalls the list at the end of Stanza E and the second is reminiscent of the nouns from פלא in Stanzas C and F
(matched sections). In the Hodayot, the opening stanza, normally two bicola, takes up two column lines on the average.
Slim as this evidence is, it seems fairly certain that this
poem had the standard thanksgiving opening, in which certain
general terms or constructions were repeated in more specific
contexts later in the poem.

There remain two lines at the bottom of column 9 and one
line at the top of column 10 that are virtually unreadable.
There were also between one and four lines at the bottom of 9
and the top of 10 which are now completely missing. The evidence from the scroll photographs suggests that it is prudent
to accept the original existence of at least two additional

lines (those that would match the top lines of column 9) and we
will work with this hypothesis. Calculating at the standard
rate (for the Hodayot) of one bicolon for each column line,
this would mean that, in addition to the Opening Stanza, five
bicola (ten poetic lines) are largely or completely missing.
In addition, there are the three poetic lines in 10:2-3 which
have not yet been placed in the poem (a total of thirteen lines
or six and a half bicola). Taking into account the hypothetical nature of some of the missing lines and allowing for error,
we would still have to conclude that one stanza is missing; in
view of the lengths of the other units of this poem, the longest of which is seven poetic lines (three column lines), it
seems more likely that two stanzas (A and B) are missing almost
entirely.

The arrangement of the poem, as well as the number of
missing lines, offers two slim lines of evidence for the existence of two such stanzas. It has been previously noted that
Stanzas C and F are matched in vocabulary and style (having
also a link with the Opening Stanza). The correspondence of a
line in Stanza F with 10:2 has also been noted. Lines 10:1-3
can be analyzed as follows.

זמת לבכה [--------] ל [-----]
ובלוא רצונכה לא יהיה
וְלֹא יִתְבָּרֲגוּ כּוֹל בחו[קיך]
[---]יכה לֹא יָבִיא כּוֹל

While it cannot be certain that the line repeated later in the
poem (...ובלוא רצונכה) is the second line of a bicolon, the
evidence suggests that it is. Its place in its stanza would
then correspond exactly to the place of the line in Stanza E:
there it is the second member of the bicolon, and it is followed
by a list which is approximately the same length as the second
bicolon in the above diagram. If, then, 10:1-3 represents the
same segment of a stanza as its matched portion in Stanza E, it
would be quite strange to have the short opening of E balanced
by nine lines (four and a half bicola) in the earlier section.

Furthermore, if all the lines in this poem from 9:39
through 10:3 were a single stanza, the matching sections shown
earlier would suggest that the present Stanza D is the focal

point of the poem. While this is an extremely well constructed
unit it lacks any strategic indicators of such a focus (double
lines, divine address, etc.), and also theme clues (references
to the sect, divine grace) which have marked such focal stanzas
in other poems.

The evidence, scanty as it is, suggests the original poem
had six stanzas plus the Opening Stanza.

```
Opening
Stanza A (entirely missing)
Stanza B (only two bicola left) theme: God
Stanza C theme: man--uses rhetorical questions
Stanza D theme: man and God linked--rhetorical questions
Stanza E theme: God and his attributes
Stanza F theme: man--rhetorical questions
```

If such was the case, Stanza A possibly was matched with Stanza
D by structure or theme.

Imagery and Theology

The themes of this truncated hymn are familiar from other
psalms: man's lowly estate, God's grace and salvation to man
within the covenant, the recognition of divine attributes--
wonderful deeds, good will, glory beyond all other beings. The
weaving together of these themes is quite according to the usual
plan as well. Once again, however, it is worth noting that if
the delineation of the poem's structure is accurately reflected,
the central thrust of the author's message appears at the midpoint and the close of the poem: God rescues man from his low
estate and places him in the covenant (Stanza C), and God rescues man for his own glory (Stanza F).

The divine titles of Stanza E are most interesting. They
are not formulae drawn from the OT, nor from Rabbinic Hebrew.
אלים and נכבדים seem to imply groups of heavenly beings.[20]
שר אלים brings to mind the archaic concept of בני אלים from the
OT. Some scholars, troubled by the clash of such archaic
imagery with the obvious differences of an apocalyptic system,
have sought to deny all such "polytheistic" roots, and to have
the expressions used only as superlative expressions of God's
nature. But as Holm-Nielsen points out:

This does not, however, prevent the individual expressions from giving, upon closer examination, the impression of describing God as the head of one or more
groups of heavenly beings. There cannot be much doubt
about the expression "the prince of gods," belonging
originally to the world of polytheistic ideas, where
God is described as the top god of a pantheon. From
the Late Jewish use of אלים of godlike beings, angels,
it is most natural to take the expression to be of God
as lord of the realm of angels.[21]

Once again the remnants of the older Semitic mythological system are visible in the imagery of apocalyptic writing, and are
not simply fossils, but have retained some of their original
essence in contributing to a new mythological system: in this
case, אלים are no longer gods in the ancient sense, but are the
angelic circle about the heavenly throne.

3. Hodayot 14:8-22 (Plate 48)

Column 14, like the other fragmentary columns found in the
second bundle of the Hodayot scroll (columns 13-18) is quite
badly deteriorated. Out of these six columns, only two psalms
survive whose limits can be clearly ascertained; the psalm so
delimited in column 17 has so little text remaining that poetic
analysis is not possible. This hymn in column 14 is in slightly better condition, but there are large gaps throughout the
poem; in fact, the right-hand margin is completely missing from
the column, and of the first nine column lines, less than half
of the text has been preserved. In the middle of line 8, however, the word אדוני can be clearly seen as the first word of
the line. Line 22 seems to have contained only a single word,
and line 23 now begins ---[אדוני. Lines 8 and 22 would seem,
then, to mark out a complete poem.

Lines 9-11 are missing approximately half of their text.
Lines 12-13, the only lines of the column where the ends of the
lines at both margins can be seen, nevertheless have gaps of
eighteen to nineteen spaces and fifteen to sixteen spaces respectively. The beginning of lines 14-18 can be restored with
some certainty, and these lines represent the best text in the
hymn. Lines 19-22 have gaps both at the beginning of the lines
and towards the end. There are no scribal corrections in the

text of the hymn that remains. Line 16 ends a considerable
distance before the left margin, and this coincides with a new
stanza opening in the next line, ואני ידעתי. There is also a
long space left in the middle of line 21, before the final hymn
line.

Hebrew Text of Hodayot 14:8-22

8	[אודכה] אדוני	
	הנותן בלב עב[דכה] בינה	Stanza
	[-------------------------]	A
9	ולהתאפק על עלי[לות] רשע	
	ולברך [שמך -----------]	
10	אש[ר-------------------]ר אהבתה	
	ולתעב את כול אשר [שנאתה]	
11	]-------------[ת אנוש	
11-12	כי לפי רוזות [----]ולם בין טוב לרשע	
	]-------------[חם פעולתם	
	ואני ידעתי ומבינתך	Stanza
13	כי ברצונכה בא[---------ר]וח קודשך	B
	וכן תגישני לבינתך	
13-14	ולפי קורבי קנאתי על כול פועלי רשע ואנשי רמיה	
	כי כול קרוביך לא ימרו פיך	
15	וכול יודעיך לא ישנו דבריך	
	כי אתה צדיק ואמת כול בחיריך	
15-16	וכול עולה [ור]שע תשמיד לעד	
	ונגלתה צדקתך לעיני כול מעשיך	
17	[וא]ני ידעתי ברוב טובך	Stanza
	ובשבועה הקימותי על נפשי	C
	לבלתי חטוא לך	
18	[ול]בלתי עשות מכול הרע בעיניך	
	וכן הוגשתי ביוזד כול אנשי סודי	
18-19	לפי [ש]כלו אגישנו וכרוב נוזלתו אהבנו	
	ולא אשא פני רע	
	ורש[--------] לא אכיר	
20	[ולא] אמיר בהון אמתך	
	ובשוזד כול משפטיך	
20-21	כי אם לפ[י --------אי]ש [אוהב]נו	
	וכרוזקך אותו כן אתעבנו	
21-22	ולא אביא בסוד [----------]שבי [---בר]יתך	

Translation of Hodayot 14:8-22

8   [I thank you], O Lord,

        The one who gives understanding within the heart
             of your servant,
             [In order to^A   ]
9   And to be restrained from evil [deeds],
             And to bless [your name   ]
10   [And to   ] which you love,
             And to abhor all which you [hate],
11   [And to   ] a man;
11-12   For according to the spirits of their [_____]
             between good and evil,
             you [_____] them their deeds.

        And I, I know even because of your understanding
13   That in your plan [_____] your holy spirit;
             And thus you draw me to your understanding.
13-14   And accordingly as I draw near, I am zealous
             against the deeds of the wicked
             and the men of deceit.
             For all who draw near to you do not alter your
             command,^B
15   And all who know you do not change your words.
             For you are the righteous truth of all your chosen,
15-16 1 And all evil wickedness you destroy forever;
             And you reveal your righteousness before the eyes
             of all yours works.

17   And I, I know by the abundance of your goodness,
             And by <your> oath I am established in my life,
             In order not to sin before you,
18   And in order not to do anything evil in your eyes.
             And thus I draw near in the company of all the
             men of my community:
18-19   According to his insight I will draw near to him,
             and according to the greatness of his
             inheritance I love him.
             And I will not lift up my face to evil,
             And [_____] I will not acknowledge;
20   And I will not exchange your truth with wealth,
             Or with bribes all your judgments.
20-21   But according [_____] a man I will [love] him,
             And according to your removing him, thus will I
             abhor him.
21-22   And I will not bring in the community [_____]
             of your covenant.

_____

^AThese lines are discussed on pp. 148-149.

    ^BThe verbs in this bicolon are ambiguous, but since מור is
definitely used later in the poem, the above understanding is
probably correct.

Stanza Analysis

In reading this hymn, the repeated phrase ואני ידעתי
(lines 12 and 17) immediately stands out, and suggests the
opening of two of the stanza units of the poem.[22] However,
there are other features of this psalm that are rather different from the standard pattern seen in the Hodayot. Although
אדוני in line 8 certainly suggests the customary opening formula, the usual opening stanza lines do not follow. There is
a single line of descriptive material about God, then a large
hole in the text at the beginning of column line 9. When the
text resumes, it is with an infinitive clause. These infinitive clauses appear to be used for several lines, until the
first strategic ואני is reached. Both in length and in form,
then, these opening lines do not conform to the usual pattern
in the Hodayot.

It is indeed discouraging that so few opening lines remain
in columns 13-17, which originally opened the scroll. Only
five psalm openings can be seen in this section of the scroll;
of the five, three definitely have a different opening from
that ordinarily employed, and only one of the five possibly
comes close to resembling the standard pattern (see Chapter
VI, Section 1, on opening arrangements). This psalm in 14:8-22
suggests at the outset that there is a second form employed in
the Hodayot--one substantially different from the "thanksgiving"
type, not merely thematically different.

It is difficult to say for certain whether the single line
of divine description following the opening formula should be
read as independent of what follows or not. In view of the
following reconstruction of the text of the first unit, it
seems likely that it is the opening line of the unit rather
than an independent statement. It seems probable that the six
lines (three bicola) following the divine description were all
infinitive clauses. Both standard grammar and the grammatical
pattern in the rest of the Hodayot demand the attachment of infinitive clauses to another earlier statement or to a finite
verb.

The full text of this first unit cannot be restored with
any certainty, but poetic analysis suggests much of the

structure. Six infinitive clauses appear to have followed the
opening statement. The line following the opening statement
is missing completely, but the following line begins with an
infinitive and a connective ו, implying a parallel structure
with the preceding line, and thus an infinitive clause. A
third infinitive clause began לברך. This is followed by a
twenty-nine space gap, at the end of which a two-word relative
clause appeared, which is then followed by another infinitive.
The gap must cover part of two poetic lines, and it can be inferred that an infinitive began the line following לברך. Similarly, another infinitive can be inferred for the missing opening of the sixth line, in parallel with לתעב. Three infinitives
appear in the present text, three are inferred. From these infinitives and the other surviving phrases it can be deduced
that the second pair of infinitives (the third and the fourth)
were both positive, and that the latter of this set, or possibly both of these positive infinitives, were in contrast with
the fifth infinitive clause, which also closed with a relative
phrase. This in turn suggests that the fifth and sixth infinitives were negative (positive: to bless; negative: to abhor).
The second clause is also negative in thrust. If the unit was
symmetrically balanced, the first infinitive clause would have
been positive.[23]

[---------------------]	infinitive clause #1: positive?
ולהתאפק על עלי[לות] רשע	#2: negative
ולברך [שמך] ---------- [---------]	#3: positive
אש[ר] אהבתה ---------------[-----]	#4 positive
ולתעב את כול אשר שנאתה	#5 negative
ת אנוש [------------]	#6 negative?

The unit concludes with a bicolon of summary, badly marred
by gaps. On the basis of these infinitive clauses and the rest
of the poem, it is probable that these lines stated some kind
of treatment of men according to their good or evil deeds.[24]
Here for the first time in the poem the preposition לפי is used,
a preposition which plays a larger role in the next two stanzas.
    Both Stanzas B and C are marked off by the strategic phrase
ואני ידעתי. Further, both contain a statement beginning לפי,
and in each case this statement follows a line which begins וכן.
Stanza C is slightly longer than B, but the line beginning לפי

occurs at about the midpoint of the stanza in both B and C.
Aside from this patterning, the two stanzas diverge in their
poetic organization, but the parallels appear to be important
to both the form and theme of the hymn.

Stanza B is the best preserved unit of the psalm. Only
in the opening bicolon (tricolon) is there is gap which cannot
be restored with complete certainty. The first three lines
read more or less prosaically, and are of uneven lengths syllabically (eleven, seventeen, and nine syllables).[25] The
fourth line, beginning לפי, is even more of a problem. It appears to be a double line, with parallelism confined to the end
of the line in the doubling of a single term. It is also an
unusual line because it contains both an infinitive and a
finite verb (an arrangement found only occasionally in the Hodayot). The remaining five lines of B employ more standard
parallelism. Two types of parallelism are combined in these
lines, for the opening word alternates between כי and וכול,
but each bicolon employs synonymous parallelism internally.

> כי כול קרוביך לא ימרו פיך
> וכול יודעיך לא ישנו דבריך
> כי אתה צדיק ואמת כול בחיריך
> וכול עולה ורשע תשמיד לעד

In column line 15, towards the end of the stanza, is a
somewhat ambiguous line. It is usually translated "For you are
righteous, and all your elect are truth."[26] In view of the
references to the members of the community in the preceding
lines, this translation appears possible, but a bit surprising.
It would be more usual in the Hodayot to see both צדיק and אמת
applied to God. The following line, employing complementary
parallelism, refers to God's destruction of עולה ורשע. The
appearance of these two terms, an obvious hendiadys corresponding in position and contrasting with צדיק and אמת in the previous line suggests that these terms also are a hendiadys. In
such a case the translation would be closer to "You are the
righteous truth of all your elect." The final line of the
stanza rounds off the themes introduced in the later bicola of
this stanza.

In view of the rather prosaic and unsymmetrical shape of
Stanza B, it is worth noting that all but two of the lines end
with ך, giving the stanza a kind of end rhyme that overrides
some of its more prosaic features.

The outline of Stanza C has already been traced. Here,
however, the stanza is a bit longer, having an additional bicolon both before and after the lines beginning וכן and לפי.
The "double line" beginning with לפי in Stanza C actually forms
a good bicolon here, but is shown in a single line to match its
counterpart in Stanza B. Interestingly enough, all the bicola
surrounding these strategic middle lines contain negative particles. The parallelism of the opening bicolon and that which
follows is more standard than in Stanza B, as is that of the
lines following the לפי statement. Only the two statements beginning וכן and לפי have a prosaic flavor in this stanza.

$$
\left.\begin{array}{r}
\text{ולא אשא פני רע} \\
\text{וש]-----------[} \,\,{}^{27}\text{לא } \underline{\text{אכיר}}
\end{array}\right\}
$$

$$
\left.\begin{array}{r}
\text{ולא] } \underline{\text{אמיר}} \text{ בהון אמתך[} \\
\text{ובשווד כול משפטיך}
\end{array}\right\}
$$

$$
\left.\begin{array}{r}
{}^{28}\text{בו]} \underline{\text{אוהב}} \text{ [יש א -[------- כי אם לפ]וי} \\
\text{וכרוזקך אותי כן } \underline{\text{אתעבנו}}
\end{array}\right\}
$$

ולא אביא בסוד [---] שבי [----בר] יתך

Rhythmical Balance

Because of the amount of missing text in Stanza A, it is
impossible to outline its syllabic structure. It can be said
that it appears to be approximately the same length as Stanza
B, so that originally the hymn consisted of three roughly equal
units in weight. Stanzas B and C are diagrammed as follows.

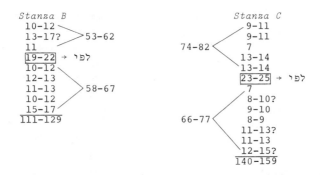

Stanza C is longer than B by about thirty syllables. The extra
weight is actually distributed in four extra lines (two bicola),
but Stanza C uses some short lines so the syllabic differences
between the stanzas are not quite as great as would be expected.
The לפי line is situated at about the midpoint of each stanza.

Imagery and Theology

Stanzas B and C have similar structural patterns, and the
thematic movement in them is also similar. Both begin with a
confident statement of God's gracious work within a man's life;
each climaxes with the declaration that because of this divine
gift, a man is "drawn near" (נגש)--first to God (Stanza B), and
then to his fellow man in the community (Stanza C). Following
this declaration in each case is the statement beginning לפי.
Although the wording is different in the two stanzas, the action
described in each לפי clause is similar. In Stanza B, the poet
declares that he is zealous for God's work according to his degree of closeness to God; in Stanza C he says that he is close
to his fellow man according to the degree his fellow is close
to God. Echoes of these important statements, using the verbs
אהב and שנא are found in the opening stanza, A, where it is
stated that God sets in men's hearts these abilities to love
righteousness and hate evil.

The לפי clauses appear to be the central affirmation of
the hymn. The early lines of Stanzas B and C lead up to this
clause, the later lines amplify the affirmation of this statement. It was noted earlier that these lines with לפי were

"double lines"; and in the case of the line in Stanza B, at
least, the לפי statement is quite prosaic. At the same time,
it may be recalled that the Manual of Discipline contains a
section (1QS 5) in which directions are set forth for the year-
ly examination of a member's religious insight, and that he receives a rank in the community according to this insight. The
similarity to the central לפי clauses in this hymn is quite
striking and suggests that these lines are creedal statements,
or are drawn from vows taken by the community. The creeds or
vows have been split up and incorporated in a poetic setting
which amplifies and illuminates their meaning.

     This possibility, the difference in the hymn form, and the
frequent references to members of the community and to the author as a member of the community, all make it extremely probable that this was a cultic psalm, written for use in public
worship, thus verifying the work of Holm-Nielsen from another
direction.

CHAPTER VI

SYNTHESIS: POETIC TECHNIQUES OF THE HODAYOT

Eight hymns, about one third of the Hodayot scroll, have
been examined. Due to the ravages of time, only one of these
was a long psalm, and this one has extremely poor text. There
appear to be several psalms which extend over two columns, and
the question remains whether or not the techniques and style
which mark the shorter, complete hymns are also characteristic
of these other sections. It would seem to be helpful to summarize the findings on poetic structures and techniques employed
in the eight hymns examined. This compilation can perhaps provide both helpful information on the state of Hebrew poetry at
Qumran and the springboard for further investigation of the Hodayot poetry itself.

The information to be summarized here can be classed under
six headings. There is first of all the opening line and stanza of these hymns, which share such common features. The summary of these features will be followed by a review of the
types of parallelism employed in the bicola and tricola, including the devices of chiasm and envelope form. A synopsis of
stylistic features present and absent in the Hodayot follows,
and special attention is then turned to the importance of certain grammatical structures in this poetry. A brief discussion
of some linguistic features which play a part in understanding
poetic technique and a summary of the patterns of stanzaic development and rhythmic balance close the chapter.

1. Opening Arrangements

In view of the great differences between many of the poems
in the Hodayot, the similarity of the opening lines of the
poems is both interesting and informative. The pattern in almost all of the opening lines (i.e., the line following the
introductory formula) is the same: כי followed by a second
person perfect verb, followed by some designation of a first
person object. In a few cases this final element is not included. Of the twenty-one opening lines[1] which can be picked

155

out with certainty in the Hodayot, thirteen follow the above
pattern; eight are different, and present several additional
patterns.

It is difficult to place 9:37 and 17:26 in this chart because of textual problems. Both lack the opening formula; in
9:37, as has already been shown, the presence of the opening
formula can be guessed with some certainty. In column 17, the
right margin is completely missing; in comparison with the
width of surrounding columns it can be calculated that twelve
to fifteen spaces are missing at the beginning of most lines
there--sufficient space for an opening formula. Since other
indications suggest that a new hymn begins in 17:26, the presence of an opening formula in the missing text can be guessed.
In this case, this psalm opening would fall where shown on the
chart.

TABLE 2

OPENING ARRANGEMENTS

Formula: Followed by	אודכה אדוני	ברוך אתה אדוני	אודכה אלי	?
2nd m.s. verb	5:5, 7:6			
1st sing. suffix	7:26, 8:4			
2nd m.s. verb, object with 1st suffix	2:20, 3:19 3:37, 4:5 7:34			
2nd m.s. verb		5:20	11:3	9:37? 17:26?
Other words	2:31			
no pattern similarity	14:8 14:23	10:14, 11:29 16:8	11:15	17:17

It can be seen that all the psalms in columns 2-8, and
probably 9, have the same formulaic opening line pattern except
for 2:31. Even here, however, the pattern has not been varied
greatly: ‏כיא עינכה ע--- על נפשי‏. (The missing word was probably
a verb.) Here is a second person designation to replace the

second person verb, a verb in the third person to agree with
the noun, and the standard first person object. The opening
patterns of the bottom line of the chart vary more dramatical-
ly, and so it can be stated with some assurance that a single
opening pattern marks the psalms in columns 2-9.
Further, in addition to the formulaic pattern of the opening line, the psalms in this section of the scroll (and in
11:3) bear other similarities. The parallelism used in the
opening stanza is quite comparable to the parallelism of the
canonical psalms; usually the lines of the stanza employ relatively complete parallelism and are arranged in synonymous bicola. Four lines (two bicola) is the most common length (2:20,
7:26, 7:6, 4:5; possibly 3:37, 7:34 and 2:31). In one case
(11:3), a single bicolon is used; in at least two cases, the
four-line pattern is augmented by a discernible "coda" line:
3:19 and 5:5. Despite this similarity of opening stanzas, the
psalms that follow are quite different, as analysis of several
has shown. 5:5-20 and 7:6-25 and 3:19-36 introduce a wealth
of apocalyptic imagery, shifting, changing, tied by link words
and various organizational features. 2:20-30 is a tightly organized, rather regular psalm. 7:26-33 and 11:3-14 are often
identified as hymns, and 9:37-10:12 shares some of their characteristics. Their disparateness suggests that the opening
stanza provided a link for their collection or use: a formal
nod to an older form or an opening antiphon.
      What of the other seven openings? What do their differ-
ences mean? We have analyzed only one of these, 14:8-22, but
the conclusions from this analysis have pertinence here. Holm-
Nielsen identified this hymn as definitely cultic from its
subject matter,[2] and this suggestion is confirmed by the poetic
analysis, which highlights the theme development and suggests
the inclusion of two creedal statements. Since the opening
stanza of this hymn was an integral part of this poem, it can
be tentatively suggested that analysis of the other fragmentary
hymns in this category will show that these too are almost certainly cultic hymns.
      The differences and similarities of the opening lines and
stanzas of the Hodayot suggest two basic forms: one employing a

standard, OT type of formal opening as a kind of antiphon, and
a second group lacking this antiphon but clearly cultic in
their themes. The "hymn" type identified by Holm-Nielsen and
Morawe is found in both categories, and the vagueness of its
description is once again demonstrated. Both of the opening
patterns, however, confirm the probable use of the Hodayot pub-
licly and cultically. The differences are perhaps an indication of different authors, or of a dramatic change in style by
a single author. On this matter, however, further work must be
done, and other criteria employed as well.

2. Parallelism and Cola Arrangements

     The extent and types of parallelism employed in the Ho-
dayot are quite comparable to those of the OT Psalter and
prophets. That is: the parallelism ranges in the same way from
quite complete to none at all. Synonymous, antithetic, chiastic, alternating line, and internal line parallelism are all
present in the Hodayot. The different flavor of this poetry is
due, not so much to differences in parallelism as to other stylistic and rhythmical devices. Nevertheless, a summary of the
salient characteristics of parallelism in the Hodayot contrib-
utes to a total understanding of the nature of this poetry.
     The most notable point in regard to parallelism in the
Hodayot is that it is generally more like the parallelism of
the prophets rather than of the Psalter--it is often loose and
incomplete. The exception is the parallelism of the opening
stanzas, which are tightly organized and employ more complete
parallelism in sets of well matched bicola. Although some of
the Hodayot follow the general thanksgiving form throughout,
many diverge from this pattern after the opening stanza (3:19-
36, 5:5-20, 7:26-33, 11:3-14). It is the opening stanza's form
and parallelism which has the greatest affinity with the Psalter; the parallelism used in the bodies of the poems is both
more incomplete and more elaborate, employing tricola, envelope
forms, alternating parallel lines.
     Tricola are used much more frequently in the Hodayot than
in canonical poetry--almost as frequently as bicola are. And
although the parallelism of the bicolon is often comparable to

that used in the Psalter, the parallelism of the tricolon shows
considerable divergence from its canonical counterpart. Rarely
are all three lines parallel, and even when they are, the parallelism is quite different from that of the early tricola in
the biblical psalms. Frequently the tricolon presents a more
ornate pattern. The first line often contains the main clause
while the second and third lines are subordinate and parallel.
Quite often there is no real parallelism in the tricolon, and
the lines are rather prosaic and divided into equal units by
the grammatical clauses. One type of "prosaic" arrangement in
the bicolon and tricolon might be mentioned especially: that in
which the second line begins with an infinitive clause subordinate to the first (or second) line.

Bicolon arrangements are occasionally marked by pattern
variations more frequently employed in tricola. The prosaic
infinitive clause arrangement has just been mentioned. Another
variation can be seen in the Opening Stanza of 7:26-33 where
the second bicolon is subordinated grammatically to the whole
first bicolon. An even greater oddity is the arrangement of
Stanza B' in 7:26-33, where what would ordinarily be a bicolon
by its length and weight is split into three lines.

One other type of parallel arrangement deserves mention.
Quite often within a stanza, parallel structures and terms are
employed over more than a bicolon or tricolon. Examples are
the list of five infinitive clauses in Stanza C in 9:37-10:12.
In these two cases the lines do not break down easily into sets
of bicola or tricola, but instead the parallel features are
arranged in elaborate patterns over the entire unit. In other
cases, such as the infinitive list in Stanza A of 14:8-22, it
would seem that the longer parallel section is composed of sets
of bicola.

TABLE 3

TYPES OF PARALLELISM IN THE HODAYOT

Synonymous Bicolon	11:3-4	כיא [הודע]תני בסוד אמתכה ותשכילני במעשי פלאכה
Other examples	2:29, 3:19, 3:24-25 3:34, 5:7, 5:12 7:28-29, 11:4-5	
Antithetic Bicolon	5:6	ולא עזבתני בזמות יצרי ותעזור משווֹת חיי
Other examples	14:20-21	
Chiastic Bicolon	3:25	ותגור נפש אביון עם מהומות רבה והוות מדהבה עם מצעדי
Other examples	7:13, 7:26, 10:4-5 10:9, 11:5-6, 9-10	
Synonymous Tricolon	11:4-5	ותתן בפי הודות ובלשוני [תהל]ה ומול שפתי במכון רנה
Other examples	5:7-8, 7:28, 7:11-12	
Tricolon with lines 2 and 3 parallel	7:30-31	וכול בני אמתכה תביא בסליחוות לפניכה [לטהרם] מפשעיהם ברוב טובכה ובהמון רוזמיכה להעמידם לפניכה לעולמי עד
Other examples	3:31-32	
Tricolon with use of infinitive clause	3:21-22	ורוח נעוה טהרתה מפשע רב להתיצב במעמד עם צבא קדושים ולבוא ביחד עם עדת בני שמים
Bicolon with infinitive	7:12	כי כול גרי למשפט תרשיע להבדיל בי בין צדיק לרשע
Other examples	7:32-33	
Alternating parallel lines	7:14-15	לנתיבות צדקה להתהלך לפניך בגבול החיים לשבילי כבוד ושלום לאין --- [ללא]ה להשבת לנצוׁ
Other examples	5:14-15, 14:14-16	
Envelope Parallelism	2:22-23 (Stanza A)	והמה סוד שוא ועדת בליעל לא ידעו כיא מאתכה מעמדי ובוזסדיכה תושיע נפשי
Other examples	5:9-11 (Stanza C)	כיא מאתכה מצעדי
Internal parallels	2:22	והמה סוד שוא ועדת בליעל
Other examples	7:16-17, 7:32, 10:3-4	

3. Stylistic Features

Some of the devices and techniques used in the Hodayot are
summarized in the chart at the end of this section. All except
the final two devices are used in canonical poetry. The exchange of prepositional objects within a bicolon is an interlocking device perhaps characteristic only of this poet. The
use of lists, especially the extensive lists in 11:3-14, is
considered to be due to foreign influence on Hebrew poetry, and
in general a mark of late poetry. While the examples in the
chart show that the Hodayot poet used his repertoire of canonical stylistic devices knowledgeably, it is perhaps significant
that the first three devices, well known in biblical poetry, are
used only rarely in the Hodayot. The refrains are used rather
differently than in canonical poetry, often placed before and
after the main section of the poem instead of being interspersed
with the stanzas.

In addition to the devices listed on the chart, other stylistic features are prominent in these psalms. As expected,
the use of divine names and addresses is more restricted in the
Hodayot than in the Psalms. The name itself is not used at all
of course, although reference to it is made. אדוני and אלי are
the two divine titles most frequently used, but even these are
used sparingly. They occur in the opening formula and in a few
strategic lines of the poem itself: כי אל עולם אתה, ואתה אלי,
כי אתה אלי. Occasionally other divine epithets occur. The
most notable of these is the list in 9:37-10:12: שר אלים,
מושל בכול מעשה, אדון לכול רוח, מלך נכבדים.

The independent pronoun, on the other hand, occurs in the
Hodayot with far greater frequency than in canonical poetry.
אתה, in reference to God, may be partial compensation for the
less frequent direct titular address, but אני, in reference to
the poet, is also frequently used. In 2:20-30, either המה or
אני is used at the opening of each unit, with המה referring to
the poet's (and God's) enemies. Both the circumscribed use of
divine titles and the frequent use of pronouns may possibly reflect more of the Hodayot poet's individual style and theology
than a pattern characteristic of the poetry of this period.

Two other stylistic phenomena may be more indicative of
current practices, however. First of all there is the poet's
use of biblical quotations and allusions. While Chapter II,
Section 2 has demonstrated that this is not as all pervasive in
the Hodayot as some have maintained, there are nevertheless
numerous examples. Scripture is freely quoted as a coda to a
poem (2:20-30), or as a catchword (in Stanza A of 7:26-33).
Ornate allusions are introduced, with the poet's own additions
to make them applicable to the situation. (Stanza C of 2:20-
30; Stanza A of 7:6-25.) These practices are in general comparable to uses made of OT scripture by NT writers.

Finally, the place of prosaic words and particles in the
Hodayot deserves note. Although את, אשר, and יש are not absent
in these poems, they are used quite sparingly. It is particularly striking how seldom את is used before the direct object;
as it will be seen in the following section, there is evidence
that the poet is moving toward the Mishnaic practice of using
ל for this function. This observation in regard to את, and to
a lesser extent, to אשר as well, is all the more important because scholars frequently fill missing text with these two
particles. In view of their infrequent use in the extant text
it would be wise to restore lacunae without their use unless
there is real evidence to the contrary.

TABLE 4

BRIEF SUMMARY OF STYLISTIC FEATURES IN THE HODAYOT

Double-duty words and particles	2:22 (verb) 2:25-26 (preposition and suffix) 7:7-8 (verbal suffix) 14:17 (noun suffix)
Splitting of stereotyped phrase	3:23-24
Hendiadys	2:27-28 (two examples) 14:15-16
Inclusio	2:20-30 (Opening and Closing Stanzas) 3:19-21 (Opening Stanza) 5:10-15 (actually uses interlocking phrases to link C, D, E) 7:22-24 (Stanza E) 7:30-31 (Stanza C, the focal stanza)

Refrains	7:6-25 9:37-10:12 11:3-14
Rhetorical Questions	3:23-24 7:28, 32-33 10:3-4, 5-7, 10-12
Repetition of single word or suffix for assonance and emphasis	3:26-34 (כול) 10:9-10 (אין) 11:7-9 (-כה)
Reversal of prepositional object	3:25 5:12-13 11:5
Lists	2:25-28 (7 symbols of destruction) 3:27-28 (5 judgment figures) 10:8 (4 divine titles) 11:7-9 (double lists: divine attri- butes and personal qualities)

4.   Some Comments on Grammatical Structure

One of the major differences between canonical poetry and
the Hodayot--far more apparent than the presence or absence of
the stylistic devices just discussed--is in the grammatical
structures of the poetic lines.   It can be seen from the chart
on the next page (Table 5) that the Hodayot consistently use
two types of grammatical structure more frequently than do the
canonical psalms: the noun sentence and the infinitive clause.
The latter difference is particularly marked.   These grammatical differences would seem to reflect more than the peculiari-
ties of a single author; all of the Sectarian writings show a
marked preference for the infinitive clause.

Further study of verbal forms highlights another important
fact: most lines employing a finite verb use only one verb.
Occasionally two verb forms are combined in a single line--that
is, two perfects or imperfects, a perfect and an imperfect, or
a finite verb and an infinitive.   Since such combinations are
not particularly frequent in canonical poetry either, this
would not seem to be a startling finding.   However, restorations
of text in the Hodayot frequently postulate lines with such verb
combinations, and a caution seems to be in order.   Moreover, the

use of a single finite verb and the relatively frequent usage
of the noun sentence may seem somewhat surprising in view of
the length of the colon in the Hodayot, which is often almost
twice as long as its canonical counterpart in Psalms.

TABLE 5

GRAMMATICAL STRUCTURES IN HEBREW POETRY

	Poetic lines (cola) with no verb	Lines with infinitive only	Lines with infinitive & finite verb	Lines with finite verb
Canonical Examples				
Psalm 29	8	0	0	15
Psalm 47	7	0	0	13
Psalm 119 (B section)	1	1	0	12
Psalm 130	4	0	0	12
Psalm 137	3	1	1	14
Isa 40:1-8	5	0	0	20
Isa 60:1-7	3	0	0	22
Hodayot Examples				
2:20-30	6	5	1	13
3:19-36	12	8	0	28
5:5-19	8	3	1	25
7:26-33	8	4	1	5
9:37-10:12	10	0	1	15
11:3-14	10	5	0	14

The following chart shows the distribution of the finite
verbs in the Hodayot analyzed. (In the case of the final three
psalms, only the lines which are now complete or where a verb
can be seen were counted.) Perfect and imperfect forms appear
with about the same overall frequency in these poems, although
some psalms seem to prefer forms of one over the other. There
are certain differences in where these forms occur, however.
While imperfect forms quite frequently are used at the beginning

of new units in the poems (are stanza indicators), perfect
forms are never used in this way. Where perfect forms occur
in the first line of a new stanza, they are invariably combined
with an independent pronoun that stands first in the line. This
difference cannot be due to subjectivity on the part of the
analyzer, since perfect verbs rarely are the first words in any
line, and in these few cases it would be difficult for anyone
to argue that they are strategically located at the beginning
of new units.

In the few instances (eighteen out of one hundred fifty-
one cases) of combinations of verb forms within a line, it is
interesting to note that three instances occur in "double
lines," and that all three use combinations of finite verbs.
The four cases in which an infinitive is combined with a finite
verb do not include any double lines. Five of the eighteen
combinations form part of a very tightly organized rhetorical
question section of 9:37-10:12 (Stanza D). Except for this
latter unit, the four Hodayot identified as "hymn" types by
Holm-Nielsen and Morawe use lines combining verb forms in sig-
nificantly fewer instances than the other Hodayot. This fact,
in combination with the listing techniques and the rhythmic
stability of lines in these poems, may be the substantive evidence for the actual existence of a hymn form in the Hodayot.

TABLE 6

FINITE VERB DISTRIBUTION IN THE HODAYOT

	perf.	imperf.	perf.+ perf.	perf.+ imperf.	imperf.+ imperf.	finite verb + inf.
2:20-30	5	6	2	1	0	1
3:19-36	6	19 (3 stanza indicators)	0	2 (1 double line)	1	0
5:5-19	14	9 (3 stanza indicators)	0	2 (1 double line)	0	1
7:26-33	2	3	0	0	0	1
11:3-14	7	7 (1 stanza indicator)	0	0	0	0
7:6-25	12	17 (3 stanza indicators)	0	0	0	0
9:37-10:12	1	9	0	5 (list)	0	1
14:8-22	7 (1 double line)	10	0	0	1 (double line)	0

5. The Use of Prepositions in the Hodayot

Prepositions are used in the Hodayot somewhat more frequently and more prominently than in the Psalter. Exact sta-
tistical information is not available here, but it would seem
that in canonical poetry prepositions occur on the average at a
rate of a little less than one per line. In the Hodayot, the
average is slightly greater--a bit higher than one preposition
per line.

More interesting than mere statistics, however, is that
frequently in the Hodayot there are two prepositions in a poetic line, a phenomenon occurring rarely in the canonical psalms.

This is to be expected in poetry that makes great use of infinitive clauses, and this grammatical feature is one of the
more distinctive differences between the Hodayot and canonical
poetry. There is also an increased use of ב and ל in other
connections as well.

In general in the Hodayot, ל is preferred to אל, and ב to
מן and על. These are the two prepositions most frequently used,
but there are many others. It is interesting for example that
the poet preferred לפי to על פי, although in the Qumran writings
as a whole על פי predominates.[3] Caution therefore has to be
exercised in drawing conclusions from the usage of prepositions
in the Hodayot, for these conclusions may not be generally applicable to other poetry of the period, but may reflect the
poet's individual style.

There are some usages of prepositions, however, that seem
to reflect grammatical practice in this late period, and other
practices which, if not characteristic of all writers, are important to the understanding of the Hodayot. The uses of ב,
in particular, appear to approach the usages of this preposition outlined by Segal for Mishnaic Hebrew.[4] ב is used to
designate the accusative of verbs more often than in the OT.

    11:5   זמר ב
    3:29   אכל ב
    7:26   שכל ב

These verbs, for example, do not use ב as a sign of the accusative in the OT. ב is often used with the infinitive in the
Hodayot in temporal clauses, while this is rarely done in
canonical poetry.

    2:28   בהתרומם גליהם
    5:5   בגורי בעט
    3:26-27   בהפתח כל פזי שחת

Compounds such as בלא, and באין, are also more frequently used
in the Hodayot than in canonical poetry.

In some cases it would seem that the Hodayot author has
deliberately used the preposition ב to enhance the style of his
poem. In 7:26-33, ב is used ten times in eighteen lines, and
the grammatical nuance of ב frequently changes in the psalm.

Most of the prepositions preface a divine attribute, yet it is
almost impossible to translate each ב in the same way because
of varying grammatical and syntactical relationships. This,
of course, was not a problem to the author who could use the
preposition in a variety of ways syntactically and still
achieve the desired repetitive effect in style.

The preposition ל is more frequently used in the Hodayot
before an indirect object or before an infinitive. Both are
standard usages, but the infinitive appears more frequently
than in canonical poetry and often in strategic positions (see
Chapter VI, Section 6). ל does not appear to be used as an
accusative particle in any of the eight psalms examined. It is
used at least once as a relative pronoun: ללוא תזעזע.

6. Linguistic Features

This poetic analysis of the Hodayot has not been concerned
with linguistic phenomena beyond the discussion of data relevant to textual problems. Two general comments emerge out of
these considerations that are worthy of note. First there is
the question of the use of Aramaic vocabulary in these psalms.
Quite frequently if the text is difficult to interpret, various
Aramaic words are suggested for the difficult expressions. This
is the case with דנח in 5:13, and with צבר in 7:29. But elsewhere, where the meaning of phrases is clear, there are no instances of Aramaic borrowing. All the vocabulary comes from
the OT, although there are many instances where substantive
forms not found in the OT are derived from verbal roots used
there. The single possible Aramaic borrowing in these eight
psalms examined--עפים in 7:9--is found in the OT itself in
Psalm 104.

On the other hand, spelling conventions may have been influenced by Aramaic; they certainly reflect late Jewish orthographical usage. That quiescent א is frequently dropped in the
Hodayot is generally recognized. Sometimes ה takes the place
of a final א or seems to compensate for its loss as in מודה =
מאוד in 11:3. Aside from such orthographical differences from
canonical forms, Aramaic seems to have had little influence on
the vocabulary and morphology of the Hodayot. Verb forms used

are consistently those of biblical Hebrew, not of Aramaic.
Solving textual problems in the Hodayot by appeal to Aramaic
would therefore seem to be quite risky.

If there is little influence from the *lingua franca* of the
poet's day, it can also be said quite definitely that archaic
linguistic influences are also absent in the Hodayot. There is
no evidence of the use of enclitic מ, nor of archaic case endings. Although this is generally recognized, there is an occasional appeal to such archaic phenomena to solve textual
problems--for example the final מ in סבבום in 2:25. Other explanations more in keeping with later canonical Hebrew can be
readily suggested in such cases. Further research may, in fact,
turn up some interesting examples of quotations or biblical
allusions in the Hodayot where archaic features have been al-
tered to conform with later classical grammar.

7. Stanzaic Development and Rhythmical Balance

As both Carmignac and Thiering maintain, the Hodayot show
clear evidence of careful structural organization, although the
patterns employed are often quite different from their biblical
counterparts. In the eight psalms analyzed the variety of
structural patterns reveals a complex picture. The opening
stanzas (except for 14:8-22) are quite clearly built on a
single pattern, as we have seen. No other single stanza pattern is as prevalent in these psalms. However, there are a
number of structural devices which frequently occur.

Stanza openings, as Carmignac correctly perceived, are
most frequently marked by the independent pronoun, often combined with other strategic particles: הנה אתה כי, אתה כי, ואתה אלי.
Of the forty stanza openings in these eight Hodayot (excluding
the opening stanzas), fifteen are indicated by independent pronouns. Other stanzas are indicated as follows.

> by interrogatives   4
> by imperfect verbs   7
> with vav consecutive
> by כי + pronoun   4
> by כי + verb   2

by הנה + pronoun	1
by substantives	5
by prepositional phrases	2

Stanzas whose beginnings fall into the final two groups have
the least distinctive openings, but their limits in all seven
cases are rather definitely marked by other rhetorical considerations (see Chapter III, Section 3, and Chapter IV, Section 1).

In the use of the imperfect verb with the vav consecutive
as a stanza indicator, it is significant that in all but one of
these seven instances the verb is second masculine singular (in
reference to God). There are twenty-one second person masculine
singular verbs with the vav consecutive in these eight psalms.
Six of these mark the beginning of stanzas, and with them must
be included the repetition of ותרם in 7:23 that marks the inclusio in Stanza E. Three others mark the beginning of subsections in 3:19-36 and 5:5-19. Two are coda line indicators
within the latter poem. Only eight of these verbs are not used
strategically. The appearance of this form in other Hodayot,
therefore, will often be an indication of the opening or closing of a unit.

Similarly, the combination of כי or הנה with a pronoun
almost invariably marks a new unit in the Hodayot. There is
but a single instance in these eight psalms where it does not
(14:15).

Two basic types of structural development seem to be used
in the poems. In the first, the poem has two roughly equal
halves (2:20-30, 9:37-10:12). In the second type, there is a
focal stanza in the middle of the poem (5:5-19, 7:26-33). There
are all sorts of variations of these two patterns: the main body
of the poem may be divided into equal halves and set off by refrains, followed by a concluding stanza in a different style
(7:6-25, 11:3-14). 14:8-22 seems to be a poem with balanced
stanzas, B and C, prefaced by a different type of opening stanza. Occasionally there is a poem like that in 3:19-36, which
has asymmetrical units building steadily toward a climax.

Special mention should be made of several methods by which
stanzas are linked structurally to give the poem graceful

cohesion. Several psalms match stanzas; that is, beyond the
consistent use of a type of stanza indicator (pronoun or imperfect verb) other grammatical or syntactical features of
stanzas are matched. In 2:20-30, Stanzas A and B both begin
והמה and close with the same phrase. In 5:5-19, Stanzas A and
B are matched by grammatical structures of the first three
lines. Stanzas A and B in 11:3-14 both have lists. It is interesting that this linking device is most frequently used in
the first two stanzas of the body of the poem, and that other
devices are used later. A second such device is the repetition
of a single line or a slight variation of it in successive
stanzas. This type of structural linkage can be seen in 7:6-
25 between Stanzas A and B with one phrase, and between B and C
with a second phrase. A more elaborate example appears in 5:
5-19, interlocking Stanzas C, D, and E. Finally, in most of
these hymns there is a link word or words found throughout the
hymn. In 11:3-14 it is כבוד; in 7:26-33 it is the suffix כה-
and the word אמה. 3:19-36 presents a more elaborate pattern in
which Stanzas A, B, and C are linked, as are the Opening and C,
and C and D, and the linkages are brought together in the final
stanza.

Rarely is the opening stanza balanced by a closing stanza
in weight or theme. In 2:20-30 there is a summary stanza and a
coda using a biblical quotation, and a similar structure can be
seen in 7:6-25. Most of the hymns, however, do not balance the
opening stanza with a unit of similar weight at the end. Usually theme or link words are carried from the opening unit all
the way to the close of the poem (see especially 3:19-36, 14:
8-22, 7:26-33), but the opening stanza still lies outside the
rhythmical balancing of the rest of the poem. The stanzas in
the body of the poem, including the final stanza, are balanced
against each other excluding the opening stanza. This phenomenon lends further weight to the suggestion that the opening
stanza is an antiphon or formalized unit from which the freer
composition of the poet depended.

This sketch of the typical stanzaic pattern already shows
a number of departures from the patterns of development seen in
the Psalter. There are two other major ways in which this

poetry differs structurally from the canonical psalms. The
change in the typical grammatical structures of the poem has
already been discussed (Chapter VI, Section 4); noun sentences
and infinitive clauses comprise a much larger proportion of the
Hodayot cola than in canonical poetry. At the same time there
is a slight increase in the number of prepositional phrases
used; these changes play their part in introducing longer lines
into Hebrew poetry. This shift in grammatical structures,
along with the decreased use of canonical devices like double-
duty words, hendiadys, and so on, mark one decisive change in
the composition of Hebrew poetry. The employment of parallelism may not be noticeably different from earlier use, but other
conventions have changed.

Another major difference between the Hodayot and canonical
poetry is rhythmical. Carmignac summed this up by saying that
there was more amplitude in the Hodayot. More precise descriptions can be given, however. The poetic line most commonly employed in the Hodayot ranges from nine to thirteen syllables in
length.[5] A bicolon normally has twenty to twenty-six syllables.
This is roughly twice the syllabic length of bicola in many of
the canonical psalms. In addition, shorter lines, particularly
in lists, were quite definitely in use; and longer lines were
used at strategic points (codas, summary lines, biblical allusions). A "double line," the length of the normal bicolon in
these hymns, occasionally appears in similar use; such a line
cannot be divided into the usual two-line structure because of
its grammatical or syntactical structure, although it can be
divided into two quite uneven lines sometimes. The effect of
poetry built on such rhythmical conventions is quite different
from biblical poetry. It is like a Rococo chapel standing next
to a Quaker meeting house. To those accustomed to the more
spartan rhythms of biblical poetry, the Hodayot do appear repetitious and chaotic. The preferred rhythmical conventions are
quite different at Qumran than in earlier, classical days.

CHAPTER VII

THEOLOGY AND POETRY

What can poetic analysis offer the study of Hodayot theology? Whether it is a bicolon, a stanza, or the whole series of poems, poetic analysis is of great assistance. Such analysis helps to solve textual problems; it enables us to understand the focus of a poem far better than line-by-line commentaries. Most of all, poetic analysis deepens appreciation for the poet at work, the range of his imagery, the subtlety of his expressions, the depth of his insights.

In the case of the Hodayot, many textual problems can be resolved by an understanding of the techniques employed by the poet, as examination of the eight complete hymns has shown. In most of these psalms the perception of the poem's organization has shown a clear purpose and movement in the theological insight presented. In this final chapter it seems appropriate to devote some attention to some of the larger themes of these psalms and the insights suggested by poetic analysis.

Three theological themes have been selected for comment here: the language and imagery connected with God; the emphasis on salvation and grace; and the vivid imagery connected with the eschatological war and the forces of Belial. Much has been written on the concept of God in the Hodayot. Although virtually every commentator has pointed out that the Hodayot do not present systematic theology (see Chapter I, especially pp. 11-13), discussions usually center around theological comment abstracted from these psalms. While such abstraction is probably unavoidable, the author's personal faith and viewpoint are often lost in this discussion. It is here that poetic analysis is valuable because the focus is continually on the author's work.

The focus of most of these discussions on God in the Hodayot is on his omnipotence. This is certainly an outstanding theme in these psalms. Coupled with this is often a comment on the deterministic viewpoint of the author. Applying these terms to the Hodayot allows scholars to compare and contrast the theology of the Hodayot with other Sectarian writings and with the

173

Old and New Testament. Unfortunately, the application of these
categories often reveals the bias of the scholar rather than
the insights of the poet. It is difficult to understand, for
example, why Hyatt states, with no further evidence, that the
determinism of the Hodayot author is more pessimistic than
other later Jewish authors.[1]

Poetic analysis tends to see the author's work from the
perspective of each poem as a whole work, rather than from theological categories. In the case of the present analysis, the
most noticeable feature of these psalms is the consistent style
of addressing God. He is addressed frequently, sometimes by
title (ואתה אלי), but more often by the pronoun alone. אתה is
by far the most frequently used independent pronoun in these
psalms; they revolve about God, his love, his wrath, his attributes, rather than about the poet's dilemmas. The use of divine names and titles in these psalms is far more sparing than
in the canonical Psalter. This, of course, is in keeping with
the religious conventions of this period. The pronoun carries
the burden of divine address; divine titles mark high points
(5:11) or formulae, or form a list for contemplation and reflection (9:37-10:12). The personal address with the pronoun
gives an intimate flavor of dialogue to virtually every psalm;
few of the canonical psalms carry such an intimate feeling of
insight into the divine plan, despite their free use of the
divine name.

The listing device is most frequently used in connection
with God's actions and attributes. The most extensive lists
are those in 11:3-14, where three well-developed lists of divine attributes are found. There is also a list of judgments
which will mark the approach of the final battle in 3:19-36.
Closely connected with the lists are sections where each line
is constructed with the same grammatical forms, usually with
the same verb form. Once again, most of these are connected
with God's attributes and actions. Examples include the third
stanza of 11:3-14 (describing the purposes of God's grace), and
Stanza D of 9:37-10:12 (contrasting God's gifts and man's
needs). These highly stylized and polished stanzas reveal both

the poet's fascination with the divine and his desire to cap-
ture in words the truths of his faith.

A second aspect of the theology of the Hodayot which poetic analysis brings into perspective is the emphasis on grace
and salvation. In almost every hymn the author's confidence
that grace triumphs over sin is seen in the arrangement of his
material. In the list of divine attributes in Stanza B of
11:3-14, it is forgiveness and compassion which culminate the
list. In the chiastically arranged poem in 7:26-33, the center
of the poem dwells on the community God establishes for his
elect. The complete dependence of man on God's grace is emphasized by the highly stylized list of God's gifts in Stanza D
of 9:37-10:12. Salvation is usually mentioned in the opening
stanza of each psalm, and this is part of the classic thanksgiving psalm form, as has long been recognized. Analysis of
the structure of other sections of the poems now reveals that
this emphasis is consistently carried throughout the poems, and
is often the focus of the poem (e.g., Stanza D of 5:5-19, pp.
91-92).

The third theme of great importance in the Hodayot is the
eschatological war. Like the other two themes mentioned in
these brief summary comments, this theme permeates these psalms.
It is woven in and out of other themes; scarcely a hymn lacks
at least a passing reference to the "sons of wickedness," and
more often the final war with Belial is mentioned as the poet
speaks of his salvation or his persecution (2:22, 3:29-34, 7:7,
11, 14:13-14). The persistency of this theme was due to the
conviction that the time until the end was short. As Holm-
Nielsen says, the community believed that "the eschatological
settlement is already in the course of preparation in the present situation."[2] Not surprisingly, then, the language and
imagery connected with every aspect of this eschatological war
are extremely vivid.

The imagery is so vivid, so concrete, and so mythological,
in fact, that commentators diverge quite widely on its interpretation. There are writers like Laurin who insist the imagery
is "allegorical" or "figurative," and that the meaning is to be
found entirely within the confines of normal human life.[3] There

are theologians like Murphy who believe that the imagery, borrowed basically from the OT, has outgrown its original meaning
entirely and has become basically metaphysical, moral terminology.[4] There are those who may be termed the "literalists" who
in varying degrees insist that the image or metaphor means exactly what it says: heaven, hell, eternal life--the only question is the meaning of these terms in this historical period.

It would seem that a great deal remains to be done in this
area of struggling with the theological import of the imagery
in the Hodayot. If, however, poetic analysis is taken seriously, one of the conclusions which must be reached is that imagery and its setting in the poem is basic to any theological
understanding of the poem. Two prominent examples of the
necessity for structural analysis are Hodayot 3:19-36 and 5:
5-19. In the former poem, debate has raged around certain
phrases isolated from the poem as a whole; in the latter poem,
several successive images are meant to convey a single theological theme. In both cases, traditional commentaries have
neglected the setting of the imagery in the total poem, and
have as a result misunderstood the theological insights
presented.

Since it is not possible to explore all of the eschatological imagery used in the Hodayot at this time, discussion here is
limited to šaḥat and its connection with the eschatological war,
and to one subsidiary point, God's use of such evil forces for
his own purposes. It is well to keep in mind at the outset the
comments of D. S. Russell on such imagery in apocalyptic
writings.

> Some of this symbolism is taken over directly
> from the Old Testament, whose imagery and metaphors
> are adapted and used as material for graphic figura-
> tive representation. Much of it, however, has its
> origin in ancient mythology. This influence is
> traceable even in the Old Testament itself, but in
> apocalyptic it is much more fully developed....More
> often than not the original significance of the sym-
> bol or figure is lost altogether; at other times
> only part of an originally complex picture is used
> to portray what the writer has in mind; at other
> times details are mentioned which have no direct
> bearing on the matter under discussion, but are
> given simply because they belong to the tradition

or myth which is at that moment being used. Thus,
though the imagery and language are for the most
part sterotyped, they nevertheless lend themselves
to a kaleidoscopic variation in their presentation
of the divine mysteries.[5]

The use of šaḥat in the Hodayot does draw heavily on
mythological material. It cuts across a variety of images employed in the OT, combining a number of motifs; this type of
combination of images has also been noted by Russell in other
apocalyptic books. Two hymns analyzed earlier in particular
employ extensive imagery in connection with šaḥat. In both
2:20-30 and 3:19-36, šaḥat is depicted as connected with Belial
and with evil forces at work in the world, as having traps,
arrows, nets, and other weapons with which to attack men. In
2:20-30, šaḥat is mentioned only in the introductory stanza,
but the forces of Belial appear throughout. Connected with
their depiction as an army is a second image, that of the *mayim
rabbim*. These waters are destructive waters; they are the
chaotic deeps. The poet makes no attempt to explain the exact
relationship between this mythological motif and the army of
Belial motif. It is clear, however, that the waters are both
destructive and evil and that the author is saved only because
of God's covenant.

In 3:19-36, šaḥat and the war of Belial are given more
direct description. Not only are the forces of Belial armed
with standard weaponry, but a river of fire and pitch aids
Belial. The poet vividly describes how this fiery river reaches
down as far as the great abyss, so that the monsters of the deep
themselves writhe in agony. In this poem the author uses the
terms *sheol abbadon, tehom*, and šaḥat.

כי פדיתה נפשי משחת
ומשאול אבדון העליתני לרום עולם

ויבקעו לאבדון נחלי בליעל
ויהמו מחשבי תהום בהמון גורשי רפש

These parallels make it difficult to separate the three terms
in discussing them, although some scholars have done this.
Moreover, all three are indisputably connected with the work of
Belial. The picture therefore is tremendously complicated. In

view of the comments on the play of themes involving heights
and depths in this psalm (see "Theology" in Chapter III, Section 3), it is difficult to deny completely that the poet is
operating with the mythological motifs connected with the
nether world. This obviously is not the primitive idea of
Sheol from earlier centuries, but it is a development of those
mythological ideas. This nether world is identified as *tehom*,
the watery deep, and the mountains are pillars whose foundations are in this deep. Further, this nether world is connected
with the forces of Belial and their destructive work.

It is difficult, then, to agree wholeheartedly with Murphy
that *šaḥat* and Belial are connected in this period chiefly with
moral corruption. This dimension is not absent from the depiction of *šaḥat* and Belial, but it is part of the growth of the
entire mythological complex on which the Hodayot author is
drawing. There is no question of either/or; the concept of
šaḥat is quite vast, and touches on several mythological motifs
--the nether world, the grave, the watery deep, the forces of
Belial, as well as including moral corruption.

It is both interesting and somewhat disappointing that the
language of the Hodayot bears little resemblance to that of the
War Scroll in such apocalyptic passages. Faint echoes are
there, of course, but the references to Belial's forces and
armory in the Hodayot are general terms, and rather limited:
arrows, spears, *gibborim*, weapons of battle. No specific war
maneuvers, even of the stylized type seen in 1QM, appear at all.
Yet in one passage the theology behind the War Scroll comes
quite close to the central statement of Hodayot 5:5-19.

> They do not know that from the God of Israel is all
> that is and that will be, and He will annihilate
> Belial in all future times of eternity. Today is his
> appointed time to subdue and to humble the prince of
> the dominion of wickedness....And justice shall re-
> joice on high, and all sons of His truth shall be
> glad in eternal knowledge. But ye, sons of His cove-
> nant, be ye strong in God's crucible, until He shall
> lift up His hand and shall complete His testings
> through His mysteries with regard to your existence.[6]

Here the War Scroll author says quite clearly that persecutions
and difficulties are for the testing and purification of the
elect. This is the same theme as that of 5:5-19, where the
poet chooses three judgment motifs--lions, hunters, and metal
refinement--to convey the same insights. Clearly the "dualism"
of the Hodayot is not an ultimate dualism; at the most profound
level, God is seen as the author of everything, including the
testing and trial of the eschatological war.

NOTES

CHAPTER I

[1]Detailed accounts of the discovery of the Dead Sea
Scrolls, a story which has fascinated both scholars and the
public, can be found in most introductions to the scrolls. Two
of the best accounts by scholars are *The Ancient Library of
Qumran* by Frank Moore Cross (New York: Doubleday, 1958) and
The Dead Sea Scrolls by Millar Burrows (New York: Viking, 1958).

[2]Millar Burrows, *More Light on the Dead Sea Scrolls* (New
York: Viking, 1958) 380.

[3]The Ben-Sira scroll found in the Cairo Geniza is shown
by Yadin to be basically close to the original Hebrew in *The
Ben-Sira Scroll from Masada* ([Jerusalem: Israel Exploration
Society, 1965] 7).

[4]Hermann Gunkel, *The Psalms* (trans. Thomas M. Horner;
Philadelphia: Fortress, 1967) 17-19. This is a translation of
Gunkel's article on Psalms in the second edition of *Die Reli-
gion in Geschichte und Gegenwart*.

[5]Ibid., 36-37.

[6]Günter Morawe, *Aufbau und Abgrenzung der Loblieder von
Qumrân* (Berlin: Evangelische Verlagsanstalt, 1960); Svend Holm-
Nielsen, *Hodayot: Psalms from Qumran* (Aarhus: Universitetsforlaget, 1960). Morawe actually terms his second category "hym-
nische Bekenntnislieder"; I have chosen "hymn" as the name for
this category because both men consider hymnic qualities to be
the principal characteristic of these passages.

[7]Those passages assigned to the hymn category by both
Morawe and Holm-Nielsen are: 1:3-39, 7:26-33, 9:37-10:13, 10:14-
11:2, 11:3-14, 11:15-28, and 11:29-12:36 (Holm-Nielsen; Morawe
includes the latter two passages, but divides them at 12:1),
14:8-22, 15:1-26, 16:8-20, 17:17-26, and 18:1-33. Morawe also
includes 7:34-8:3, 14:23-28 and 17:26-28, sections which Holm-
Nielsen considers too short to determine their type. Holm-
Nielsen includes in the hymn list 13:1-21, a poorly preserved
column which Morawe does not discuss.

[8]This occurs in the discussion of 11:3-14 and 11:15-28 in
Holm-Nielsen (*Hodayot*, 188-89 and 195-96).

[9]Ibid., 343-44.

[10]Morawe, *Aufbau und Abgrenzung*, 162. Compare also the
tables on the thankoffering type and the hymn type (pp. 133 and
159). Morawe has carefully analyzed each element belonging to
these two types, and has admirably summed them up in these
tables. Unfortunately his final conclusions, toward which he
has obviously worked in his book, are marred by a basic

misunderstanding of the ordering of the columns of the scroll.
He accepts the current column numbering, known to be imposed
by Sukenik and not original, as somehow important to understanding the arrangement of the psalms. Accordingly, he finds
a neat arrangement with all the thankoffering songs in columns
2-7 and the hymns in columns 7-18, with a hymn in column 1
introducing the collection. Since this arrangement simply
never existed when the scroll was in use (see Chapter II),
Morawe's analyses of individual psalms must be treated with
some attention to his bias.

[11]Menahem Mansoor, *The Thanksgiving Hymns* (Grand Rapids:
Eerdmans, 1961). This book contains material published earlier
in the following articles: J. Baumgarten and M. Mansoor,
"Studies in the New *Hodayot* (Thanksgiving Hymns) I, II, and
III," *JBL* 74 (1955), 115-24, 188-95, and *JBL* 75 (1956) 107-13;
M. Mansoor, "Two More New Psalms as Translated from the Dead
Sea Scrolls," *Commentary* (1955) 368-69.

[12]The three passages are 7:26-33 and 11:3-14, discussed
in Chapter IV, and 9:37-10:12, discussed in Chapter V.

[13]Holm-Nielsen, *Hodayot*, 316.

[14]Ibid., 316-20, 330-48.

[15]Both Hans Bardtke ("Considérations sur les cantiques de
Qumrân," *RB* 63 [1956] 220-33) and Georg Molin (*Die Söhne des
Lichtes* [Munich: Verlag Herold, 1952] 103) are strong adherents
of this view. It is not surprising, I believe, that they also
have a low opinion of the poetic ability of the author. The
two views are used in their discussions to reinforce each
other. Jacob Licht ("The Doctrine of the Thanksgiving Scroll,"
IEJ 6 [1956] 1-13, 89-101) might also be included in this group
since he holds similar views, although he does not deal directly with either form criticism or Sitz im Leben.
    Tomas Arvedson in "De s.k. Tacksagelsepsalmerna från Qum-
ran" (*Svensk Exegetisk Årsbok* 22-23 [1957-1958] 208-18) represents a view which is radically different from both Holm-Nielsen
and Bardtke. He attempts to demonstrate that the Hodayot are
actually an adaptation of the Israelite royal psalms, written
to instruct the Qumran community in a salvation achieved by a
"mystagogue" who is the subject of the psalms (the Teacher of
Righteousness). In view of the extraneous material he cites as
evidence, and the way in which the Hodayot are forced to fit
the royal ideological pattern, his theory can be dismissed with
Holm-Nielsen's comment (*Hodayot*, 342), that "it touches on the
fantastic."

[16]Cross, *Ancient Library*, 122.

[17]Licht, "Doctrine," 1.

[18]Holm-Nielsen, *Hodayot*, 45.

[19]Charles F. Kraft, "Poetic Structure in the Qumran Thanksgiving Psalms," *Biblical Research* 2 (1957) 1-18.

[20]E. L. Sukenik (ed.), *'wsr hmgylwt hgnwzwt* (Jerusalem: Magnes, 1954). In this study, the English edition (*The Dead Sea Scrolls of the Hebrew University* [Jerusalem: Magnes, 1955]) has been used. The plates and transcriptions in both editions are the same (including the numbering).

[21]Jacob Licht (ed.), *mgylt hhwdywt* (Jerusalem: Bialik Institute, 1957); A. M. Habermann (ed.), *mgylwt mdbr yhwdh* (Jerusalem: Machbaroth Lesifruth, 1959); M. Delcor, *Les Hymnes de Qumran* (Paris: Letouzey et Ané, 1962). Delcor's text is a photographic reproduction of Sukenik's transcription.

[22]Eduard Lohse, *Die Texte aus Qumran* (Munich: Kösel, 1964).

[23]Geza Vermes, *The Dead Sea Scrolls in English* (Harmondsworth: Penguin, 1968); André Dupont-Sommer, *Les Ecrits esséniens découverts près de la mer Morte* (Paris: Payot, 1959); this has been translated by Geza Vermes into English, *The Essene Writings from Qumran* (New York: World, 1962). The translation of the Hodayot in this collection is taken from earlier work done by Dupont-Sommer in *Le Livre des Hymnes découvert près de la mer Morte (I QH)* (*Semitica* VII; Paris, 1957), and this earlier work, with its fuller footnotes is the one usually cited in this work. Theodor Gaster, *The Dead Sea Scriptures in English Translation* (New York: Doubleday, 1956); Millar Burrows, *The Dead Sea Scrolls*.

[24]A more complete listing of those who have translated all or part of the Hodayot is given in the Bibliography.

[25]Already cited in these notes are the works by Holm-Nielsen (*Hodayot*), Mansoor (*Thanksgiving Hymns*, "Two More New Psalms," and with Baumgarten, "Studies in the New *Hodayot*"), Delcor (*Les Hymnes de Qumran*), and Molin (*Die Söhne des Lichtes*). A. van Selms, *De Rol der Lofprijzingen* (Baarn, Netherlands: Bosch & Kenning, 1957); Meir Wallenstein, *Hymns from the Judean Scrolls* (Manchester: University Press, 1950); idem, "A Striking Hymn from the Dead Sea Scrolls," *BJRL* 38 (1955-1956) 241-65; idem, "A Hymn from the Scrolls," *VT* 5 (1955) 277-83; A. S. van der Woude, *De Dankpsalmen* (Amsterdam: Proost en Brandt, 1957); J. Carmignac, in *Les Textes de Qumran* (trans. J. Carmignac and P. Guilbert; Paris: Letouzey et Ané, 1961); and Hans Bardtke, "Die Loblieder von Qumran," *TLZ* 81 (1956) cols. 149-54, 589-604, 715-24, and *TLZ* 82 (1957) cols. 339-48.

[26]The chief proponent of the Messianic view of this passage is Dupont-Sommer. His interpretation first appeared in *Le Livre des Hymnes* (p. 35) and has been carried forward in his translation of the collected Qumran writings, *Les Ecrits esséniens*, and in his article "La Mère du Messie et la Mère de l'Aspic dans un hymne de Qoumran" (*RHR* 147 [1955] 174-88). The most decisive evidence against this view is presented by J. V. Chamberlain,

"Another Qumran Thanksgiving Psalm," *JNES* 14 (1955) 32-41,
181-82; and Lou H. Silberman, "Language and Structure in the
Hodayot," *JBL* 75 (1956) 96-106.

[27]Bardtke, "Considérations sur les cantiques," 232; J. P.
Hyatt, "The View of Man in the Qumran 'Hodayot,'" *NTS* 2 (1955-
1956) 276; G. S. Glanzmann, "The Sectarian Psalms from the
Dead Sea," *TS* 13 (1952) 490; Molin, *Die Söhne des Lichtes*, 103;
Jean Carmignac, "Les Eléments historiques des Hymnes de Qumrân,"
RQ 2 (1959-60) 205-22.

[28]Cross, *Ancient Library*, 86-87.

[29]Holm-Nielsen, *Hodayot*, 327-28.

[30]Licht, "Doctrine," 2.

[31]Ibid., 3.

[32]Friedrich Nötscher, *Zur Theologischen Terminologie der
Qumran-Texte* (Bonn: P. Hanstein, 1956); Helmer Ringgren, *The
Faith of Qumran* (trans. Emilie T. Sander; Philadelphia: For-
tress, 1963).

[33]Licht, "Doctrine," 7, 89-90.

[34]There is still some debate as to whether the Qumran
community was actually Essene or not. Those who still disagree
(a minority now) base their case largely on the differences
between Josephus' account of the Essenes in his autobiography
and *Wars of the Jews*, and the type of community revealed by the
scrolls and the archaeological finds. Most scholars believe
the community is either the Essene group described by Josephus
or a closely related group.

[35]This work is *Hodayot: Psalms from Qumran*, already cited
in connection with other topics.

[36]Holm-Nielsen, *Hodayot*, 74.

[37]Kraft, "Poetic Structure."

[38]Kraft's list of complete poems (p. 3): 2:20-30, 3:19-36,
4:5-38, 5:5-19, 7:26-32 and 11:3-14.

[39]Kraft, "Poetic Structure," 17.

[40]Ibid., 16-17.

[41]This analysis of strophe is summarized on p. 2 of this
article, and is based on work done by Kraft in two earlier
books: *The Strophic Structure of Hebrew Poetry as Illustrated
in the First Book of the Psalter* (Chicago: University of Chicago, 1938); and "Some Further Observations Concerning the
Strophic Structure of Hebrew Poetry," pp. 62-89 in *A Stubborn
Faith: Papers on Old Testament and Related Subjects Presented*

to Honor William Andrew Irwin (ed. Edward C. Hobbs; Dallas: Southern Methodist University, 1956) 62-89.

[42]Kraft, "Poetic Structure," 11, 17.

[43]Ibid., 6.

[44]There is a slight problem with Kraft's translation of חצים ויפרו. Most scholars take חצים as the subject of the verb and translate with the meaning "And arrows rend (shatter)...." Kraft has taken חצים as the object, and understood the pronoun of the verb as a reference to the warriors in the previous lines. In this case he must change the meaning of the verb, and he does not note his evidence for this; apparently he either extended the meaning of פרר to include the definition "loose" or he emended the text to ויגרו, root נגר ("to hurl down"), as Wallenstein does (*Hymns*, 12).

[45]Jean Carmignac, "Etude sur les Procédés Poétiques des Hymnes," *RQ* 2 (1959-1960) 515-32.

[46]Ibid., 517, 522-23.

[47]Ibid., 522.

[48]Ibid., 523-25.

[49]Malachi Martin lists fourteen places where large spaces (not marginal fitting) have been left in the text which do not coincide with the end of a thought. Thirteen of these spaces (in cols. 1, 2, 11 and 13) he believes were due to flaws in the surface of the leather. The other space, col. 12:20-21, he believes is due to the irregularity of ruling the column. Martin also has found evidence of marginal fitting in fifty-one lines in the scroll; Malachi Martin, *The Scribal Character of the Dead Sea Scrolls* (Louvain: Publications Universitaires, 1958) 1.110-11, 118.

[50]Barbara Thiering, "The Poetic Forms of the Hodayot," *JSS* 8 (1963) 189-209.

[51]Ibid., 189.

[52]Ibid.

[53]Nils W. Lund, "The Presence of Chiasmus in the Old Testament," *AJSL* 46 (1929) 104-26; and "Chiasmus in the Psalms," *AJSL* 49 (1932) 281-312.

[54]Thiering, "Poetic Forms," 190.

[55]Ibid., 195.

[56]Ibid., 194.

[57]As in 2:20-30, 10:1-12, 11:3-14--all analyzed by Thiering.

[58]For example, Thiering's analysis of 1:21-27 (pp. 192-93) outlines a poem whose "*chiasmus*" is based on single-word repetitions.

[59]Thiering, "Poetic Forms," 202; 10:1-12 is the section in question.

NOTES

CHAPTER II

[1]Sukenik, *The Dead Sea Scrolls*, 37-38, figs. 14-17, 22-25.

[2]Ibid., 37.

[3]Left-hand margin missing: cols. 6, 16; right-hand margin missing: cols. 13, 14, 17.

[4]Descriptions of the archaeological work at Khirbet Qumran and Cave 1 can be found in Cross (*Ancient Library*, 38-52), Roland de Vaux ("Exploration de la Region de Qumran," *RB* 60 [1953] 540-61); James L. Kelso ("The Archaeology of Qumran," *JBL* 74 [1955] 141-46); D. Barthélemy and J. T. Milik (eds.), (*Discoveries in the Judean Desert*, Vol. 1: *Qumran Cave I* [Oxford: Clarendon, 1955] 3-41).

[5]Between 167 B.C. and 237 A.D., according to Barthélemy and Milik (*Qumran Cave I*, 27).

[6]A. A. Birnbaum, "How Old Are the Cave Manuscripts? A Paleographical Discussion," *VT* 1 (1951) 91-109.

[7]Burrows, *More Light*, 409.

[8]Sukenik, *The Dead Sea Scrolls*, 37-38.

[9]I have given here an extremely short summary of Martin's argument, which is found piecemeal throughout his two-volume work, *The Scribal Character of the Dead Sea Scrolls*. Of particular interest to this point are 1.59-64, 84, 98-99, 101-102, 105, 110-11, 117, 387-88. Some of his more specific observations are noted in the description of the texts of the various hymns.

[10]Holm-Nielsen, *Hodayot*, 10-12.

[11]Martin, *Scribal Character*, 309.

[12]Carmignac's argument is developed in a series of articles: "Remarques sur le texte des Hymnes de Qumran," *Biblica* 39 (1958) 138-55; "Localisation des fragments 15, 18 et 22 des Hymnes," *RQ* 1 (1958-1959) 425-430; "Les Eléments historiques," 205-22.

[13]Barthélemy and Milik, *Qumran Cave I*.

[14]Carmignac, "Les Eléments historiques."

[15]2:30-31, 5:4-5, 5:19-20, 7:33-34, 8:3-4, 11:2-3, 11:14-15, 14:22-23.

[16]2:19-20, 3:18-19, 3:36-37, 7:5-6, 7:25-26, 14:7-8.
Martin (*Scribal Character*, 1.119), believes these differences
within Copyist A's work are part of the evidence for a compiled document.

[17]Mansoor, *The Thanksgiving Hymns*, 33-34.

[18]Holm-Nielsen does not number these units as he does the
earlier hymns because of the difficulties in the order of the
columns as now numbered, but he does call his units "individual
psalms" (*Hodayot*, 212). He delineates twelve units in cols.
13-18, six of which begin with line 1 of a column (one hymn
beginning each column).

[19]Kraft also believed that poetic exploration must begin
with complete hymns, and he used roughly the same criteria for
determining completeness ("Poetic Structure," 3). He excluded
the hymns from cols. 14-17 apparently because of the number of
lacunae. He also excluded the hymn in 7:6-25 for undiscernible
reasons. He included one hymn in the complete category which I
have placed in the incomplete category: 4:5-? This has the
standard opening but, due to the missing lines at the bottom of
col. 4 and the top of col. 5, its end is not certain. It is an
example of a longer hymn, however, and therefore worthy of the
attention he gives it.

[20]Robert Lowth, *Isaiah* (1st ed.; Boston: T. Buckingham,
1815) x.

[21]George Buchanan Gray, *The Forms of Hebrew Poetry*, with a
prolegomenon by David Noel Freedman (The Library of Biblical
Studies; n.p.: KTAV, 1972) 49, 59-83.

[22]David Noel Freedman, in the Prolegomenon to Gray, *The
Forms of Hebrew Poetry*, xxv-xxvi.

[23]Carmignac, "Procédés Poétiques," 523-25.

[24]James Muilenburg gives a list of strategically used
words in biblical poetry in "The Linguistic and Rhetorical
Usages of the Particle כי in the Old Testament" (*HUCA* 32 [1961]
135).

[25]Habermann, *mgylwt*; Lohse, *Die Texte aus Qumran*.
Syllable counts in this study are made from Lohse's text,
except where he differs in the consonantal text from transcriptions shown here.
     A comparison of sample texts of Habermann and Lohse reveal
the following differences: in 2:20-30 (eleven lines), there are
eight differences in the two texts. In four instances, Habermann vocalizes with a *dagesh forte* in the first letter of a
word following a word ending in a long open syllable. In two
places, Habermann has copied the text incorrectly, and in two
cases the two scholars disagree on the interpretation of a word,
marking vowels for different roots or different forms. In only
one of these cases is there a difference in syllable count as a

result. In 3:19-36 (eighteen lines) there are fourteen differences between the two texts.   Three differences are due to
Habermann's use of the *dagesh* noted above; three are copying
errors on the part of Habermann, two are due to interpretation
from different roots, three are due to interpretation of different forms of the same root, and three simply involve the use
of long vowels by Habermann where Lohse uses short vowels.
Discounting the copying errors, there would be a difference of
three syllables in the total syllable count of the poem between
Habermann and Lohse.

NOTES

CHAPTER III

[1]Both Carmignac and Kraft recognized the strategic use of
the independent pronouns in this poem. Kraft's division of the
psalm's "strophes" corresponds exactly to the stanzas outlined
here, although his analysis of the inner arrangement of each of
these strophes is quite different (Kraft, "Poetic Structure,"
5-9). Carmignac commented generally on the importance of pronouns as strophe indicators in "Procédés Poétiques" (524-25).
In his translation of this psalm, however, he is content to
recognize only a single division within the poem, dividing it
into two equal halves at ואני אמרתי (Les Textes, 188).

[2]Among those who restore כי in the text are Mansoor (The
Thanksgiving Hymns, 107), Bardtke ("Die Loblieder," 591), Lohse
(Die Texte aus Qumran, 116), Carmignac (Les Textes, 188), Delcor (Les Hymnes de Qumran, 102), and van der Woude (De Dankpsalmen, 22). Holm-Nielsen (Hodayot, 41) believes that possibly a space was left in the text before עריצם indicating a
pause, and Dupont-Sommer (Le Livre des Hymnes, 33) and Vermes
(Dead Sea Scrolls, 155) apparently based their translations on
similar analysis, since they make the first major division
within the poem at this point. This second clause, on other
poetic evidence (e.g., the independent pronoun beginning the
next clause), more likely belongs with the opening statement,
whatever the missing text.

[3]Wallenstein, Hymns, 10.

[4]Thiering, "Poetic Forms," 193-94.

[5]Kraft, "Poetic Structure," 5.

[6]Carmignac is doubtful of this text (Les Textes, 189).
Bardtke is unhappy with the expression, but ultimately accepts
it, despite its awkwardness ("Die Loblieder," 591).

[7]Bardtke, "Die Loblieder," 591; Licht, mgylt, 71; Dupont-
Sommer, Le Livre des Hymnes, 34; Delcor, Les Hymnes de Qumran,
105. Holm-Nielsen believes "that a careless writing of כי
might become ם," but careful study of the copyist's hand does
not bear this out (Hodayot, 42). However, it is possible that
כי in the autograph of the Hodayot was mistaken by the later
copyist, but this is only a speculative explanation.

[8]Mansoor, The Thanksgiving Hymns, 19-20, 108-109.

[9]Carmignac, Les Textes, 189.

[10]David Noel Freedman suggested such a reading to Silberman, who dealt briefly with this passage in his article "Language and Structure in the Hodayot" (JBL 75 [1956] p. 98 n. 15).

[11]Wallenstein, *Hymns*, 12.

[12]See p. 185 n. 44. Kraft, "Poetic Structure," 6.

[13]Bardtke, "Die Loblieder," 591.

[14]For further comments on this "double line," see the discussions of 3:19-36, 5:5-19 and 14:8-22.

[15]See, for example, Vermes, *Dead Sea Scrolls*, 154; Mansoor, *The Thanksgiving Hymns*, 109; Burrows, *The Dead Sea Scrolls*, 402; Bardtke, "Die Loblieder," 591.

[16]Silberman, "Language and Structure," 104.

[17]Burrows, *The Dead Sea Scrolls*, 402.

[18]This is the solution adopted by Holm-Nielsen (*Hodayot*, 40, 42-44) and Gaster (*Dead Sea Scriptures*, 132, 209).

[19]See, for example, Holm-Nielsen, *Hodayot*, 44.

[20]Ibid., 45.

[21]Standard 3 + 3 or 3 + 2 meter can be detected in the opening and closing stanzas (see Kraft, "Poetic Structure," 10, and Holm-Nielsen, *Hodayot*, 46), but these calculations break down in the body of the poem.

[22]Delcor, *Les Hymnes de Qumran*, 103.

[23]Carmignac, *Les Textes*, 189-90.

[24]Delcor, *Les Hymnes de Qumran*, 106.

[25]Holm-Nielsen, *Hodayot*, 45.

[26]This does not mean that the author did not "deliberately" choose to use these words, too; the matter of conscious and purposive choice of words is not the question here. "Deliberate" here means that a specific type of literary form or imagery (e.g., eschatological imagery) can be discerned in the poem and presumably reflects the interest of the poet, while "free use" indicates that the biblical language is not so specific in recalling either a particular passage or a special literary form.

[27]Almost everyone follows the restorations suggested by Sukenik in *The Dead Sea Scrolls*, in the transcription of Plate 37. These are noted in the transcription on p. 57.

[28]Martin (*Scribal Character*, 1.118) says that the usual space left to indicate paragraphs is three to four letter spaces, a slightly larger space than is left in these two places.

[29]Vermes, *Dead Sea Scrolls*, 159; Dupont-Sommer, *Le Livre des Hymnes*, 39; Holm-Nielsen, *Hodayot*, 65; Licht, *mgylt*, 85. Carmignac (*Les Textes*, 200) has a more awkward arrangement of these lines:

ואני יצר החומר מח
אני מגבל במים למי נחשבתי

In all these arrangements the final question is shown as an extra half line. Holm-Nielsen explains all usages of this expression except this one as a noun in construct with מים (*Hodayot*, 25). This one is identified by most scholars as a pual participle rather than a noun, due to the prepositional phrase which follows. While the sense is almost the same as the construct chain used elsewhere, and there is no translation problem, it may be that in 3:24 there is an interrupted construct chain, a phenomenon known in canonical poetry.

[30]J. C. Greenfield, "The Root 'GBL' in Mishnaic Hebrew and in the Hymnic Literature from Qumran," *RQ* 2 (1959-1960) 155-62. Greenfield notes the complementary parallelism of this phrase in passing (p. 160).

The breakup of stereotyped expressions in canonical poetry is discussed by David Noel Freedman in his Prolegomenon in Gray's *The Forms of Hebrew Poetry* (p. xxx).

[31]Compare the following: Vermes, *Dead Sea Scrolls*, 158; Mansoor, *The Thanksgiving Hymns*, 116-17; Delcor, *Les Hymnes de Qumran*, 125-26; Dupont-Sommer, *Le Livre des Hymnes*, 39; Carmignac, *Les Textes*, 199; Holm-Nielsen, *Hodayot*, 64; Bardtke, "Die Loblieder," 593; Wallenstein, *Hymns*, 15. All are agreed on the *translation* of the first term as "eternal height"; on the second term, Dupont-Sommer believes the reference is to the eternal assembly, while the others take this as a standard term for the Qumran community. Although the third term מישור לאין חקר is translated by a variety of phrases, all keep to the idea first delineated by F. M. Cross in "The Newly Discovered Scrolls in the Hebrew University Museum in Jerusalem" (*BA* [1949] 36-46): a plain without limits or obstructions where one is free to roam.

[32]Robert B. Laurin, "The Question of Immortality in the Qumran 'Hodayot,'" *JSS* 3 (1958) 344-55. Holm-Nielsen is inclined toward this view (*Hodayot*, 66-69).

[33]Mansoor, *The Thanksgiving Hymns*, 84-87; Matthew Black, "Theological Conceptions in the Dead Sea Scrolls," *Svensk Exegetisk Årsbok* 18-19 (1953-1954) 82; J. van der Ploeg, "L'immortalité de l'homme d'après les textes de la mer Morte," *VT* 2 (1952) 171-75; and idem, "rum ᶜolam," *VT* 3 (1953) 191-92.

[34]Such an arrangement is shown by Holm-Nielsen (*Hodayot*, 66), Carmignac (*Les Textes*, 199-200), and Licht (*mgylt*, 84-85). Dupont-Sommer (*Le Livre des Hymnes*, 39) and Vermes (*Dead Sea Scrolls*, 158-59) show a different arrangement, dividing the poem at לאין חקר and again at ואני.

[35]See Kittel's note in *Biblia Hebraica* on Isa 14:4; the RSV follows this emendation.

[36]1QIsa^a 14:4.

[37]Wallenstein, *Hymns*, 15 ("wrath"); Vermes, *Dead Sea Scrolls*, 159 ("torment"); Bardtke, "Die Loblieder," 593 ("oppression"); Mansoor, *The Thanksgiving Hymns*, 118 ("calamity"); Holm-Nielsen, *Hodayot*, 65, 70 ("tribulation").

[38]Vermes, *Dead Sea Scrolls*, 159; Holm-Nielsen, *Hodayot*, 65; Wallenstein, *Hymns*, 15; Delcor, *Les Hymnes de Qumran*, 129. Dupont-Sommer (*Le Livre des Hymnes*, 40) says the first, רבה, is an adverb and the second, מדהבה, an adjective; but his translation makes sense only if the adverb is attached to the verb. Bardtke ("Die Loblieder," 593) also identifies the first as an adverb, but translates it as an adjective, modifying the noun. He also treats the second as an adjective. Carmignac (*Les Textes*, 200) and Mansoor (*The Thanksgiving Hymns*, 118) translate both words as adjectives.

[39]Licht, *mgylt*, 85; Mansoor, *The Thanksgiving Hymns*, 118; Gesenius 124e.

[40]Holm-Nielsen (*Hodayot*, 65), Vermes (*Dead Sea Scrolls*, 159), and Mansoor (*The Thanksgiving Hymns*, 118) attach this unit to the preceding material. Bardtke ("Die Loblieder," 593) and Wallenstein (*Hymns*, 15) attach it to the following material. Dupont-Sommer (*Le Livre des Hymnes*, 40) divides the section at וחבלי and Carmignac (*Les Textes*, 200) at רקץ.

[41]Although the destruction of the abyss and the underworld themselves by the fiery river of Belial may seem somewhat peculiar, there are parallels. In the Nag Hammadi text "On the Origin of the World" (Codex 2, Tractate 5, as translated by Graduate Theological Union student David Johnson) appear the following lines:
"the gods of chaos will be thrown into the abyss. They will be wiped out through their own wickedness. For they will become like fire-vomiting mountains and devour one another until they are destroyed by their own archigenitor. When he has destroyed them, he will turn against himself and destroy himself....His world will fall down to earth so that it cannot bear them and they will fall into the abyss and the abyss will be destroyed."

In Revelation, the destruction comes from God, but it is interesting to note that the final act before the new creation is the casting of Death and Hades into the lake of fire (Rev 20:14).

[42]Holm-Nielsen, *Hodayot*, 75.

[43]Ibid., 73-75.

[44]van der Ploeg, "L'immortalité," 171-75; also idem, "rum
^{c}olam," 191-92; Delcor, *Les Hymnes de Qumran*, 125-29.

[45]Laurin, "The Question of Immortality," 344-55.

[46]Roland Murphy, "Ṣaḥat in the Qumran Literature," *Biblica*
39 (1958) 61-66.

[47]Cf. Ringgren's comments in *The Faith of Qumran* (pp. 84-
85).

[48]Licht, *mgylt*, 99-100.

[49]Sukenik, *The Dead Sea Scrolls*, transcription of Plate 39.

[50]See, for example, the hymn in 9:37-10:12, which uses the
construction several times (see Chapter V). Kuhn also reads
בלוא in 5:15 (*Konkordanz zu Qumrantexten* [Göttingen: Vanden-
hoeck und Ruprecht, 1960] 33 n. 1).

[51]Sigmund Mowinckel, "Some Remarks on Hodayot 39:5-20
IQH5," *JBL* 75 (1956) 266.

[52]ותוסף in line 14 is usually understood as a second person imperfect hiphil of אסף, with the א omitted. However, the
poetic analysis of the surrounding lines suggests that it is
the third feminine singular pual instead. See p. 93.

[53]Gaster, *Dead Sea Scriptures*, 148; Dupont-Sommer, *Le Livre
des Hymnes*, 46; Carmignac, *Les Textes*, 213; Mowinckel, "Some
Remarks," 270; Meir Wallenstein, "A Hymn from the Scrolls,"
VT 5 (1955) 278.

[54]Licht, *mgylt*, 99-100. His restoration:
כי לא עזבתני בגורי בעם [כבד עון רחטא]
[ולא כפשעי] וכאשמתי שפטתני

[55]Licht's restoration can be further criticized stylistically. A three-word description of עם, employing a construct
chain extended by an adjective is not in keeping with the author's style in the opening stanzas. Such a lengthy description is found only in lists or in the apocalyptic sections of
the poems.

[56]Dupont-Sommer, *Le Livre des Hymnes*, 46.

[57]Gaster, *Dead Sea Scriptures*, 148; Carmignac, *Les Textes*,
213; Delcor, *Les Hymnes de Qumran*, 155.

[58]1QH 2:20-21.

[59]Holm-Nielsen believes that שחת as a reference to the
nether world is impossible here because עזר is never used in
the OT with the meaning "to help up from" (*Hodayot*, 92). However, elsewhere he always translates שחת by the traditional
"Pit," and even notes the contrast effected with "life" (p. 41).

Roland Murphy ("Šahat," 61-66) has also objected in general to
the rendering of שׁוחה as "Pit" in the Hodayot and other Qumran
literature. He attempts to show that at Qumran the term referred less to the grave and the nether world than to moral
corruption (the noun can be derived from either שׁוח or שׁחח).
He maintains that although the word is still used in biblical-
sounding phrases recalling the nether world, the term actually
is connected to the evil-doers, those belonging to Belial and
therefore primarily with corruption/destruction. Murphy's evidence, however, testifies to the fact that the mythology of the
nether world is still very much alive at Qumran, and that it
has been woven into the cosmological and eschatological schemes
of the Qumran writers. Although "Pit" may be somewhat ana-
chronistic (and perhaps linguistically incorrect), its traditional connotation of the underworld is that invoked throughout
the Hodayot.

[60]Gaster restores נפשׁי (*Dead Sea Scriptures*, 148); Wallenstein restores את נפשׁ עבדכה, but את is used very rarely in the
Hodayot ("A Hymn from the Scrolls," 278).

[61]Dupont-Sommer restores נפשׁי למשׁפט (*Le Livre des Hymnes*,
46); Licht: את עבדכה לפליט (*mgylt*, 100).

[62]Bardtke, "Die Loblieder," 597; Mansoor, *The Thanksgiving
Hymns*, 133.

[63]Wallenstein, "A Hymn from the Scrolls," 278; he further
emends the expression to ומיה ברוח which he believes is equivalent to מי בארות. The orthographic changes are due to Aramaic
influence and syncopation of gutturals at Qumran (p. 280).

[64]Dupont-Sommer, *Le Livre des Hymnes*, 47; Holm-Nielsen,
Hodayot, 94.

[65]Wallenstein, "A Hymn from the Scrolls," 278.

[66]Holm-Nielsen, *Hodayot*, 94-95.

[67]Bardtke, "Die Loblieder," 597; Wallenstein, "A Hymn from
the Scrolls," 281.

[68]Holm-Nielsen, *Hodayot*, 94; Vermes, *Dead Sea Scrolls*,
165; Dupont-Sommer, *Le Livre des Hymnes*, 47; Mansoor, *The
Thanksgiving Hymns*, 133; Carmignac, *Les Textes*, 214.

[69]Wallenstein, "A Hymn from the Scrolls," 281.

[70]Holm-Nielsen, *Hodayot*, 95; Dupont-Sommer, *Le Livre des
Hymnes*, 47.

[71]I am indebted to David Noel Freedman for this suggestion.

[72]So reads Dupont-Sommer (*Le Livre des Hymnes*, 47) and
Bardtke ("Die Loblieder," 597); Licht (*mgylt*, 102) believes the
verb is כרת.

[73]Licht (*mgylt*, 102) restores כצ]דקחכה וחצל נ[טרף; Bardtke
("Die Loblieder," 597) suggests כ]הציל רועה[טרף.

[74]Holm-Nielsen, *Hodayot*, 95; Dupont-Sommer, *Le Livre des Hymnes*, 47.

[75]Jer 16:16, Hab 1:14-17, Mal 3:3.

[76]Compare this statement with 1QS 2:25-3:12.

[1]Sukenik, *The Dead Sea Scrolls*, Plate 41 and transcription.

[2]The transcription here reflects the scroll reading, where the copyist used final ך in a medial position.

[3]The missing word in this second bicolon modified איש and there is no doubt that the meaning must have been close to "sinful." Licht suggests הוה (*mgylt*, 128); Mansoor suggests רשע (*The Thanksgiving Hymns*, 151). Although either of these would fit in terms of size and general meaning, Licht's suggestion introduces the "punch line" of the final stanza into the opening, which is unlikely, and Mansoor's term is usually applied to the community's enemies rather than to men in general. Possibly the missing word was אשמה or פשע.

[4]Burrows, *The Dead Sea Scrolls*, 410; E. Parish Sanders, "Chiasmus and the Translation of I Q Hodayot VII 26-27," *RQ* 6 (1968) 427-32.

[5]Sanders, "Chiasmus," 428-29.

[6]Sanders is concerned with ב only in the opening quatrain of the psalm, but ב attached to divine attributes reappears in Stanza C and also Stanza A'. Whatever the decision in regard to its syntactical use, there is little doubt that its repetition drew the poem together artistically, whether or not all of the prepositional phrases shared the same syntactical function.

[7]Thiering, "Poetic Forms," 201-202. The terms she finds significant in her analysis are the divine attribute phrases discussed here.

[8]Holm-Nielsen, *Hodayot*, 140. He says that several places in Isaiah 40-55 come to mind as a possible locus, but it is difficult to determine what he had in mind beyond the rhetorical question style which is prominent there.

[9]Translated thus by Holm-Nielsen, *Hodayot*, 138; Dupont-Sommer, *Le Livre des Hymnes*, 61; Carmignac, *Les Textes*, 233; Bardtke, "Die Loblieder," 602.

[10]Martin, *Scribal Character*, 2.481.

[11]כול צבי רוח is taken as an aside by Holm-Nielsen (*Hodayot*, 138), Bardtke ("Die Loblieder," 602), Carmignac (*Les Textes*, 233), and Dupont-Sommer (*Le Livre des Hymnes*, 61). Another group has rejected צבי without comment: Burrows (*The Dead Sea Scrolls*, 410), Gaster (*Dead Sea Scriptures*, 162), and Mansoor (*The Thanksgiving Hymns*, 152). Thiering wishes to excise the whole phrase ("Poetic Forms," 201). Martin's solution

is to transfer צבי to the second כול in the bicolon, but he offers no suggestions on how to obtain sense from the resulting stanza (*Scribal Character*, 2.481).

[12]Licht, *mgylt*, 129.

[13]Kuhn, *Konkordanz zu den Qumrantexten*, 184.

[14]See Mowinckel's comments on this in "Some Remarks on Hodayot 39:5-20 (pp. 265-66) where he criticizes Wallenstein's arrangement of lines in 5:5-19.

[15]Burrows, *The Dead Sea Scrolls*, 413; Licht, *mgylt*, 161; Bardtke, "Die Loblieder," 722; Mansoor, *The Thanksgiving Hymns*, 167; Holm-Nielsen, *Hodayot*, 186; Carmignac, *Les Textes*, 254.

[16]Dupont-Sommer (*Le Livre des Hymnes*, 78), Licht (*mgylt*, 161), Holm-Nielsen (*Hodayot*, 167) all read תהלה here; Burrows (*The Dead Sea Scrolls*, 413) and Bardtke ("Die Loblieder," 722) suggest שמחה.

[17]Carmignac shows this same three-unit structure in *Les Textes* (pp. 255-56) but does not note the presence of a refrain.

[18]Those who derive this word from ידה include: Burrows (*Dead Sea Scrolls*, 413) and Bardtke ("Die Loblieder," 722) who both attach the phrase to ואני מה; and Vermes (*The Dead Sea Scrolls*, 185) who attaches it to the opening bicolon.

[19]Carmignac,(*Les Textes*, 255) and Dupont-Sommer (*Le Livre des Hymnes*, 78) both so interpret מודה. מאד is doubled in Gen 17:2,6,20, Ezek 9:9 and 16:13.

[20]1QS 10:16; also, the variant spelling מואדה appears in 1QM 19:5.

[21]Thiering has also noted these lists in her analysis ("Poetic Forms," 202-203). Although she comments that the main interest in this psalm is in the lists, she nevertheless attempts to impose a chiastic pattern on the poem as well. As a result, she once again is left with two lines extraneous to her organization of the poem, which actually present the final attributes in the second list of seven. Her units are completely out of balance: she matches all of Stanza C against the introductory bicolon in her chiastic pattern, solely on the basis of the repetition of עפר in column line 12.

[22]These lines are shorter than the "standard line" in the Hodayot, but the three parallel elements suggest an understanding as a tricolon rather than as a line with internal parallelism or as a list.

[23]Holm-Nielsen, *Hodayot*, 188.

[24]Not all the matched attributes in this doulbe list have OT counterparts, but most do. פה and אמת (of Yahweh) are linked

in 1 Kgs 17:24, and אמח is frequently connected with the spoken
word. כוח and גבורה are linked in 1 Chr 29:12 and 2 Chr 20:6.
Judgment due to God's wrath is a common motif. טוב as an attribute of God is linked to forgiveness of sin in Psa 25:7
(although the word סליחות does not appear there). רוחמים, which
appears alone in this list, seems to be peripherally linked to
סליחות which just precedes it, and these terms are linked in
Dan 9:9. The statements of Psalm 145 also provide a number of
parallels to the thoughts expressed in this list.

NOTES

CHAPTER V

[1]Holm-Nielsen, *Hodayot*, 131. He translates, for example,
"Thou hast not made (me) dejected (that I wander) from Thy
covenant."

[2]The syllable count of this second refrain can be based
on either the text reconstructed by Licht (*mgylt*, 126) or upon
that of Dupont-Sommer (*Le Livre des Hymnes*, 60). The syllable
counts are the same. However, Licht restores:
..כירנ[קים/וישמחתר] כשעשע עולול, while Dupont-Sommer restores:
כירנ]ק לשדי אמר]. The latter type of reconstruction seems more
likely, since the final line beginning וכשעשע already is of
standard length.

[3]Dupont-Sommer, *Le Livre des Hymnes*, 58; Bardtke, "Die
Loblieder," 601; Holm-Nielsen, *Hodayot*, 129.

[4]See Licht, *mgylt*, 124; Vermes, *Dead Sea Scrolls*, 173.

[5]Vermes, *Dead Sea Scrolls*, 173; Bardtke, "Die Loblieder,"
601. Dupont-Sommer also believes the reference is to branches
or foliage, but interprets this to be the Teacher of Righteousness rather than the community (*Le Livre des Hymnes*, 68).

[6]Interpreting עפים this way are Carmignac (*Les Textes*,
229-30) and Holm-Nielsen (*Hodayot*, 131-32).

[7]Licht restores לבי (*mgylt*, 124); Bardtke, נ (("Die Loblieder," 601); Dupont-Sommer, ג (*Le Livre des Hymnes*, 58);
Holm-Nielsen, לבי (*Hodayot*, 129); Vermes, פי (*Dead Sea Scrolls*,
173).

[8]Dupont-Sommer, *Le Livre des Hymnes*, 58; Holm-Nielsen,
Hodayot, 130; Bardtke, "Die Loblieder," 601; Licht, *mgylt*, 124;
Carmignac, *Les Textes*, 230.

[9]Licht, *mgylt*, 125; Mansoor, *The Thanksgiving Hymns*, 150;
Vermes, *Dead Sea Scrolls*, 173. Others wish to read רשעה or
רשעים, but the size of the gap and the slice of the final let-
ter of the word which can be seen do not support this (see
Bardtke, "Die Loblieder," 601; Dupont-Sommer, *Le Livre des
Hymnes*, 59).

[10]Licht, *mgylt*, 125; Mansoor, *The Thanksgiving Hymns*, 150;
Dupont-Sommer, *Le Livre des Hymnes*, 59; Carmignac, *Les Textes*,
230.

[11]The following scholars suggest this restoration: Licht,
mgylt, 125; Dupont-Sommer, *Le Livre des Hymnes*, 59; Holm-
Nielsen, *Hodayot*, 130.

[12]This fact was not taken into consideration by Licht
(*mgylt*, 125), who restores a longer phrase (eleven spaces).

[13]Mansoor (*The Thanksgiving Hymns*, 150), Vermes (*Dead Sea Scrolls*, 174) and Dupont-Sommer (*Le Livre des Hymnes*, 59) all have phrases close to this employing פשע or equivalent, and בלוא.

[14]Licht, *mgylt*, 125-26.

[15]Licht, *mgylt*, 127; Dupont-Sommer, *Le Livre des Hymnes*, 60. The final word, after במישור, is disputed.

[16]Holm-Nielsen, *Hodayot*, 136-37.

[17]כרוה is almost universally restored here. Licht, *mgylt*, 153; Carmignac, *Les Textes*, 250; Mansoor, *The Thanksgiving Hymns*, 164; Bardtke, "Die Loblieder," 720.

[18]Sukenik, *The Dead Sea Scrolls*, transcription of Plate 44. Licht, *mgylt*, 151; Carmignac, *Les Textes*, 248; Bardtke, "Die Loblieder," 720; Holm-Nielsen, *Hodayot*, 173.

[19]Everyone is agreed on the restoration of אמתכה in the second bicolon. There are some vociferous dissenters on the two common restorations suggested in the first bicolon, however. Bardtke and Carmignac believe that the line was left blank after הוא. Carmignac (*Les Textes*, 249) then construes הוא with קרוץ; Bardtke ("Die Loblieder," 720) treats קרוץ as an independent phrase linked with the following words for sense. Since considerable space is left at the end of line 3 in the MSS, and since the identical expression employing מזמר at its beginning is found in 1QS 11:21, this is commonly restored here. See Holm-Nielsen, *Hodayot*, 171. Licht suggests the variant מעפר (*mgylt*, 151).

[20]Holm-Nielsen, *Hodayot*, 173-74.

[21]Ibid., 174.

[22]Both Dupont-Sommer (*Le Livre des Hymnes*, 88-89) and Carmignac (*Les Textes*, 154-55) follow these same stanza indicators in arranging the poem, although Carmignac separates the final line (col. line 21) as a coda.

[23]Carmignac, Licht, and Dupont-Sommer have all attempted to show the outline of these clauses. Licht restores infinitives in col. lines 9 and 10, but failed to perceive the continuation of the pattern (*mgylt*, 189). Carmignac (*Les Textes*, 154) shows eight infinitive clauses, arranged in eight lines, rather than the six shown here. Apparently he felt that the size of the gaps in line 9 and 11 (about thirty-two to thirty-four spaces) were too large for a single colon. However, they are rather short for *two* lines (one bicolon), since the clauses which do remain take up twenty-one to twenty-three spaces. Dupont-Sommer shows five infinitive clauses in his restoration, with a space left for one missing line before the summary lines at the end of the stanza (*Le Livre des Hymnes*, 88-89).

[24]The restorations of this summary bicolon are quite disparate, although the general idea is clear. Licht (*mgylt*, 189)
restores: פלגתם עבודתם וימלאו כאותותם...גורלם. Dupont-
Sommer (*Le Livre des Hymnes*, 89) restores: הפלתה...העולם רוחות
גורל לכול בני אדם ותחתו.

[25]Licht's restoration is probably best in the second
stanza line: באןיש תמהרנו בר[רוח] (*mgylt*, 189), but the line has
a slightly awkward feeling to it. In any case, Dupont-Sommer's
restoration, involving two finite verbs in different forms,
seems completely out of character for the Hodayot (*Le Livre des
Hymnes*, 89).

[26]Vermes, *Dead Sea Scrolls*, 193; Dupont-Sommer, *Le Livre
des Hymnes*, 89; Holm-Nielsen, *Hodayot*, 219; Carmignac, *Les
Textes*, 154.

[27]Several scholars restore the first word of this gap as
שרוד: Licht, *mgylt*, 191; Dupont-Sommer, *Le Livre des Hymnes*, 90;
Holm-Nielsen, *Hodayot*, 222.

[28]Holm-Nielsen is probably correct in his decision to support the restoration of Gaster and Licht (*Hodayot*, 222). This
line is undoubtedly parallel to the next line and contrasting
rather than synonymous parallelism is suggested by the summary
character of these final lines.

[1]All these opening lines are noted by both Licht and
Dupont-Sommer, whose psalm delineations are commonly used.

[2]Holm-Nielsen, *Hodayot*, 224, 319.

[3]In the Hodayot, פי על is used twice, לפי appears eleven
times. In 1QS, on the other hand, פי על is used thirteen
times, and לפי eleven times.

[4]M. H. Segal, *A Grammar of Mishnaic Hebrew* (Oxford:
Clarendon, 1927) 171-72.

[5]Nine to thirteen syllables is designated as the "standard
line" in the Hodayot because lines having as few as nine syllables and as many as thirteen are set in parallel cola. Lines
that definitely have more than thirteen or less than nine syllables are rarely (only a half dozen times in these eight hymns)
paralleled with a standard line. They stand by themselves, or
in a list, or are paralleled by other long or short lines.

NOTES

CHAPTER VII

[1]J. Philip Hyatt, "The View of Man in the Qumran Hodayot," *NTS* 2 (1955-56) 278, 283.

[2]Holm-Nielsen, *Hodayot*, 296.

[3]Laurin's views are discussed in the section "Theology" of Chapter III, Section 3.

[4]Murphy's views are discussed on p. 195 n. 59.

[5]D. S. Russell, *The Method and Message of Jewish Apocalyptic* (Philadelphia: Westminster, 1964) 122-23.

[6]1QM 17:5-9, quoted from the translation of Yigael Yadin in *The Scroll of the War of the Sons of Light against the Sons of Darkness* ([London: Oxford University, 1962] 340).

GLOSSARY OF TERMS FOR HEBREW POETRY

(See also the discussion of Hebrew poetry on pp. 30-31.

ballast variant:
   a term whose weight balances a synonym as well as a
   double-duty term in a bicolon.

chiasm (*chiasmus*):
   basically, a reverse matching of items (ABCBA). In
   Hebrew poetry, there may be chiastic bicola, in which
   the elements of the second line of a bicolon are reversed in order. There are also chiastic poems in
   which whole sections are matched stylistically in
   reverse order, usually with a focal stanza at the
   center of the poem.

double-duty term:
   a verb, verbal suffix, pronoun, or occasionally a
   noun, which is used only once in a bicolon, but which
   is understood to apply to the other half of the bicolon as well.

envelope structure:
   a structure in which the first and last lines of a
   section complement each other (form a bicolon), while
   the material in the center also has its own interrelationships (are bicola or tricola).

hendiadys:
   two words combined in a single expression, usually
   connected by "and." The terms in such an expression
   lose their ordinary connotations and combine to form
   a new idiom. (English example: good and true = really
   true.)

inclusio:
   a phrase or word which is used at the beginning of a
   section of a poem and is repeated at the end of the
   section as a device to signal the poem's organization
   to the reader/listener.

internal parallelism:
   synonymous phrases, words, or forms within a single
   line of Hebrew poetry.

BIBLIOGRAPHY

General Works Pertinent to the Study of the Hodayot

Birnbaum, S. A. "How Old Are the Cave Manuscripts? A Paleo-
    graphical Discussion." *VT* 1 (1951) 91-109.

Burrows, Millar. *The Dead Sea Scrolls.* New York: Viking, 1955.

_____. *More Light on the Dead Sea Scrolls.* London: Secker
    and Warburg, 1958.

Cross, Frank Moore. *The Ancient Library of Qumran.* New York:
    Doubleday, 1958.

_____. "The Newly Discovered Scrolls in the Hebrew Univer-
    sity Museum in Jerusalem." *BA* (1949) 36-46.

Goshen-Gottstein, M. H. *Text and Language in Bible and Qumran.*
    Jerusalem: Orient Publishing, 1960.

Hooke, S. H. "Symbolism in the Dead Sea Scrolls." *Studia
    Evangelica* (1959) 600-612.

Kuhn, Karl Georg. *Konkordanz zu Qumrantexten.* Göttingen:
    Vandenhoeck & Ruprecht, 1960.

Martin, Malachi. *The Scribal Character of the Dead Sea Scrolls.*
    2 vols. Louvain: Publications Universitaires, 1958.

Nötscher, Friedrich. *Zur Theologischen Terminologie der Qumran-
    Texte.* Bonn: P. Hanstein, 1956.

Ringgren, Helmer. *The Faith of Qumran.* Trans. Emilie T.
    Sander. Philadelphia: Fortress, 1963.

Segal, M. H. *A Grammar of Mishnaic Hebrew.* Oxford: Clarendon,
    1927.

Editions of the Hebrew Text of the Hodayot

Barthélemy, D. and J. T. Milik (eds.). *Discoveries in the
    Judean Desert.* Vol. 1: *Qumran Cave I.* Oxford: Clarendon,
    1955.

Habermann, A. M. (ed.). *mgylwt mdbr yhwdh.* Jerusalem: Mach-
    baroth Lesifruth, 1959.

Licht, Jacob (ed.). *mgylt hhwdywt.* Jerusalem: Bialik Insti-
    tute, 1957.

Lohse, Eduard. *Die Texte aus Qumran.* Munich: Kösel, 1964.

Sukenik, E. L. *'wsr hmgylwt hgnwzwt.* Jerusalem: Magnes, 1954.

Translations of the Hodayot

Bardtke, Hans. "Die Loblieder von Qumran." *TLZ* 81 (1956) col.
149-54, 589-604, 715-724; and *TLZ* 82 (1957) col. 339-48.

Baumgarten, Joseph, and Menahem Mansoor. "Studies in the New
Hodayot (Thanksgiving Hymns)." *JBL* 74 (1955) 115-24,
188-95; and *JBL* 75 (1956) 107-13.

Carmignac, Jean and P. Guilbert. *Les Textes de Qumran*. Trans.
J. Carmignac and P. Guilbert. Paris: Letouzey et Ané,
1961.

Delcor, M. *Les Hymnes de Qumran (Hodayot)*. Paris: Letouzey
et Ané, 1962.

Dupont-Sommer, Andre. *Les Ecrits esséniens découverts près de
la mer Morte*. Paris: Payot, 1959.

_____. *The Essene Writings from Qumran*. Trans. Geza Vermes.
New York: World, 1962.

_____. *Le Livre des Hymnes découvert près de la mer Morte
(IQH)*. *Semitica* VII. Paris: Librairie d'Amérique et
d'Orient Adrien Maisonneuve, 1957.

Gaster, Theodor. *The Dead Sea Scriptures in English Translation*. New York: Doubleday, 1956.

Holm-Nielsen, Svend. *Hodayot: Psalms From Qumran*. Aarhus:
Universitetsforlaget, 1960.

Mansoor, Menahem. *The Thanksgiving Hymns*. Grand Rapids:
Eerdmans, 1961.

_____. "Two More New Psalms as Translated from the Dead
Sea Scrolls." *Commentary* (1955) 368-69.

Molin, Georg. *Die Söhne des Lichtes*. Munich: Verlag Herold,
1952.

Rotenberry, Paul Wilson. "A Translation and Study of the
Qumran Hodayot." Unpublished Ph.D. dissertation, Vander-
bilt University, 1968.

Selms, A. van. *De Rol der Lofprijzingen*. Baarn: Bosch and
Kenning, 1957.

Vermes, Geza. *The Dead Sea Scrolls in English*. Harmondsworth:
Penguin, 1968.

Wallenstein, Meir. "A Hymn from the Scrolls." *VT* 5 (1955)
277-83.

_____. *Hymns From the Judean Scrolls*. Manchester: Univer-
sity Press, 1950.

Wallenstein, Meir. "A Striking Hymn from the Dead Sea
    Scrolls." *BJRL* 38 (1955-56) 241-65.

Woude, A. S. van der. *De Dankpsalmen*. Amsterdam: Proost en
    Brandt N.V., 1957.

Other Materials on the Hodayot

Arvedson, Tomas. "De s.k. Tacksagelsepsalmerna från Qumran."
    Svensk Exegetisk Årsbok 22-23 (1957-58) 208-18.

Bardtke, Hans. "Considérations sur les cantiques de Qumrân."
    RB 63 (1956) 220-33.

Carmignac, Jean. "Les Eléments historiques des Hymnes de
    Qumrân." *RQ* 2 (1959-60) 205-22.

_____. "Etude sur les Procédés Poétiques des Hymnes."
    RQ 2 (1959-60) 515-32.

_____. "Localisation des fragments 15, 18, et 22 des
    Hymnes." *RQ* 1 (1958-59) 425-30.

_____. "Remarques sur le Texte des Hymnes de Qumrân."
    Biblica 39 (1958) 138-55.

Chamberlain, J. V. "Another Qumran Thanksgiving Psalm."
    JNES 14 (1955) 32-41, 181-82.

Dupont-Sommer, André. ""La Mère du Messie et la Mère de l'Aspic
    dans un hymne de Qoumran." *RHR* 147 (1955) 174-88.

Ehrhardt, A. A. T. "A Penitentiary Psalm from the Dead Sea
    Scroll and its Allies." *Studia Evangelica* (1959) 582-91.

Glanzmann, G. S. "The Sectarian Psalms from the Dead Sea."
    TS 13 (1952) 490.

Greenfield, Jonas C. "The Root 'GBL' in Mishnaic Hebrew in the
    Hymnic Literature from Qumran." *RQ* 2 (1959-60) 155-62.

Hyatt, J. P. "The View of Man in the Qumran 'Hodayot.'" *NTS*
    2 (1955-56) 276-84.

Kraft, Charles F. "Poetic Structure in the Qumran Thanksgiving
    Psalms." *Biblical Research* 2 (1957) 1-18.

Laurin, Robert B. "The Question of Immortality in the Qumran
    'Hodayot.'" *JSS* 3 (1958) 344-55.

Licht, Jacob. "The Doctrine of the Thanksgiving Scroll."
    IEJ 6 (1956) 1-13, 89-101.

Morawe, Gunter. *Aufbau und Abgrenzung der Loblieder von Qumran*.
    Berlin: Evangelische Verlagsanstalt, 1960.

Mowinckel, Sigmund. "Some Remarks on Hodayot 39.5-20."
    JBL 75 (1956) 265-76.

Murphy, Roland. "*Šaḥat* in the Qumran Literature." *Biblica* 39
    (1958) 61-66.

Ploeg, J. van der. "L'immortalité de l'homme d'après les
    textes de la mer Morte (1QS, 1QH)." *VT* 2 (1952) 171-75.

_____. "rum ᶜolam (1QH 3:20)." *VT* 3 (1953) 191-92.

Sanders, E. Parish. "Chiasmus and the Translation of I Q
    Hodayot VII 25-27." *RQ* 6 (1968) 427-32.

Schirmann, Jefim. "Hebrew Liturgical Poetry and Christian
    Hymnology." *JQR* 44 (1953-54) 123-61.

Silberman, Lou R. "Language and Structure in the Hodayot
    (1QH3)." *JBL* 75 (1956) 96-106.

Thiering, Barbara. "The Poetic Forms of the Hodayot." *JSS* 8
    (1963) 189-209.

INDEX OF QUMRAN MATERIALS CITED

Column 5	23, 24, 157, 182 n. 10, 188 n. 19
5:4	187 n. 15
5:5-19	26, 33, 42, 80-97, 103, 131, 157-158, 164, 166, 170, 171, 175, 176, 178-179, 184 n. 38, 192 n. 14, 200 n. 14
5:5	156-157, 167, 187 n. 15
5:6	160
5:7	160
5:8	160
5:9	160
5:10	160, 162
5:11	160, 162, 174
5:12	160, 162, 163
5:13	162, 163, 168
5:14	160, 162
5:15	160, 162, 195 n. 50
5:19	187 n. 15
5:20	82, 156, 187 n. 15
Column 6	23, 24, 157, 182 n. 10, 187 n. 1
Column 7	21, 23, 24, 157, 182 n. 10
7:5	188 n. 16
7:6-25	26, 33, 52, 121-136, 157, 162, 163, 166, 170, 171, 188 n. 19
7:6	156-157, 188 n. 16
7:7	162, 175
7:8	162
7:9	168
7:11	160, 175
7:12	160
7:13	160
7:14	160
7:15	160
7:16	160
7:17	160
7:22	162
7:23	162, 170
7:24	162
7:25	188 n. 16
7:26-33	26, 33, 99-108, 112, 118, 121, 140, 142, 157, 158, 159, 162, 164, 166, 167, 170, 171, 174, 175, 181 n. 7, 182 n. 12, 184 n. 38
7:26	156-157, 160, 188 n. 16
7:28	160, 163
7:29	160, 168
7:30	160, 162
7:31	162
7:32	160, 163
7:33	160, 163, 187 n. 15
7:34-8:3	181 n. 7
7:34	156-157, 187 n. 15
Column 8	21, 23, 24, 157, 182 n. 10
8:3	187 n. 15
8:4	156, 187 n. 15

INDEX OF BIBLICAL PASSAGES CITED